THE FAMILY Handyman ®

Toys, games,
and furniture

THE FAMILY Handyman ®

Toys, games,
and furniture

Over 30 Woodworking Projects You Can Make for Children

Reader's Digest

THE READER'S DIGEST ASSOCIATION, INC.
Pleasantville, New York/Montreal

First printing in paperback August 2005
A READER'S DIGEST BOOK

Produced by Roundtable Press, Inc.
Directors: Susan E. Meyer, Marsha Melnick
Executive Editor: Amy T. Jonak
Project Editor: William Broecker
Editor: Dave Kirchner
Assistant Editor: Megan Keiler
Design: Sisco & Evans, New York
Production: Steven Rosen

For The Family Handyman
Editor in Chief: Gary Havens
Special Projects Editor: Ken Collier
Associate Editor: Gregg Carlsen

For Reader's Digest
Executive Editor: James Wagenvoord
Editorial Director: John Sullivan
Design Director: Michele Italiano-Perla
Managing Editors: Diane Shanley, Christine Moltzen
Editorial Associate: Daniela Marchetti

Library of Congress Cataloging in Publication Data
The Family handyman toys, games, and furniture.
        p.   cm.
    Includes index.
    ISBN 0-89577-790-8 (hardcover)
    ISBN 0-7421-0682-4 (paperback)
    1. Wooden toy making. 2. Children's furniture. I. Reader's
Digest Association.   II. Family handyman.
TT174.5.W6F36   1995
745.592—dc20   95-30437

Printed in China
3 5 7 9 10 8 6 4 2 (hardcover)
1 3 5 7 9 10 8 6 4 2 (paperback)

A Note
from the Editor

What need is there for wooden games and toys in a world full of fast-moving, exciting, electronic gizmos? Why would we want to build and own throwbacks to another era? And why would the children of today want to play with them? (And make no mistake about it, they do.)

We all have our private answers to those questions, but for me the answer is easy: This old-fashioned stuff exists and is worth re-creating because it is uniquely beautiful, practical, useful, and adaptable.

Beautiful? You bet. Nothing else beats the look, feel, and touch of wood.

Practical? And how. Drop one of those electronic marvels on the sidewalk and it'll break—for good. Drop our toy fish, our doll's cradle, or our table hockey game and it'll probably break too. But you can fix it in a few minutes with common tools.

Useful and adaptable? There's none better. No batteries needed, ever. These toys run on imagination.

The toys that you build from the plans in this book might well be cherished for years—cleaned, polished, and held dear until they wind up on display shelves in your children's homes. More than likely, though, they'll be thrown around the basement playroom, left in the rain, bashed, buried, bruised, and busted.

Either way, the toys you build will be loved, becoming the building blocks for memories of a happy childhood. Enjoy!

Gary Havens

Editor, *The Family Handyman*

Contents

Toys

Introduction

As a child, were you lucky enough to be given a hand-crafted toy or piece of furniture that was a favorite of a parent or even a grandparent when they were young? Whether it was a rollicking rocking horse, a steam-engine locomotive, or an heirloom doll's cradle, it likely was lovingly and durably crafted from wood. That's because with a useful life measured in generations, not just years, no other material lasts as long or looks as good.

When you build any of the 33 projects in *The Family Handyman Children's Toys, Games, and Furniture,* you'll be immediately proud of the results. But more than that, you'll recognize that these are timeless project designs that your children and grandchildren would be proud to hand down to *their* children and grandchildren. Here are projects you can undertake with confidence whether you're a seasoned woodworker with a shopful of power tools or a novice who's still building up the shop arsenal. For each one, we tell you the tools and skills you'll need before you start. Then step-by-step instructions and photographs, detailed exploded-view drawings, and bills of materials and shopping lists lead you through all the stages of cutting, assembly, and finishing.

These projects were designed to be fun to make and fun to use. Don't let an accident mar that fun. Make your shop a safe place to work by clearing it of clutter and obstructions, and by keeping your tools and blades clean and sharp. Wear eye protection, not just when using power tools but also when using hand tools such as hammers and chisels. And when you apply paints and other finishes, do so only in a well-ventilated area; wear a face mask, if possible, to avoid breathing potentially harmful fumes. Finally, before starting a project, read the important information about building safely for children, on the next pages.

Building Safely for Children

The aim of every do-it-yourselfer is to make home "homier." An important part of that is to make sure home is safe as well, which means never building anything that might be hazardous for children. Following are some of the areas recognized as posing risks to children, along with some suggestions for avoiding the risks.

Head entrapment

A child's head can become entrapped in openings that are greater than 3-1/2 inches and less than 9 inches, sometimes with disastrous consequences. To avoid that hazard, keep distances between slats, railings, and any other spaces young children are likely to peek into less than 3-1/2 inches wide.

Part size

Small parts can be a choking hazard for children under age three. While most choking deaths have occurred on objects 1-5/8 inches or less in diameter, fatalities can also occur with larger objects. Be very cautious; make sure that where children under three are concerned, no toy or removable part of furniture (such as a knob) is less than 1-3/4 inches in size.

Nontoxic finishes

Even children several years old will put toys into their mouths, quite unconsciously. For this reason, the finish on a toy must be nontoxic. Aside from no finish at all, the simplest safe finish to use on wooden toys is a coat of mineral oil, the grade sold in pharmacies as safe for human consumption. Raw linseed oil, fresh shellac, and waxes containing either carnauba or beeswax are also considered safe. If you want to paint the toys you make, examine the labels and choose carefully. Stay away from finishes containing such metallic driers as lead, manganese, and cobalt, which are used in boiled linseed oil and oil-base (alkyd) paints. Water-base finishes are not necessarily safe just because they have no oils or volatile ingredients. Many contain toxic pigments, fungicides, and other additives. The safest choice is one of the specially developed nontoxic paints that are sold in arts and crafts stores. Look for the seal of the Arts and Crafts Materials Institute or the words "Conforms to ASTM D-4236" on the label. Of course, you should keep young children out of your workshop, so they can't explore the many other toxic materials stored there.

Corners and edges

Sharp corners and thin, sharp edges are not only painful to fall against or run into, but can cause permanent injury to a young child. Remember that children are shorter than you—a hazard that might jab you in the thigh is at a child's head and eye level. Round over all exposed corners and edges that children might encounter. This certainly applies to toys, but it also applies to furniture parts, such as the corners of drawers and coffee and end tables, and the like.

Pinch and crush points

Although generally less serious than other hazards, pinch and crush points can cause painful injuries. These are often tricky to assess, simply because adults don't have tiny fingers and wouldn't think of grabbing things the way children often do. To prevent finger pinching, any opening that might admit a 3/16-inch diameter rod (or finger) should be made large enough for a 1/2-inch rod. A good example of a pinch point is a wagon with wheels mounted too close to the wagon bed, where fingers could be caught when the rider grabs the sides of the wagon.

Chests and boxes

Falling lids, pinching hinges, and entrapment leading to suffocation are the leading causes of child injury from toy chests and boxes. Always equip a lid with positive support mechanisms—and never with an automatic locking device. Drill ventilation holes so that a trapped child could breathe. And make the gap between the front edges of the box and the lid at least 1/2 inch wide, so small fingers can't be crushed by a closing lid.

Stability

The biggest danger to children from an unstable large toy or piece of furniture is that they might pull it over on themselves. Remember: Children will climb—even up the front of a dresser, using the drawers as steps. Bolt large items such as dressers and bunk beds to the baseboard or to studs in the wall. Keep the design of riding and climbing toys such as wagons, hobby horses, and the like relatively wide and low, to reduce side-to-side tippability. Test such toys on a slight incline and in their "worst case" positions. Often you can add stops to rockers, or "outrigger" supports at the sides of a toy to eliminate instability.

Entanglement

The chief danger from entanglement is that children might strangle if collars, drawstrings, or hoods get caught on protrusions. Make sure that cribs, bunk beds, railings, outdoor play equipment, and similar items are free of protrusions on which clothing might become entangled. It's also a good idea to avoid dressing children in clothing that is oversize or that has a drawstring.

Additional information

Further information on avoiding these and other hazards is available in the publication "Standard Consumer Safety Specification for Toy Safety" (F963), available from the American Society for Testing and Materials, 1916 Race Street, Philadelphia, PA 19103.

Toys

Race Car

This 1957 Maserati model is as fast to make as it is to drive. Its aerodynamic body will give a novice woodworker good practice cutting curves.

38

Doll's Cradle

Every would-be parent knows that dolls like to be rocked to sleep. This toy cradle looks like the real thing and can be made of pine or hardwood.

42

Doll's Chair

This Shaker design is both simple and elegant; it's likely to find admirers among folk art collectors as well as among doll lovers. Building it takes intermediate skills and plenty of patience and care.

46

School Bus

You don't have to be old enough for school to love a big yellow bus. This ride-on toy will delight any preschooler.

50

Airplanes

Send your junior pilot on a flight through aviation history with these authentic-looking replicas.

54

Steam Shovel

This sandbox workhorse is easy for children to operate and easy for a basic woodworker to build.

62

Working Toys

Realistic details make this bulldozer, grader, and flatbed truck just the tools for hard-working play.

68

Freight Train

Train buffs of any age will love the beauty and craftsmanship of these collector-quality rail cars.

76

A wiggly fish pull toy

Here's a lively fish—when you pull it, the whole body wiggles and the tail flaps from side to side. The secret of this wonderful animation is off-center wheels.

Getting ready

If you have basic woodworking skills you can build this toy. The materials are staples at any lumberyard. You'll need a jigsaw, electric sander, and drill. A router would be helpful but is not essential. Draw 1-inch grid lines on the pieces of pine. Transfer the outline of the fish body (A) to the 1-1/2 inch pine, and the fins (B, C, J) to the 3/4-inch pine.

Step-by-step instructions

1 • Cut out all parts except the axle spacers (H) and eyes (F) with a jigsaw. Use a 1-1/2-inch hole saw to cut out the spacers and eyes.

2 • Round over the edges of the body (A) and the fins (B, C, J). Use a router with 1/4- and 3/8-inch round-over bits, or a wood file and sandpaper. Smooth all other sharp edges with medium-grit sandpaper.

3 • Drill 1/2- and 1/8-inch holes for the rope. Then drill 9/16-inch eye holes in parts A and F and 7/16-inch axle holes in parts A, H, and D. Drill pilot holes for the screw eyes in the body (A) and the tail fin (B).

4 • Paint the body with thinned latex paint so the wood grain will show through, and stain the exposed ends of the eye dowel with a dark wood stain. Insert the eye dowel in its hole so it sticks out equally on both sides of the body.

5 • Attach the top and bottom fins (C, J) and the eyes (F) to the body with finish nails and carpenter's glue.

6 • Insert the axle dowel in its hole so it sticks out equally on both sides of the body. Thread on the spacers (H), but don't glue them. Glue the wheels (D) onto the axle so they're offset from each other 180 degrees.

7 • Apply nontoxic oil finish to all parts.

8 • Attach two screw eyes to the body and two more to the tail fin as shown. Pry open the screw eyes on the tail fin and then squeeze them closed around the screw eyes on the body. Thread the pull rope through the jaw and tie a knot in each end.

Off-center axle holes in the wheels give this fish its wiggle. Glue the wheels to the axle so they're offset 180 degrees from each other.

Pattern Pieces   Each square = 1"

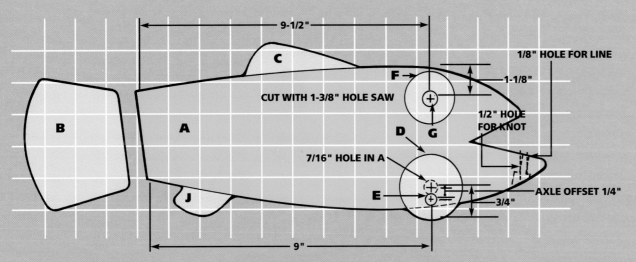

9-1/2"

1/8" HOLE FOR LINE

C

F

1-1/8"

CUT WITH 1-3/8" HOLE SAW

1/2" HOLE
FOR KNOT

B

A

D   G

7/16" HOLE IN A

AXLE OFFSET 1/4"

E

3/4"

J

9"

CONSTRUCTION TIP

If you don't have a
1-1/2 inch hole saw
to cut parts F and H,
buy 1-1/4 inch or
larger dowel or
closet-rod stock and
cut off four 3/4-inch
sections.

Assembly Plan

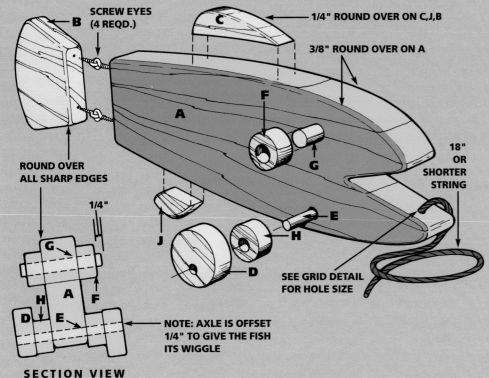

SCREW EYES
(4 REQD.)

B

1/4" ROUND OVER ON C,J,B

C

3/8" ROUND OVER ON A

F

A

18"
OR
SHORTER
STRING

ROUND OVER
ALL SHARP EDGES

1/4"

G

G

H

J

E

D

H

SEE GRID DETAIL
FOR HOLE SIZE

A

F

D   E

NOTE: AXLE IS OFFSET
1/4" TO GIVE THE FISH
ITS WIGGLE

SECTION VIEW

Cutting List

Key	Pcs.	Size and Description
A	1	1-1/2" x 4-1/2" x 13 3/8" pine
B	1	3/4" x 3-1/4" x 4-1/8" pine
C	1	3/4" x 1" x 5/8" pine
D	2	2" diameter pine or birch
E	1	3/8" x 4-5/8" dowel
F	2	3/4" x 1-3/8" diameter pine
G	1	1/2" diameter x 3-1/2" dowel
H	2	3/4" x 1-3/8" diameter pine
J	1	3/4" x 1" x 2" pine

Materials List

18" length of 1/8" diameter rope

3/8" screw eyes

Latex paint, dark stain, Danish oil

A good old-fashioned **piggy bank**

This *woodworker's version of the classic piggy bank is perfect for a quick evening in the shop. And the pig's smile is bound to put one on the face of any youngster who receives it.*

Getting ready

This is an easy project to build, but it requires a band saw, scroll saw, or jigsaw and a router—preferably mounted in a router table. The jigsaw will give you smoother cuts and shorten the time you spend sanding.

This bank was built from cherry, with pieces of leather from an old handbag for the ears.

Step-by-step instructions

1 • Glue and clamp together three pieces of 3/4-inch cherry to get the thickness required for the body (A). Mark a grid of 1-inch squares on A and on pieces of cherry for the sides (B, C). Transfer the outlines from the pattern plan and cut out the pieces. Or photocopy the patterns to size and trace the shapes on the wood. Note that the leg positions are slightly different on the right and left sides.

2 • Mark the leg and foot kerf cuts in the sides (B, C) and the mouth kerf cut in the body (A). Make all kerf cuts.

3 • Drill a 1-1/4 inch hole in the underside of the body (A) with a Forstner bit or a hole saw. The hole makes it possible to remove coins. Plug it with a cork shaped to fit.

4 • Transfer the outlines of the interior opening and the coin slot to the body (A), then cut them out (photo, below right).

5 • Round over all outside edges of the body (A) and all outside edges of the sides (B, C) except on the bottoms of the feet. Use a router with a 1/4-inch round-over bit. Sand all edges smooth.

6 • Drill a 3/16-inch hole in the body (A) for the eye dowel. Cut and glue the dowel in place and sand it flush with the body.

7 • Drill a 1/8-inch hole in the body (A) for the tail. Tie a knot in one end of the tail and thread the other end through the hole from inside the body cavity.

8 • Glue the sides (B, C) onto the body (A).

9 • Wrap masking tape around the tail and apply a safe oil finish.

10 • Cut the ears from scrap leather; nail them to the head of the pig with 1/2-inch brads.

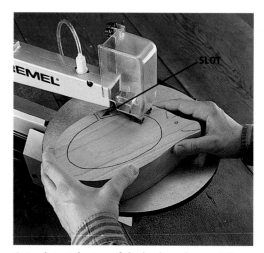

Cut a slot at the top of the body and cut out the middle to hold coins. The pig's mouth is just a slightly curved saw kerf.

Assembly Plan

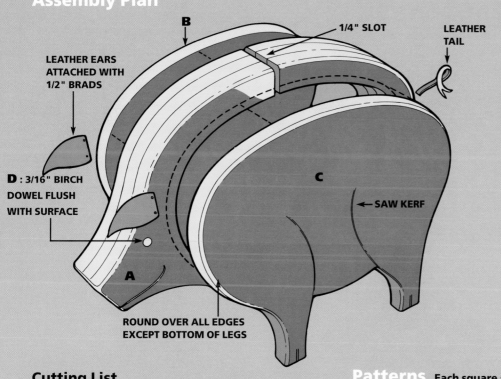

B

1/4" SLOT

LEATHER TAIL

LEATHER EARS ATTACHED WITH 1/2" BRADS

D : 3/16" BIRCH DOWEL FLUSH WITH SURFACE

C

← SAW KERF

A

ROUND OVER ALL EDGES EXCEPT BOTTOM OF LEGS

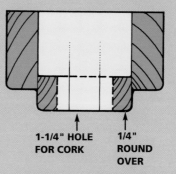

1-1/4" HOLE FOR CORK

1/4" ROUND OVER

DETAIL: COIN HOLE

CONSTRUCTION TIP

Cut the leather ears from an old handbag, coin purse, or thin leather glove. They can be brown or black. Cut a thin strip for the tail or use a scrap of leather boot lace.

Cutting List

Key	Pcs.	Size and Description
A	3	3/4" x 5-3/8" x 9-1/2" cherry
B	1	3/4" x 6-1/4" x 6-7/8" cherry
C	1	3/4" x 6-1/4" x 6-7/8" cherry
D	1	3/16" x 2-1/4" birch dowel

Materials List

1/2" brads

Scraps of dark brown leather (ears)

6" leather string (tail)

Nontoxic oil finish

Patterns Each square = 1"

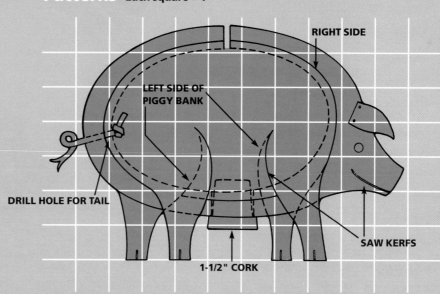

RIGHT SIDE

LEFT SIDE OF PIGGY BANK

DRILL HOLE FOR TAIL

SAW KERFS

1-1/2" CORK

snowflake ornaments

to make by the dozen

If your Christmas gift list is a mile long, here's a charming solution to your problem.
You can turn out these unusual snowflake-shaped holiday ornaments by the boxful with just a few hours in the shop.
The trick is to rout lengthwise grooves in four strips, glue them together, and rout them again. Then you just slice off the snowflakes and drill a few holes!

Getting ready

Although this project isn't difficult, it does require a router and a router table as well as a power miter box, table saw, or radial arm saw fitted with a fine-tooth blade. Using a router table is the only safe way to rout such narrow strips. And without the fine-tooth saw blade, you'd need to spend too much time sanding.

Assembly Plan

1/2"

1/2"

GLUE

3/16" DEEP
QUARTER-ROUND
V-GROOVE

GLUE

3/32" DEEP
V-GROOVE

1/4"

1/4" ROUND OVER

CONSTRUCTION TIP

Experiment with
different species of
wood—it's half the
fun of this project.
Pine and walnut
almost always will
give good results.
If you use fir, expect
some splitting with
the thin slices, espe-
cially when you do
the final drilling.

Materials List

Wood stock 3/4" x 3/4" or larger

Danish oil finish or equivalent

String for hanging

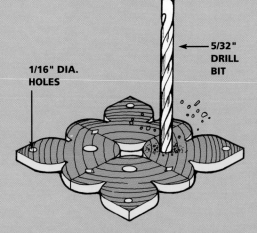

5/32"
DRILL
BIT

1/16" DIA.
HOLES

Drilling Pattern

Plan is oversize; each square = 1/4"

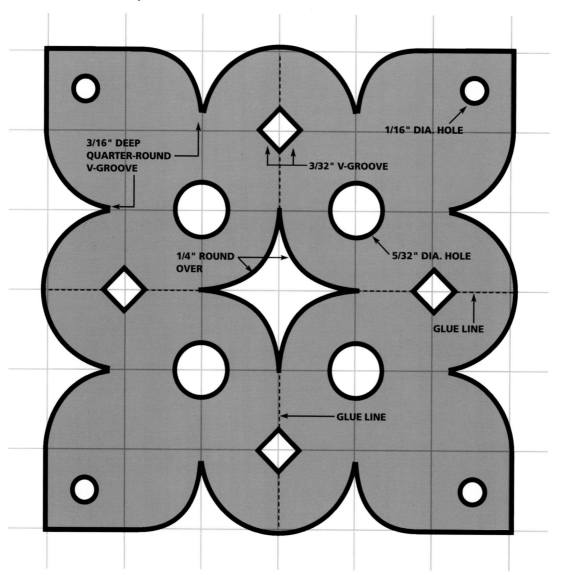

3/16" DEEP QUARTER-ROUND V-GROOVE

1/16" DIA. HOLE

3/32" V-GROOVE

1/4" ROUND OVER

5/32" DIA. HOLE

GLUE LINE

GLUE LINE

Make the ornaments

1 • Select your lumber and rip 3/4- x 3/4-inch strips from it.

2 • Round over one corner of each strip on the router table, using a 1/4-inch round-over bit.

3 • Rout 3/32-inch V-grooves on the two sides of each strip that are adjacent to the round over (Photo 1). Locate each groove 1/4 inch from the square edge of its side.

4 • Glue and clamp strips together in pairs, aligning the V-grooves exactly (Photo 2). Run a continuous bead of glue on each side of the V-groove, being careful to avoid squeeze-out into the groove.

5 • In the same way, glue and clamp pairs of strips together to form larger 1-1/2 x 1-1/2 inch sticks as shown in the plans.

6 • Sand the sides of the sticks with 100-grit sandpaper so they're flush and smooth.

7 • Rout two 3/16-inch deep quarter-round V-grooves in each side of all the glued-up sticks. Use a 3/16-inch point-cut quarter-round bit. Or use an ordinary fine V-groove bit and sand the round overs by hand. Position the grooves 1/2 inch from the square corners of the sticks.

8 • Crosscut the stick into slices 1/8 inch thick. If you use a power miter box or radial arm saw, make an auxiliary table from scrap wood to support the slices as they fall from the stick (Photo 3). Otherwise they'll fall into the table slots or old saw cuts.

9 • Drill four 5/32-inch holes around the center of each snowflake, and a 1/16-inch hole in each corner (see the Drilling Pattern, left). A drill press and 90-degree jigs to hold the snowflakes will speed your work.

10 • Dip each snowflake in Danish oil and let it dry on newspaper. Then sand it lightly with 100-grit sandpaper, dip it again, and let it dry completely. Attach a hanging string to one of the corner holes.

MAKE THE ORNAMENTS

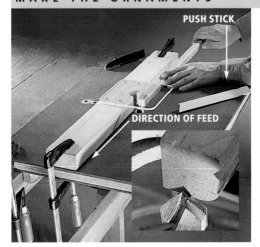

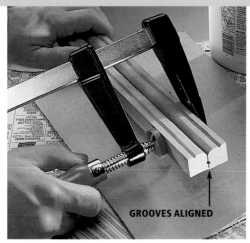

Photo 1 • Use a router table to cut V-grooves 3/32 inch deep on two sides of 3/4-inch square sticks. Other grooves are cut after gluing-up.

Photo 2 • Glue pairs of sticks together. Align the V-grooves exactly and be careful to avoid glue squeeze-out; it will be hard to clean up.

Photo 3 • Rout the glued-together stick, then crosscut it into slices. Use an auxiliary table to support the slices.

a circular saw *for your young helper*

All apprentice carpenters need their own tools. Start a collection for your child with this beautifully detailed toy circular saw. It has the look and feel of the real thing. The solid walnut and oak construction means it will last through lots of pretend projects.

Getting ready

You'll need 3/8-inch thick lumber for this toy, so a planer is helpful. If you don't have one, ask a local cabinet shop or woodworker's store to plane your stock to thickness. A band saw or scroll saw is best for cutting the curved parts, but a jigsaw with a narrow blade will do. A small sanding drum that fits in your electric drill will speed smoothing out the curves.

Mark a grid of 1-inch squares on your pieces of wood. Use oak for parts D, E, F, G, K, and L, and walnut for the other parts. Transfer the outlines of the parts from the patterns in the plans to the wood. Flop the pattern for the blade (D) to get the lower half.

Build the saw

1 • Cut three oversize pieces of 3/4-inch oak, and glue and clamp them together to make the motor (G). When the glue is dry, cut a block 3-1/2 x 4 x 2-1/4 inches.

2 • Bevel the motor block on the front, back, and left side. Start the bevel 1 inch up from the bottom and slant it in 3/4 inch from the top edges. Use a band saw, or screw the motor to a piece of plywood and cut the bevels with a radial arm saw or a table saw.

3 • Cut out a rectangle for the base (K), and then cut the opening for the blade. Round over the four outside corners with a wood file. Sand the base with 100-grit sandpaper.

Assembly Plan

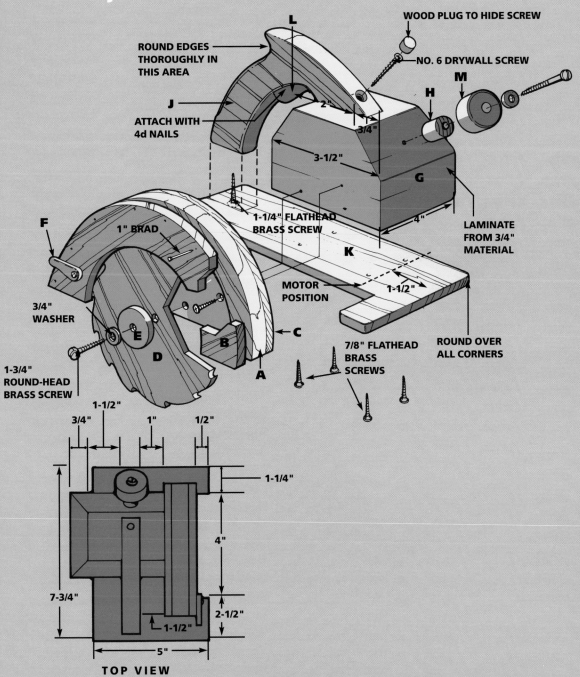

WOOD PLUG TO HIDE SCREW

ROUND EDGES THOROUGHLY IN THIS AREA

L

NO. 6 DRYWALL SCREW

1-3/4" ROUND-HEAD BRASS SCREW AND 3/4" WASHER

J

ATTACH WITH 4d NAILS

M

2"

3/4"

H

3-1/2"

G

4"

LAMINATE FROM 3/4" MATERIAL

F

1" BRAD

1-1/4" FLATHEAD BRASS SCREW

K

3/4" **WASHER**

E

MOTOR POSITION

1-1/2"

ROUND OVER ALL CORNERS

C

1-3/4" ROUND-HEAD BRASS SCREW

D

B

A

7/8" FLATHEAD BRASS SCREWS

TOP VIEW

3/4"   1-1/2"   1"   1/2"

1-1/4"

4"

7-3/4"

1-1/2"   2-1/2"

5"

TOP VIEW

Cutting List

Key	Pcs.	Size and Description
A	1	1/2" x 2-3/4" x 5-1/2" walnut
B	1	3/8" x 2-3/4" x 5-1/2" walnut
C	1	3/8" x 2-3/4" x 5-1/2" walnut
D	1	3/8" x 3-3/4" diameter oak
E	1	1/4" x 1" diameter walnut
F	1	1/4" x 3/8" x 1" oak
G	1	2-1/4" x 3-1/2" x 4" oak
H	1	1/2" x 1/2" diameter walnut
J	1	3/4" x 4-1/8" x 4-7/8" walnut
K	1	3/8" x 5" x 7-3/4" oak
L	1	1/4" x 3/8" x 3/4" oak
M	1	1/2" x 1-1/4" diameter walnut

Materials List

Flathead brass screws

No. 8 x 1-1/2" round-head brass screws and washers

No. 6 drywall screw

1" wire brads

4d finish nails

Nontoxic oil finish

Pattern Pieces

Each square = 1"

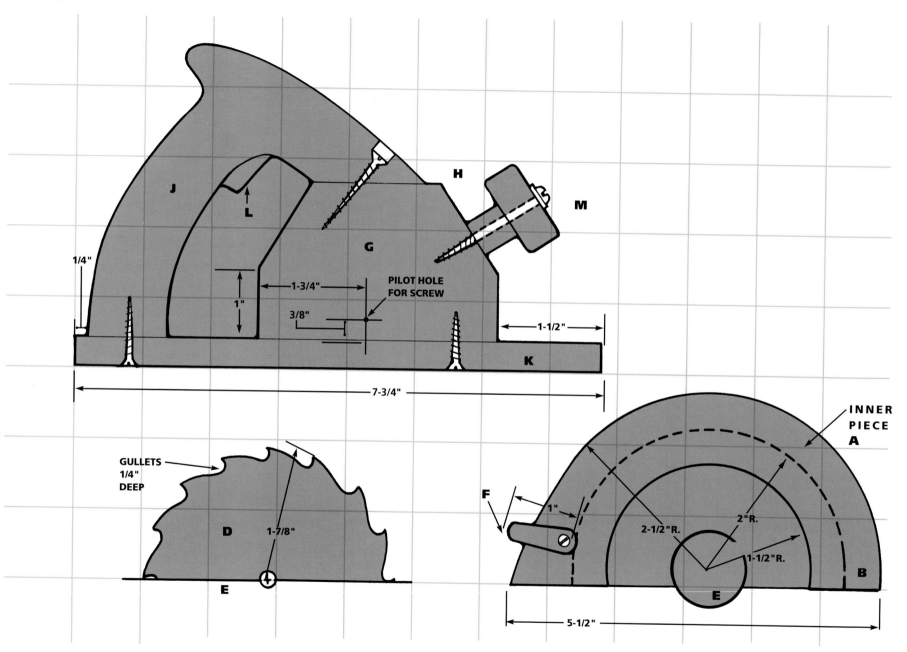

J

H

M

L

G

1/4"

1-3/4"

1"

PILOT HOLE
FOR SCREW

3/8"

1-1/2"

K

7-3/4"

GULLETS
1/4"
DEEP

D

1-7/8"

E

F

INNER
PIECE
A

1"

2-1/2"R.

2"R.

1-1/2"R.

E

B

5-1/2"

4 • Cut out the parts for the blade guard (A, B, C), and glue and clamp them together (Photo 1). Tack the pieces together with 1-inch brads to keep them from shifting as you tighten the clamps. When the glue is dry, sand the edges flush and the sides smooth.

5 • Screw and glue the blade guard to the motor. Countersink the screws; they will be concealed by the blade. Secure the motor in place with glue and four countersunk screws driven up through the bottom of the base.

6 • To make the blade (D), first drill a series of 16 equally spaced 1/4-inch diameter holes just inside the circumference of a 1-7/8 inch radius circle. These holes will form the gullets of the blade teeth. Saw a curve from the top of one

hole to the bottom of the next for each tooth (Photo 2). Slightly round the points and edges of the teeth with sandpaper for safety.

7 • Use a 1-1/8 inch hole saw to cut out the blade washer (E) (Photo 3). Screw it and the blade to the motor with a No. 8 x 1-1/2-inch round-head brass screw and washers.

8 • Cut out the handle (J), round over the edges, and sand smooth with 100-grit paper.

9 • Cut out the trigger switch (L), and glue and nail it to the handle with 4d finish nails. Drill pilot holes for the nails to avoid splitting the narrow trigger.

10 • Glue and screw the handle (J) in place. Counterbore the hole for the screw that holds it to the motor, cut a plug to fit, and glue it in place. Countersink the screw that comes up through the base into the handle.

11 • Cut out the knob (M) with a 1-3/8 inch hole saw to get a piece 1-1/4 inches in diameter (Photo 3). Use a 5/8-inch hole saw to cut the 1/2-inch diameter post for the knob. Round the edges of the knob and screw it and the post (H) to the face of the motor block with a round-head brass screw and washer.

12 • Finish-sand all parts with 100-grit sandpaper, and apply a child-safe oil finish.

BUILD THE SAW

THIS SIDE ATTACHES TO MOTOR

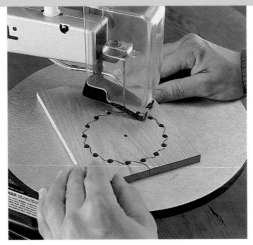

HOLE SAW

SCRAP WOOD

Photo 1 • Glue and clamp together three pieces of walnut stock to make the blade guard. Use brads to keep the pieces in line.

Photo 2 • Drill a series of 1/4-inch holes to make uniform gullets in the blade. They also make the piece easy to turn when cutting it out.

Photo 3 • Cut out the knob and its post with hole saws. The pilot drill bit in the saws makes a convenient hole for screwing the knob to the motor.

An heirloom Advent calendar

Start a new family tradition
with this Advent calendar.
Behind each door is a small
compartment that's just right
for holding candy or a small
toy, one for each of the 24 days
before Christmas.

Getting ready

This project requires pine pieces less than 3/4
inch thick, so you'll need access to a planer or
the services of a local cabinet shop. A table
saw or a radial arm saw also is handy for cutting out the many small and angled pieces
used in the project.

Mark a grid of 1-inch squares on two pieces of
rough cedar and transfer the outline of the
boughs (F) from the pattern (page 28). Each
strip is 32-3/8 inches long; repeat the pattern
for a total of eight boughs per strip. Similarly,
transfer the outline of the star (G) to a 3- to
4-inch square piece of 1/4-inch pine.

Assembly Plan

1" HOLE FOR HANGING

4d FINISH NAILS

F G

E

1" BRADS

L

C

E

SEE DOOR DETAIL

H

Cutting List

Key	Pcs.	Size and Description
A	36	1/4" x 2" x 2-1/2" pine
B	32	1/4" x 2-1/2" x 3" pine
C	2	1/2" x 3" x 32-3/8" pine
D		11' x 1/2" x 3" pine
E		1/2" x 2-1/2" pine, cut to fit
F	2	3/4" x 1-1/2" x 32-3/4" rough cedar
G	1	1/4" x 3" diameter pine
H		3/4" x 1-1/2" x 9" rough cedar
J		11' x 1/4" x 1/2" pine
K	36	Knobs
L	1	1/4" x 21-1/2" x 30-1/2" plywood

Materials List

1" brads

3/4" brads

4d finish nails

Latex paint, clear varnish or lacquer, metallic paint, red paint

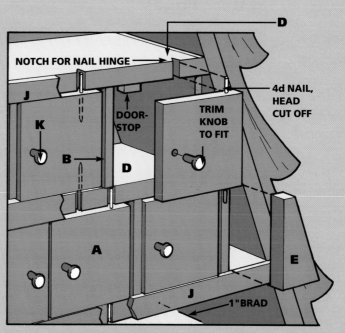

NOTCH FOR NAIL HINGE

D

4d NAIL, HEAD CUT OFF

J

K

DOOR-STOP

TRIM KNOB TO FIT

B

D

A

J

E

1" BRAD

DETAIL: DOOR HINGES

Build the Advent calendar

1 • Lay out the shape of the back (L) on 1/4-inch plywood and cut it out. The back is a triangle 21-1/2 inches wide and 30-1/2 inches tall. The slanted sides measure 32-3/8 inches.

2 • Cut the two side pieces (C) to length and miter their top edges to match the apex of the triangular back. Glue and nail the back to the sides with 1-inch brads, and fasten the top joint with brads as well.

3 • The shelves (D) are different lengths because the sides converge at the top. Measure the lowest shelf and cut it with the ends angled to match the slant of the sides. Glue and nail it in place with brads driven through the back and sides.

4 • Mark and drill a 1-inch diameter hole at the top of the back, between the sides at the peak, for hanging the calendar.

5 • Cut out all 32 vertical dividers (B). They are 3 inches wide and 2-1/2 inches high.

6 • Stand three or four dividers on the bottom shelf as temporary spacers and measure across their tops to get the length of the next shelf. Cut the shelf, again angling the ends to match the slanted sides. Work for a snug fit, but don't worry about small gaps at the joints; facing strips (J) will cover them later. Nail and glue the shelf in place.

7 • Now position dividers between these first two shelves according to the plan. Allow 2-1/8 inches of space between them for single doors, and 4-3/16 inches for double doors. Try to make the triangular openings at the ends roughly equal in size. Fasten the dividers in place with glue and 3/4-inch brads driven through the shelves (Photo 1).

8 • Cut filler pieces (E) for the triangular spaces at each end of this first level of compartments. They won't be exactly the same, so measure and cut each filler piece individually. Glue them into the openings.

9 • There are seven more levels of compartments. Working one level at a time, install a shelf (D), the number of dividers (B) shown in the plans, and filler pieces (E) at the ends. When all levels are completed, sand the front of the assembled frame so all pieces are flush.

Pattern Pieces

Each square = 1"

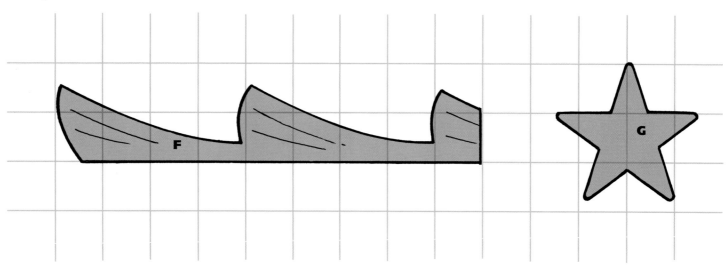

10 • Cut out the doors (A), drill holes in their fronts for attaching knobs, and drill pilot holes in their top and bottom edges for nails that will form the hinges.

11 • Drive 4d finish nails into the pilot holes in the door edges, leaving just over 1/2 inch exposed. Clip off the nailheads with diagonal-cutting pliers. Wear goggles or safety glasses to protect your eyes as you clip the nails.

12 • Working on one compartment at a time, lay a door in place and tap the nails with a hammer to dent the front edges of the shelves above and below; this marks the hinge locations. Chisel a recess at each location just wide and deep enough for the nail shank (Photo 2). Also trim the doors to fit with a chisel, if necessary. Identify each compartment and its door(s) with marked pieces of masking tape. Do all the compartments on one level, then move up to the next, until all levels have been completed.

13 • Measure the lengths of the trim strips (J) that cover the edges of the shelves (Photo 3). Cut them a bit long. Lay the calendar on its back and put the doors in position with the hinge nails in their grooves. Use brads and glue to fasten the trim strips in place, covering the hinges. When all the strips have been attached, pare them at their ends as necessary and sand them flush with the sides.

14 • Cut out the boughs (F) and the star (G), which you marked on pieces of rough cedar earlier. Also cut out the bottom trunk piece (H) from rough cedar.

15 • Apply watered-down latex paint to the trunk, boughs, and sides. Apply clear varnish or lacquer to the trim strips, doors, and filler pieces on the front of the calendar. Leave the compartment interiors unfinished. Paint the star with metallic paint.

16 • Miniature knobs are available from some woodworking specialty suppliers and model shops. The ones shown in the photos are actually wooden wheel axles. Trim the knobs to an appropriate length, push them through slits in a piece of cardboard, and spray with red paint.

17 • Nail on the boughs, the star, and the trunk. Glue the knobs in their holes in the doors. Cut doorstops from scrap wood, and glue one to the underside of the top shelf in each compartment.

BUILD THE ADVENT CALENDAR

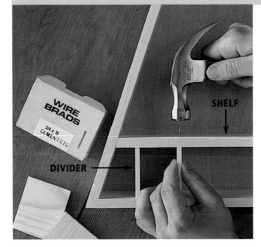

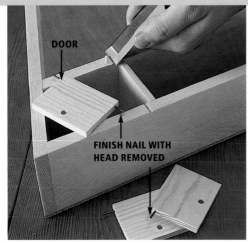

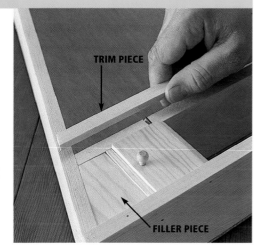

Photo 1 • Attach dividers with glue and small brads driven through the shelves. Some compartments have one door, others two.

Photo 2 • Make hinges for the doors from finish nails with the heads cut off. Cut shallow chiseled notches to hold them.

Photo 3 • Attach a trim strip to each shelf edge to cover the hinge nails. Install filler pieces in the triangular end openings first.

Fancy, easy-to-build **push sled**

Projects like this are a delight for a weekend woodworker. You'll have a tremendous amount of fun, but spend just a little time in the shop. You can assemble this sled with a few brass screws. And those fancy turned uprights are actually ready-made stair spindles, right off the home center shelf. So build the sled, bundle up, and take your favorite youngster out for a winter stroll.

Getting ready

All you need to build this sled is a drill, jigsaw, miter box, circular saw, and beginning-level woodworking skills. The wood is stock sizes, but you will need 1/2-inch thick oak for the slats. Ask your lumberyard or a local cabinet shop to plane down 3/4-inch stock.

When you're ready to apply the finishing touches, take your time with the painting. It's not difficult, but it can make or break the final appearance of your sled.

Assembly Plan

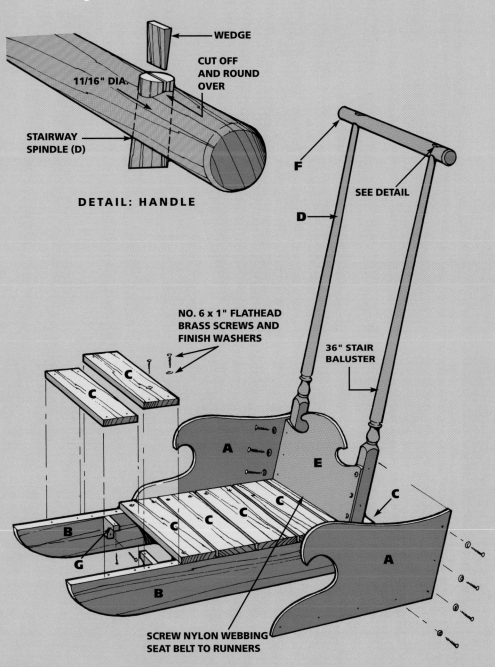

WEDGE

CUT OFF
AND ROUND
OVER

11/16" DIA.

STAIRWAY
SPINDLE (D)

DETAIL: HANDLE

F

SEE DETAIL

D

36" STAIR
BALUSTER

NO. 6 x 1" FLATHEAD
BRASS SCREWS AND
FINISH WASHERS

C

C

A

E

B

G

C

C

C

C

C

A

B

SCREW NYLON WEBBING
SEAT BELT TO RUNNERS

Cutting List

Key	Pcs.	Size and Description
A	2	1/2" x 8" x 17-3/8" birch plywood
B	2	3/4" x 3-1/2" x 33" oak
C	7	1/2" x 3-1/2" x 16" oak
D	2	36" stair balusters, oak
E	1	1/2" x 7-9/16" x 16" birch plywood
F	1	1-1/4" dia. x 19-1/2" dowel
G	6	3/4" x 1-3/4" x 1-3/4" oak

Materials List

No. 6 x 1" flathead steel screws

No. 6 x 1" flathead brass screws and matching finish washers

Wood filler, red paint, varnish, paste wax

Nylon webbing for seat belt

Pattern Pieces

Each square = 1"

Working Tip

To cut the curved parts of the sled, you need to draw them to size on the wood. Start by drawing 1-inch grids on your plywood or stock. Then, following the patterns shown here, mark the approximate spots on the wood where a pattern outline intersects each grid line. Smoothly connect the marks to create the cutting outline.

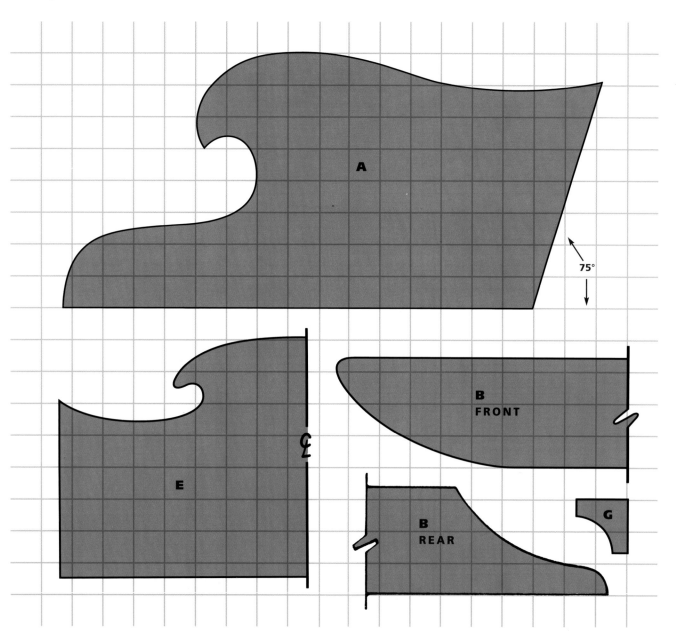

Build the sled

1 • Cut out the oak sled runners (B) and slats (C). Use the grid pattern to transfer the curved runner ends. Sand the parts smooth.

2 • Use clamps or wooden blocks to hold the runners (B) upright as you attach the slats (C) with steel screws. Then sand the ends of the slats flush with the runners.

3 • Lay out and cut the six braces (G). Attach them under the second, fourth, and sixth slats, counting from the front.

4 • Lay out the curved side and back pieces (A, E) on birch plywood. The pattern for E is for the left half only; flop and duplicate it to lay out the right half. Cut out these pieces with a jigsaw and sand all edges smooth (Photo 1).

5 • Bevel the bottom edge of the back (E) to match the angle of the rear edges of the sides.

Drill 1/8-inch pilot holes in all three pieces. Offset the holes in the sides from those in the back so the screws will clear.

6 • Attach the sides (A) to the runners (B) with No. 6 x 1-inch steel screws.

7 • Angle-cut the ends of the uprights (D) so they will stand at the same slant as the rear edges of the sides. Drill 1/8-inch pilot holes in the uprights to match the holes in the sides and screw the sides to the uprights (Photo 2).

8 • Drill 1/8-inch pilot holes in the uprights that match the holes in the back (E) and screw the back to the uprights.

9 • Cut the handle (F) to 19-1/2 inches, and chamfer the ends.

10 • Measure between the centers of the uprights (D) and mark hole locations on the handle (F). Drill 1-1/16 inch holes and fit the handle over the uprights. Trim the uprights so just 1/4 inch protrudes through the handle.

11 • Remove the handle, and cut wedge slots in the ends of the uprights (D), running across the wood grain. Cut two tapered wedges from scrap wood to fit the slots (see the detail in the assembly plan).

12 • Glue the handle to the uprights and drive the wedges into their slots with glue. When the glue is dry trim away the protruding ends with a coping saw and sand them to match the curve of the handle (Photo 3).

13 • Disassemble the sled, fill cracks and plywood edges with wood filler, and finish-sand all parts. Paint the sides and back—spraying gives the smoothest results. Apply varnish to the other parts with foam-brush applicators.

14 • Reassemble the sled with brass screws and finish washers. Pass the ends of a nylon webbing seat belt between the rear slats and screw them to the runners. Then wax the runners and take your child for a winter ride.

Safety Tip

Always fasten the seat belt around your passenger, and do not let children use this sled without supervision.

BUILD THE SLED

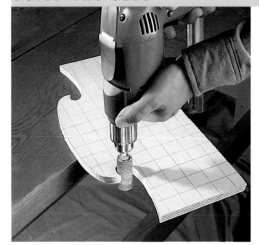

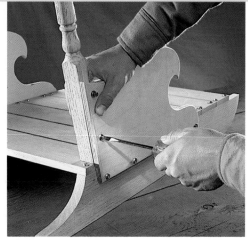

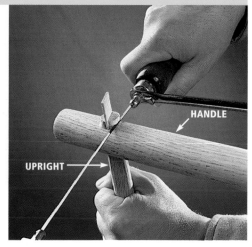

Photo 1 • Sand curved edges with a small sanding drum in an electric drill. Use a belt sander or a sanding block for straight edges and flat surfaces.

Photo 2 • Test-assemble the sled with steel screws. Disassemble it to apply the paint and varnish to the parts and reassemble with brass screws.

Photo 3 • Use glue and wedges to secure the uprights in the handle. Cut off their ends and sand them flush with the curve of the handle.

A toddler-size **toy minivan**

Just about every two-year-old loves cars. But if your family vehicle is a minivan, this reduced-scale version will be especially appealing to your youngster.

This project incorporates authentic minivan details yet is relatively simple to build. It's also rugged enough to stand up to toddlers, and it might even outlast the real thing!

Getting ready

Although this project requires only intermediate craft skills, some power tools are essential: a drill press, a table saw or radial arm saw, and a belt sander. A scroll saw or jigsaw will simplify cutting out the windows, but you could use a coping saw.

Since the minivan doesn't require much material, you can choose as fancy a wood as you like. The van shown here is made of oak. A softwood could be painted instead of stained.

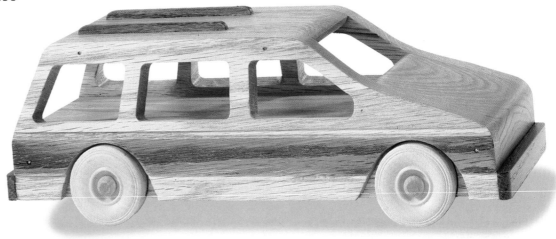

Assembly Plan

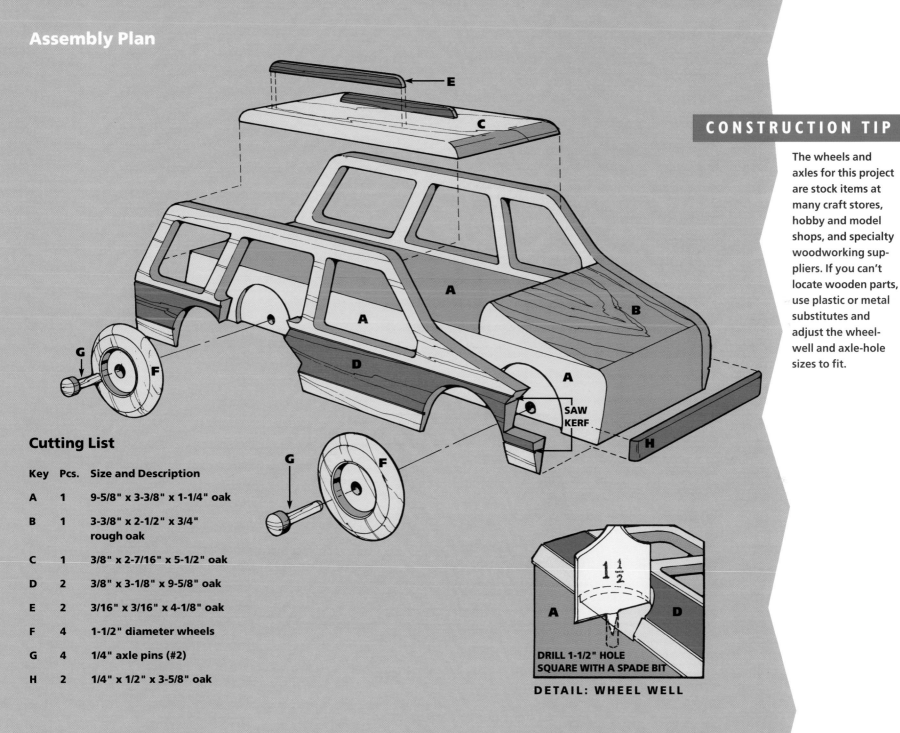

CONSTRUCTION TIP

The wheels and axles for this project are stock items at many craft stores, hobby and model shops, and specialty woodworking suppliers. If you can't locate wooden parts, use plastic or metal substitutes and adjust the wheel-well and axle-hole sizes to fit.

SAW KERF

Cutting List

Key	Pcs.	Size and Description
A	1	9-5/8" x 3-3/8" x 1-1/4" oak
B	1	3-3/8" x 2-1/2" x 3/4" rough oak
C	1	3/8" x 2-7/16" x 5-1/2" oak
D	2	3/8" x 3-1/8" x 9-5/8" oak
E	2	3/16" x 3/16" x 4-1/8" oak
F	4	1-1/2" diameter wheels
G	4	1/4" axle pins (#2)
H	2	1/4" x 1/2" x 3-5/8" oak

$1\frac{1}{2}$

DRILL 1-1/2" HOLE SQUARE WITH A SPADE BIT

DETAIL: WHEEL WELL

Pattern Pieces

Each square = 1"

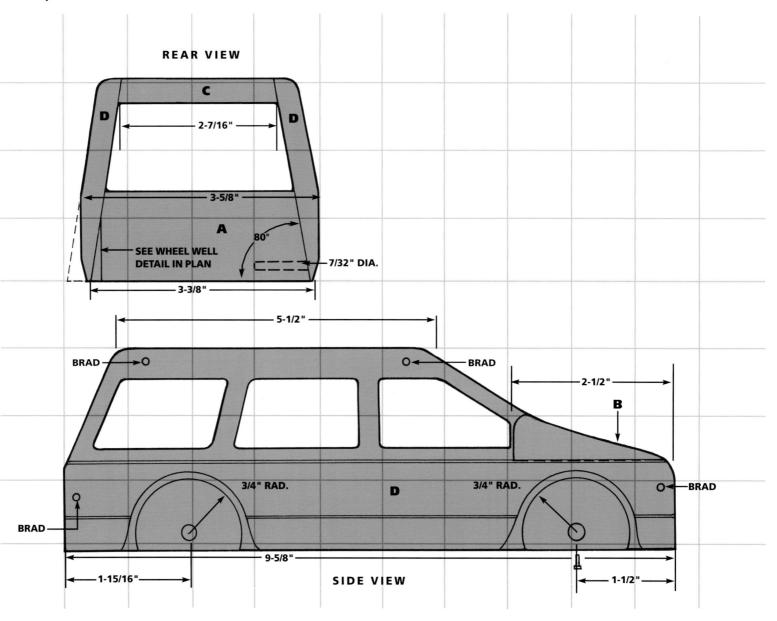

REAR VIEW

C

D   D

2-7/16"

3-5/8"

A

80°

SEE WHEEL WELL
DETAIL IN PLAN

7/32" DIA.

3-3/8"

5-1/2"

BRAD

BRAD

2-1/2"

B

3/4" RAD.

D

3/4" RAD.

BRAD

BRAD

9-5/8"

1-15/16"

SIDE VIEW

1-1/2"

Build the minivan

1 • Cut out body piece A about 1/16 inch over-size in width and length.

2 • Cut out body piece B, round over the dash-board edge, and glue it to piece A. Trim A to 9-5/8 inches long and round over the nose.

3 • Rip 80-degree angled edges on the sides of A. Use the same saw setting to cut the roof (C) to width. Then make 90-degree cuts to trim the roof to length.

4 • Cut two oversize rectangles for the sides (D). Transfer the front and back angles, the wheel openings, and the window outlines from the patterns to these pieces, then cut along the marked outlines with a jigsaw.

5 • Predrill four pilot holes for the brads in each side (D). The hole locations are shown on the side view pattern.

6 • Glue and nail the sides (D) and roof (C) to piece A with 3/4-inch brads (Photo 1). Clamp the pieces with angled blocks or hand screws. Use a nail set to sink the brads 3/16 inch when the glue is completely dry.

7 • Sand the sides (D) flush with the body block (pieces A and B).

8 • Rip vertical faces on the lower portions of the sides (D) (rear view pattern and Photo 2). Rip two saw-kerf grooves along each side, one at the top of the flat section, the other near the bottom (see plan and side view pattern). Cut the small angled faces along the lower edges of the sides (see rear view pattern).

9 • Use a 1-1/2 inch spade bit to flatten the insides of the wheel wells (Photo 3 and plan detail). Use a wheel to mark a starting point for the bit. Keep the drill square with piece A—perpendicular to the bottom. Use a larger bit if the wheels are bigger than 1-1/2 inches.

10 • Drill holes in the body (A) for a snug fit with the axles. If necessary, enlarge the holes in the wheels so the wheels can turn on the axles without binding.

11 • Cut the bumpers (H) and roof-rack pieces (E) with a jigsaw or coping saw.

12 • Finish-sand all parts with 100-grit sand-paper. Apply stain, using a darker color for the vertical faces of the sides and the roof-rack pieces to provide visual accent. If you prefer to paint the van, apply a prime coat of enamel undercoater to all parts. Fine-sand it when dry and add a finish coat of child-safe enamel.

13 • Insert the axles through the wheels and glue the axles into the body holes. Glue on the bumpers and roof-rack pieces.

BUILD THE MINIVAN

Photo 1 • Fasten the sides with brads to keep them from slipping when you glue them to the angled body piece.

Photo 2 • Rip the sides to make a vertical face on the lower half. This gives the minivan a distinctive, more realistic look.

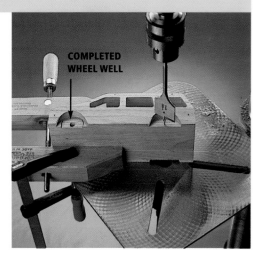

Photo 3 • Drill the inside of the wheel wells with a spade bit to provide a flat surface for the wheels. Let wheel diameter determine well size.

A sporty toy **race car**

This sporty little race car is a takeoff on one of the fastest cars of the past, the 1957 Maserati.

It's also fast to build—just a sleekly shaped wood body with a few holes drilled in it for the axles and details. If you've never cut out a shape that's curved in all dimensions, you'll learn how to do it here.

Getting ready

To cut the curves in the body, a band saw is best. You could use a saber saw or a coping saw, but not nearly as easily. To make perfectly straight holes for the axles, nothing beats a drill press. If you don't have one, you can use an electric drill with a guide attachment.

This car was cut from pine. You could substitute a hardwood—and perhaps use a clear finish rather than racing colors—but it will take longer to shape and sand.

The hardest part of this project may well be achieving a new-car finish. To get it, you'll need to apply several coats of spray-can enamel, masking between color areas and sanding thoroughly between coats.

Assembly Plan

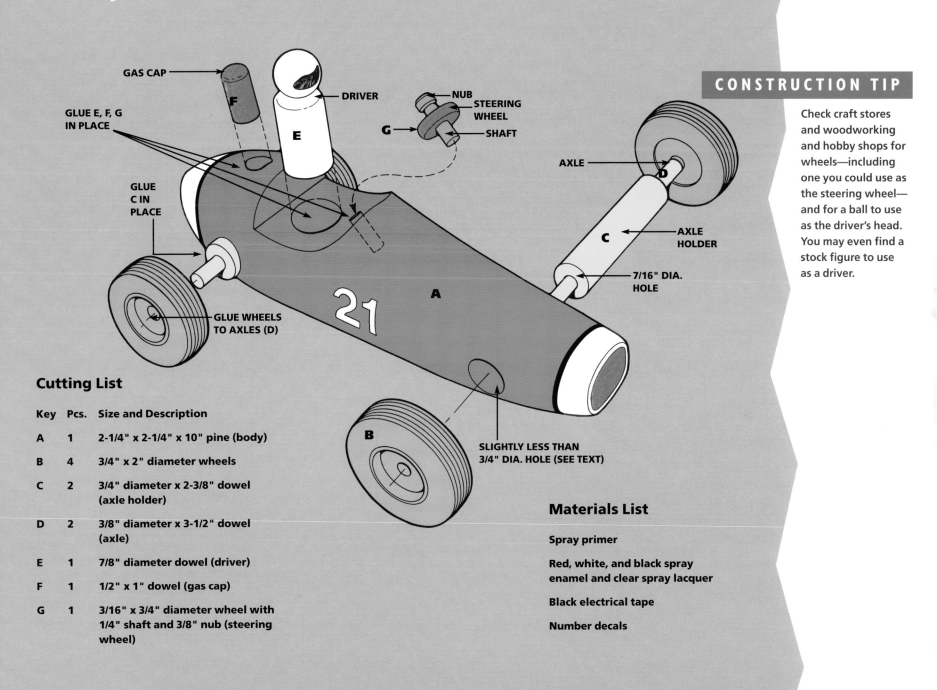

GAS CAP

GLUE E, F, G IN PLACE

DRIVER

NUB
STEERING WHEEL
SHAFT

GLUE C IN PLACE

F

E

G

AXLE

D

C

AXLE HOLDER

7/16" DIA. HOLE

GLUE WHEELS TO AXLES (D)

21

A

B

SLIGHTLY LESS THAN 3/4" DIA. HOLE (SEE TEXT)

CONSTRUCTION TIP

Check craft stores and woodworking and hobby shops for wheels—including one you could use as the steering wheel—and for a ball to use as the driver's head. You may even find a stock figure to use as a driver.

Cutting List

Key	Pcs.	Size and Description
A	1	2-1/4" x 2-1/4" x 10" pine (body)
B	4	3/4" x 2" diameter wheels
C	2	3/4" diameter x 2-3/8" dowel (axle holder)
D	2	3/8" diameter x 3-1/2" dowel (axle)
E	1	7/8" diameter dowel (driver)
F	1	1/2" x 1" dowel (gas cap)
G	1	3/16" x 3/4" diameter wheel with 1/4" shaft and 3/8" nub (steering wheel)

Materials List

Spray primer

Red, white, and black spray enamel and clear spray lacquer

Black electrical tape

Number decals

Pattern Pieces

Each square = 1"

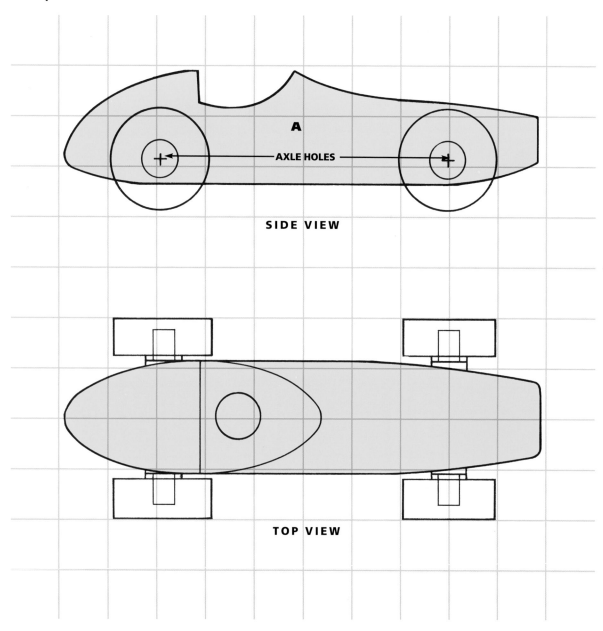

A

← AXLE HOLES →

SIDE VIEW

TOP VIEW

1 • Cut out a piece of stock 2-1/4 inches square and trim it to a 10-inch length for the body (A). Use a length of 4x4 or glue together three lengths of 1x4.

2 • Draw a grid of 1-inch squares on the top and on one side of the block. Then transfer the top view and side view shapes from the patterns to the wood.

3 • Drill holes slightly less than 3/4 inch diameter in the body for the axle holders (C) (Photo 1). Drill test holes in scrap wood first to be sure the axle holders fit snugly. You may need to file or grind the sides of a 3/4-inch spade bit to make the right size hole.

4 • Cut the axle holders (C) 2-3/8 inches long and drill a 7/16-inch axle hole in each one. Stand them upright in one of the test holes you drilled in Step 3. Drill halfway into the axle holder from each end.

5 • Cut out the top view profile marked on the body (A). Follow the lines precisely.

6 • Tape the cut-off pieces back onto the block or hold them with a few spots of hot-melt glue, so you again have flat surfaces to rest on the band-saw table. Now cut out the side view profile (Photo 2).

7 • Shape the body with a rasp, then with a file, and finally with progressively finer sandpaper, from 80- to 120-grit.

8 • Glue the axle holders into the body.

9 • Cut 3/8-inch dowels 3-1/2 inches long for the axles (D); test-fit them in the axle holders (C). If necessary, sand the axles so they turn freely in the holders. Test-fit the wheels (G) on the axles; they should fit snugly.

10 • Drill a hole in the body for the gas cap, a hole for the driver, and a hole for the steering wheel—see Step 11. Size the holes so these parts fit snugly.

11 • Cut a 1-inch length of 1/2-inch dowel for the gas cap (F) and round the edges at one end. Cut a 2-inch length of 7/8-inch dowel for the body of the driver (E) and round the top edges. Use a 7/8- or 1-inch diameter wooden ball for the driver's head. Drill the head and the body for a short length of dowel and glue them together with the dowel.

12 • Use a 3/4-inch diameter wood disk for the steering wheel (G), and a 1/4-inch dowel for the wheel shaft. Use a bit of 3/8-inch dowel for the head of the shaft.

13 • Apply a coat of spray-can primer to all surfaces you plan to paint. Fill any imperfections with wood filler, and fine-sand all surfaces with 150-grit sandpaper. Apply another coat of primer and fine-sand when the paint is dry.

14 • Spray-paint the body, steering wheel, and driver with white enamel. Sand with 150-grit paper and spray again. Repeat as needed for a fine, smooth finish.

15 • Spray-paint the gas cap, steering-wheel pin, and driver's mask black.

16 • Mask off the front and back of the body and spray-paint them with red enamel.

17 • Glue the gas cap, driver, and steering wheel assembly in their holes in the body.

18 • Cut pieces of black electrical tape for the pinstripes and front grille (Photo 3). Stick the tape to a hard, smooth surface in order to cut the shapes with a razor knife. Apply number decals to the sides of the body.

19 • Spray the completed body with two coats of clear lacquer. Test the lacquer on painted scrap wood first to be sure it's compatible with the finishes you're using.

20 • Insert the axles (D) through the body (C), and glue the wheels to the ends of the axles.

BUILD THE RACE CAR

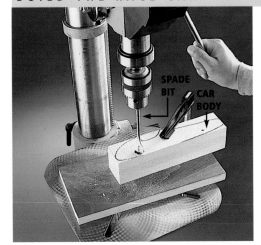

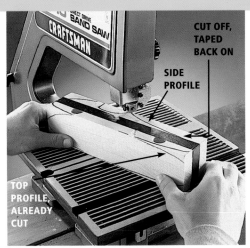

Photo 1 • Drill the body for the axle holders before cutting out its shape. For a tight dowel fit, file down both sides of the spade bit to make a slightly smaller hole.

Photo 2 • Cut the top body profile first, then tape or hot-melt glue the cutoff pieces back in place to cut the side profile. Pry glued pieces apart with a putty knife or other thin blade.

Photo 3 • Use electrician's tape for the black pinstripes and front grille. Use a razor knife and straightedge to cut the tape on a smooth board or a pane of glass.

A *classic* doll's cradle

Babies like to be rocked to sleep, and so do dolls. If you know someone who dotes on a doll, this fancy cradle would make a perfect gift.

Safety Tip

This cradle is designed only for dolls. It will not meet safety requirements for human infants, even if built in a larger size.

Getting ready

If you own a scroll saw or jigsaw, this project is a natural. It's assembled from only seven parts, which are just screwed or nailed together. You could use a saber saw, but even if you fit it with a narrow, fine-tooth blade you'll get a rougher cut than with a scroll saw.

To minimize sanding—especially on the curves—you can build the cradle from pine. But if you don't mind a bit more work, it would look great made from a hardwood.

Assembly Plan

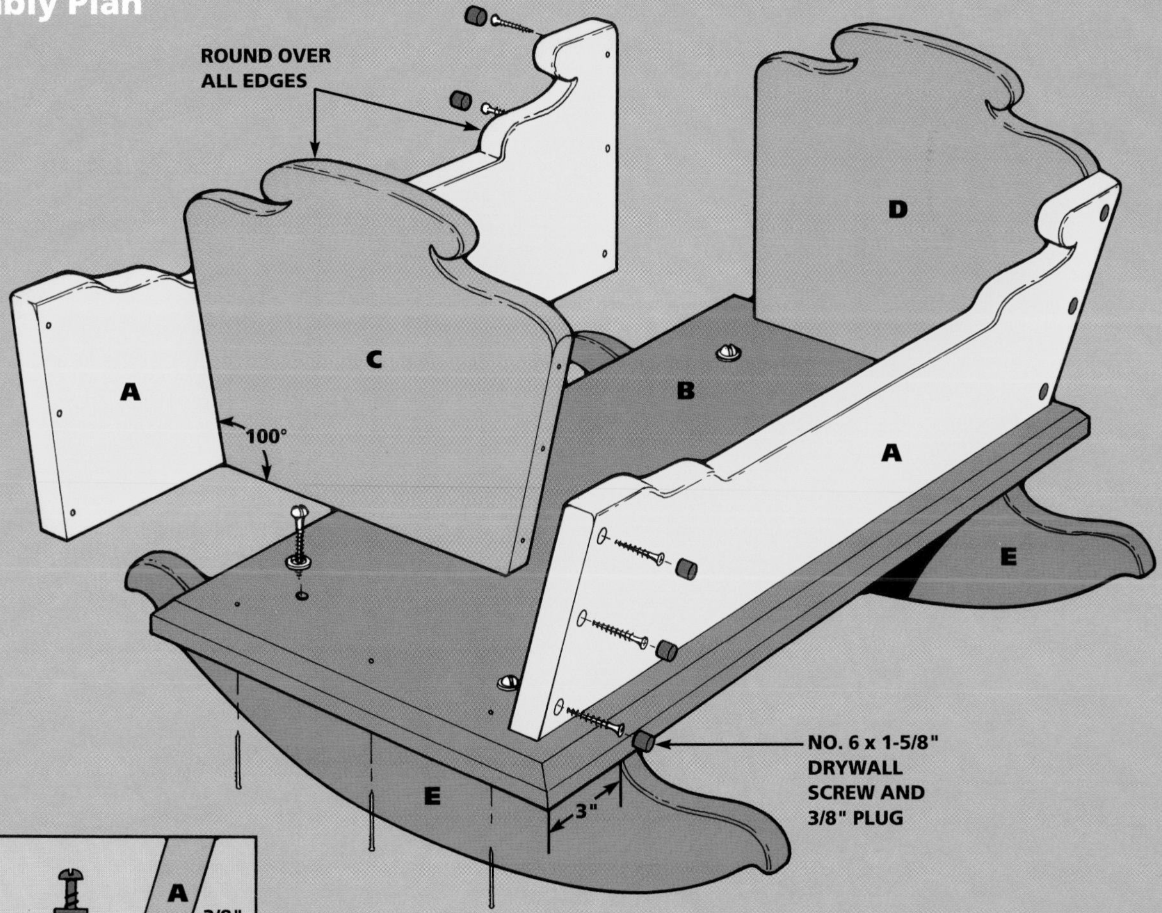
ROUND OVER
ALL EDGES
D
C
A
B
A
100°
E
E
3"
NO. 6 x 1-5/8"
DRYWALL
SCREW AND
3/8" PLUG

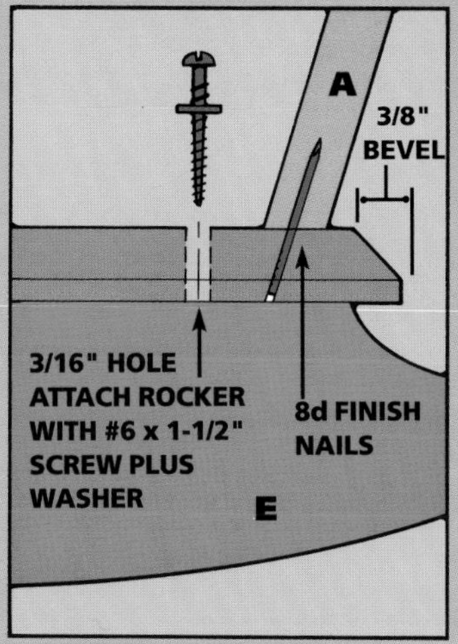
A
3/8"
BEVEL
3/16" HOLE
ATTACH ROCKER
WITH #6 x 1-1/2"
SCREW PLUS
WASHER
8d FINISH
NAILS
E

ROCKER ATTACHMENT

Cutting List

Key	Pcs.	Size and Description
A	2	3/4" x 6" x 20" pine (sides)
B	1	3/4" x 10" x 21-1/2" pine (bottom)
C	1	3/4" x 6-3/4" x 8-3/4" pine (footboard)
D	1	3/4" x 7-3/4" x 9" pine (headboard)
E	2	3/4" x 4" x 17" pine (rockers)

Materials List

8d finish nails

No. 6 x 1-1/2" screws and flat washers

No. 6 x 1-3/8" drywall screws

Stain controller, stain, polyurethane varnish

CONSTRUCTION TIP

Screw heads in the sides of the cradle are hidden under wood plugs. You can get a plug cutter bit for your drill from woodworking tool suppliers or many tool and hardware stores. You can also cut ordinary dowel stock to length for plugs.

Pattern Pieces

Each square = 1"

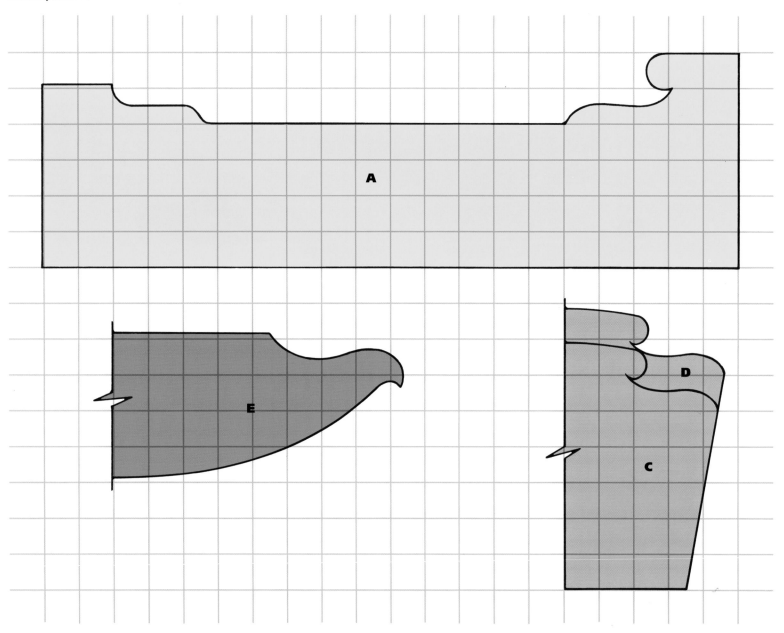

Build the cradle

1 • Draw a grid of 1-inch squares on the boards you've chosen for parts A, D, and E, and copy the outlines from the patterns onto the wood. The patterns for the rocker (E), the headboard (D), and the footboard (C) are for the right-hand halves of their parts; flop them to get the left-hand halves. For E and A, mark just one piece of wood each; you can trace the second piece from the first after cutting it out. Also, mark D but not C—you can trace C from D after cutting it out; they are the same except for their heights.

2 • Cut out the curved pieces (Photo 1), and sand all cut edges smooth. Trace their outlines onto other pieces of wood as explained in Step 1. Then cut out the traced shapes and sand the edges smooth.

3 • Cut the bottom (B) from 3/4-inch pine. Bevel the edges with a router, table saw, or plane (see Rocker Attachment Detail in the plans), and sand the edges smooth.

4 • Drill pilot holes for No. 6 drywall screws in the sides, then counterbore the holes for 3/8-inch diameter plugs that will cover the screw heads. Finally, mark and drill pilot holes in the edges of the headboard (D) and footboard (C) that match the holes in the sides.

5 • Bevel the bottom edges of the sides (A) so they sit flush on the bottom when placed against the edges of the headboard and footboard (Photo 2).

6 • Screw and glue the sides to the footboard and headboard, using No. 6 x 1-5/8 inch drywall screws (Photo 3).

7 • Glue wood plugs into the holes to hide the heads of the drywall screws. After the glue dries, trim the plugs with a sharp chisel and sand them flush with the sides.

8 • Stain and finish all parts. Apply a stain controller followed by an oil-base stain. Then apply a polyurethane varnish.

9 • Nail the bottom to the assembled sides, headboard, and footboard, using 8d finish nails. Keep the bottom overhang equal around all the edges.

10 • Determine where you'll attach the rockers (E) to the cradle bottom (B), and drill 3/16-inch holes in the bottom, two at each end. The holes are oversize to allow the bottom to expand and contract without splitting. Screw the bottom to the rockers, using No. 6 x 1-1/2 inch round-head screws and flat washers (see detail in the plans).

BUILD THE CRADLE

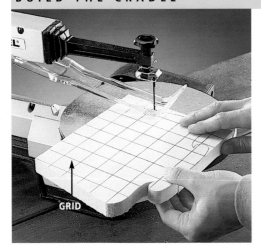

Photo 1 • Cut out one of each curved part and sand the edges. Trace the duplicate parts from the first, for an exact match.

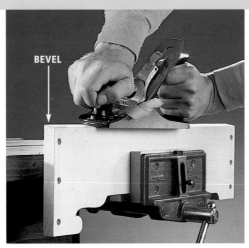

Photo 2 • Bevel the bottom edges of the sides with a block plane. This lets them sit flush on the bottom of the cradle.

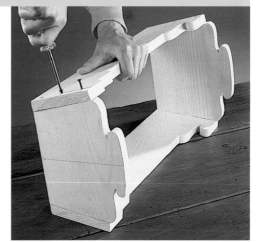

Photo 3 • Glue and screw the sides to the headboard and footboard. Cover the screw heads with glued-in wood plugs.

A Shaker doll's chair

At just 18 inches tall, this delicate, perfectly proportioned chair is just right for that special doll, or perhaps for display as a folk-art replica.

Getting ready

The simple and graceful Shaker design has been scaled down to let you make all the parts from ordinary dowels. That means you don't need a lathe for the small amount of turning the posts require.

You must use a drill press to build this project in order to keep all the rungs straight and tight-fitting. You'll also need a 1/8-inch wide chisel to cut the slat mortises, and furniture clamps to hold the forms that bend the slats.

Although the chair requires only intermediate woodworking skills, it's still complicated to build. Fortunately, the materials are so inexpensive that you can afford to build a practice chair to work out the details.

Safety Tip

This chair was not designed for children to sit upon—even small children. As a doll's chair, it's an appropriate toy only for children who are six or older.

Assembly Plan

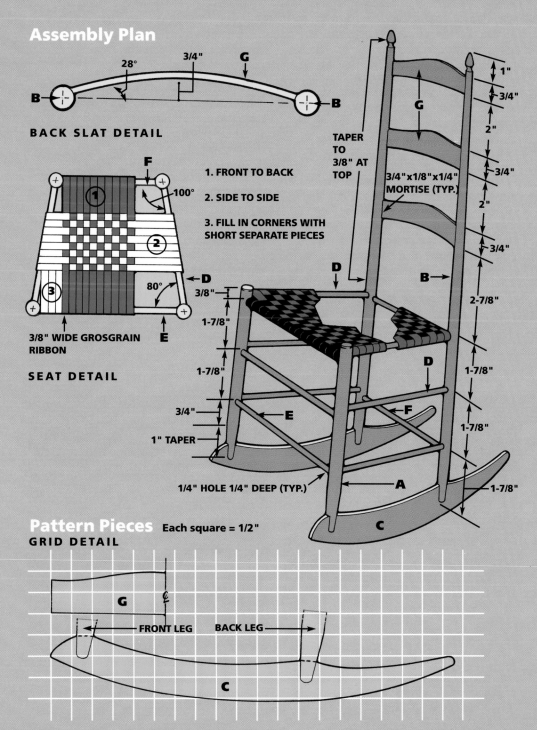

BACK SLAT DETAIL

28°   3/4"   G

B   B

SEAT DETAIL

1. FRONT TO BACK

2. SIDE TO SIDE

3. FILL IN CORNERS WITH SHORT SEPARATE PIECES

100°

80°

3/8" WIDE GROSGRAIN RIBBON

TAPER TO 3/8" AT TOP

3/4"x1/8"x1/4" MORTISE (TYP.)

1"
3/4"
2"
3/4"
2"
3/4"
2-7/8"
1-7/8"
1-7/8"
1-7/8"

3/8"
1-7/8"
1-7/8"
3/4"
1" TAPER

1/4" HOLE 1/4" DEEP (TYP.)

Pattern Pieces   Each square = 1/2"
GRID DETAIL

FRONT LEG   BACK LEG

Cutting List

Key	Pcs.	Size and Description
A	2	1/2" diameter x 6-1/4" dowel
B	2	1/2" diameter x 15-3/4" dowel
C	2	1/8" x 1-1/2" x 9-3/4" birch
D	6	1/4" diameter x 5-3/8" dowel
E	3	1/4" diameter x 7-1/4" dowel
F	2	1/4" diameter x 5-1/2" dowel
G	3	1/8" x 1" x 5-3/4" birch

Materials List

4 feet	1/2" diameter dowel
6 feet	1/4" diameter dowel
3-1/2 feet	1/8" x 1-1/2" or 2" birch
5 yards	3/8" grosgrain ribbon (first color)
5 yards	3/8" grosgrain ribbon (second color)
	Hot-melt glue
	Wood stain
1 can	Spray varnish or lacquer

Build the doll's chair

1 • Cut the front posts (A) and back posts (B) 2 inches longer than specified in the Cutting List, so the posts can be held for turning.

2 • Turn the posts in your drill press. Use a board with a slightly oversize hole to support one end of each dowel. Clamp the board to the bed of the drill press and hold the other end of the dowel in the drill press chuck (Photo 1). Run the drill at its lowest speed and use a file to create the bottom tapers and, on the back posts, the top tapers and the finial details. Always wear a face mask and safety glasses whenever you turn wood.

3 • Trim the posts to the final lengths given in the Cutting List and sand them. If you're building a practice chair, skip the sanding.

4 • Make a V-block to hold the posts for drilling (see box, Drilling Rung Holes). Use 2x4 or similar stock about 18 inches long. Mark a vertical reference line in the center of one end of the block and 80-degree reference lines on each side of the vertical line. Then rip a 90-degree V-groove along the top of the block, centered on the vertical line. The V should be 3/4 inch wide and 3/8 inch deep.

5 • Mark the posts for rung holes spaced 1-7/8 inches apart (see Assembly Plan).The front and back rungs are located 3/8 inch lower than the side rungs. Also draw a diameter line across the bottom end of each post. You can use these diameter lines and the reference lines on the V-block to get the required 80- or 100-degree offsets between rung holes in the posts (see Seat Detail in the plans).

6 • Refer to the box Drilling Rung Holes (opposite page) to position the posts for each set of rung holes. Tape each post in the V-block for drilling (Photo 2). Use a 1/4-inch brad-point or Forstner bit and make all the holes 1/4 inch deep.

7 • Also drill a series of 1/8-inch diameter holes 1/4 inch deep in the back posts to rough out the mortises for the ends of the slats (see Back Slat Detail in the plans). Complete the mortises with a 1/8-inch wide chisel.

8 • Cut the rungs (D, E, F) to length and sand them smooth.

9 • Make a full-size template from the grid pattern for the back slats. Note that each grid square equals 1/2 inch. Flop the pattern left to right to get the complete shape. Trace the outlines of the slats onto 1/8-inch birch, cut them out, and sand them smooth.

BUILD THE DOLL'S CHAIR

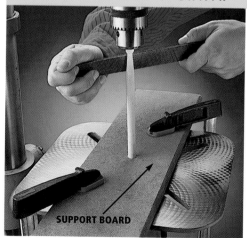

Photo 1 • Shape the turned parts on a drill press or lathe, using a file. Clamp the support board to the bed of the press. Wear a face mask.

SUPPORT BOARD

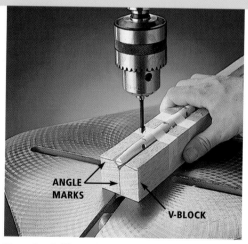

ANGLE MARKS

V-BLOCK

Photo 2 • Drill rung holes using a V-block for support. Tape each post for drilling. Reference lines on the post and block help you set the hole angles.

BENDING FORM

Photo 3 • Bend the slats by boiling them for half an hour and then clamping them overnight in two-part bending forms.

10 • Make three pairs of bending forms with a radius of about 16 inches (Photo 3). This is twice as tight a radius as you need, to allow for spring-back. Boil the slats for 30 minutes, clamp them in the bending forms while still soft, and let them dry overnight. Test-fit the slats between the back posts. Because of differences in wood characteristics, you may need to alter the radius of the bending forms and repeat the procedure.

11 • Test-assemble the chair and make any adjustments necessary. Then glue the parts together. Be sure to keep everything square and all four posts level—feet touching the floor—as the glue dries.

12 • Mark rocker slots 1/8" wide in the post bottoms. Cut them 1/2 inch deep with a fine-tooth handsaw, then clean out with a chisel.

13 • Make a template for one rocker using the pattern grid. Trace the outline onto 1/8-inch birch and cut out the rocker. Use the first rocker to trace the outline of the second. Cut it out and sand both rockers smooth. Glue the rockers into the post slots.

14 • Finish-sand all parts with 100-grit sand paper, stain the chair, and add a finish coat of spray-can varnish or lacquer.

15 • Weave the seat with grosgrain ribbon. Make a loop at the ribbon end and use hot-melt glue to secure it. Then weave the ribbons in and out as shown in the seat detail in the plans. A dowel with a slit cut in one end can serve as a "needle" for threading the ribbon.

Drilling Rung Holes

Here's an easy four-step technique for positioning the rung holes at just the right angles.

Step 1. V-block. Mark one end of an 18-inch 2x4 with vertical and 80-degree reference lines. Then cut a V-groove 3/4 inch wide and 3/8 inch deep along the top center.

Step 2. Align the diameter line on each post with the vertical line on the V-block to drill the first set of rung holes. Secure the post with tape for drilling.

Step 3. For the second set of holes in one front post (80° offset), align the bottom of the diameter line on the post with the left-hand reference line on the V-block, as shown. For the second set of holes in the other front post, align its diameter line with the right-hand reference line.

Step 4. For the second set of holes in one back post (100° offset), align the top of the diameter line on the post with the lefthand reference line on the block, as shown. For the other post, align the top of its diameter line with the righthand reference line.

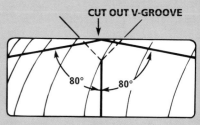

CUT OUT V-GROOVE

80°   80°

STEP 1

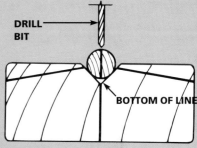

DRILL BIT

BOTTOM OF LINE

STEP 2

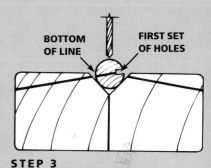

BOTTOM OF LINE   **FIRST SET OF HOLES**

STEP 3

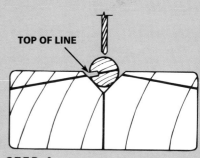

TOP OF LINE

STEP 4

Big yellow **school bus**

This ride-on school bus is guaranteed to give preschoolers a happy trip to their pretend destinations. It's fun to build too, and shouldn't take more than five or six hours spread over a few days.

Getting Ready

The bus is made of 3/4-inch birch plywood, glued and nailed together. The hood is screwed on, so you can mount the carriage-bolt "headlights" after you finish painting.

An electric drill and saber saw are all you really need to build this bus, but a table saw, router, and power sander will speed your work.

Assembly Plan

Cutting List

Key	Pcs.	Size and Description
A	1	3/4" x 8" x 22-1/2" birch plywood (top)
B	2	3/4" x 7-1/4" x 27-1/2" birch plywood (sides)
C	1	3/4" x 7-1/4" x 8" birch plywood (back)
D	1	3/4" x 6-1/2" x 27-1/2" birch plywood (bottom)
E	1	3/4" x 6-1/2" x 6-1/2" birch plywood (center)
F	1	3/4" x 5" x 8" birch plywood (hood)
G	1	2-3/4" x 3-3/4" x 8" birch plywood (front)
H	2	2-3/4" x 1" x 6-1/2" birch plywood (bumpers)

CONSTRUCTION TIP

Check local crafts stores and hobby shops or hobbyist mail-order catalogs for wheels. They should be 5-1/2 to 6 inches in diameter. Take extra care when you drill the holes for the lag screws that hold the wheels. They must line up exactly so the bus won't wobble when taken for a ride.

Materials List

1	3/4" x 48" x 48" birch plywood
4	No. 6 x 1-1/2" flathead wood screws
4	No. 6 x 1-1/4" drywall screws
40	4d finish nails
2	1/2" x 1-1/2" carriage bolts, flat washers, lock washers, and nuts
4	3/8" x 4-1/2" lag screws
4	3/8" flat washers
4	5-1/2" or 6" diameter wheels
	White spray enamel primer
	Yellow spray enamel
	Black spray enamel
	3/4" masking tape
	Wood putty

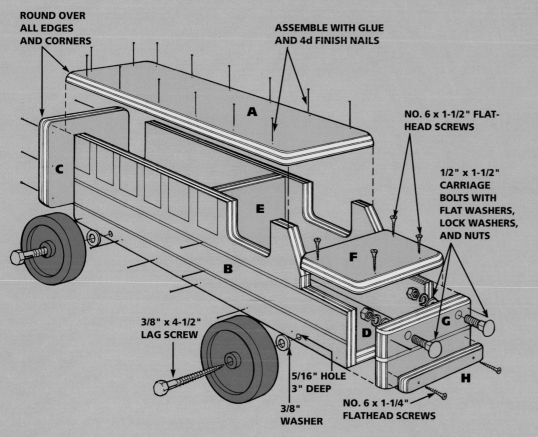

ROUND OVER ALL EDGES AND CORNERS

ASSEMBLE WITH GLUE AND 4d FINISH NAILS

NO. 6 x 1-1/2" FLAT-HEAD SCREWS

1/2" x 1-1/2" CARRIAGE BOLTS WITH FLAT WASHERS, LOCK WASHERS, AND NUTS

3/8" x 4-1/2" LAG SCREW

5/16" HOLE 3" DEEP

3/8" WASHER

NO. 6 x 1-1/4" FLATHEAD SCREWS

Dimensioned Plans

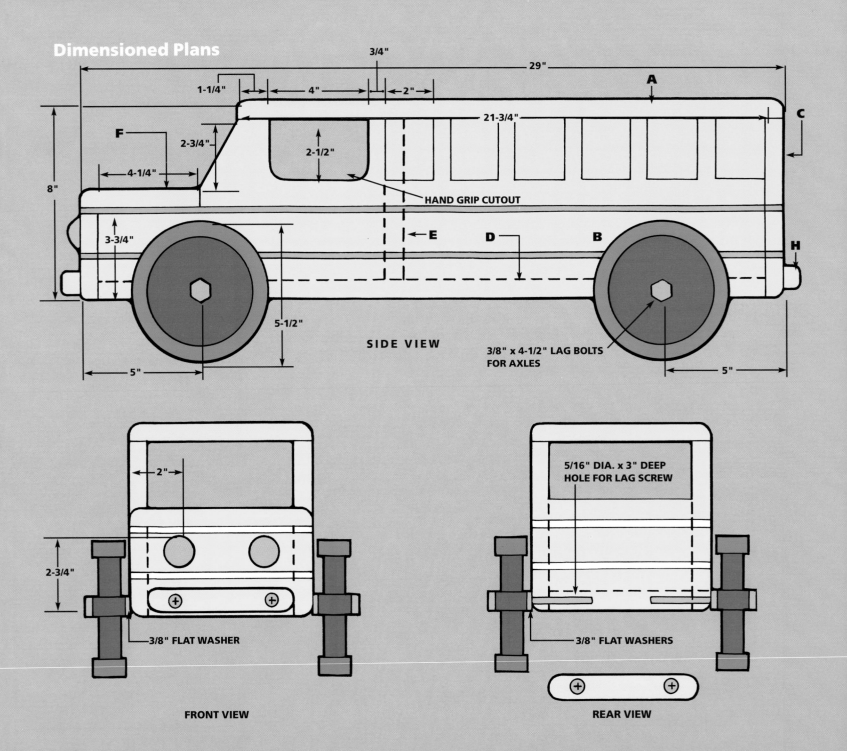

SIDE VIEW

3/4"

29"

1-1/4"

4"

2"

21-3/4"

A

C

F

2-3/4"

2-1/2"

HAND GRIP CUTOUT

4-1/4"

8"

3-3/4"

E

D

B

H

5-1/2"

3/8" x 4-1/2" LAG BOLTS FOR AXLES

5"

5"

FRONT VIEW

2"

2-3/4"

3/8" FLAT WASHER

REAR VIEW

5/16" DIA. x 3" DEEP HOLE FOR LAG SCREW

3/8" FLAT WASHERS

Build the school bus

1 • Cut all pieces to the sizes in the Cutting List. Use a clamped-on board as a cutting guide for your saber saw (Photo 1).

2 • Cut the hand grip openings (front side windows) and the windshield angles on the sides (B), and the rounded ends of the bumpers (H) (Photo 2).

3 • Countersink and drill 1/8-inch pilot holes in the hood (F) and bumpers (H) as shown in the plans. Drill 1/2-inch holes in the front (G) for the headlight carriage bolts (see Front View in the plans, opposite).

4 • Use a file to round over the exposed outside edges of the sides (B), top (A), and hood (F). Don't round over edges where the top and hood attach to the sides. Also round over the outside edges of the bumpers (H).

5 • Assemble the bus body with glue and 4d finish nails. Glue and nail the center (E) to the bottom (D) (see side view in the plans). Then attach the sides (B) (Photo 3), the front (G), the back (C), and finally the top (A). Use a nail set to sink the nailheads slightly below the surface of the wood.

6 • Screw the hood (F) in place temporarily. Sand any overhanging plywood edges flush with the sides, bottom, front, and back.

7 • Lay out and drill 5/16-inch holes 3 inches deep for the lag screws that attach the wheels (see side view in the plans and Photo 4). Drill slowly, and hold the drill as straight as you can so the wheels will align and turn smoothly when attached.

8 • Fill all nail holes and gaps in plywood edges with wood putty. After the putty hardens, sand the surfaces smooth.

9 • Round over all outside edges and corners of the bus body, using a file and sandpaper. Remove the hood (F). Then finish-sand all parts with 100-grit sandpaper.

10 • Use spray-can paints. Spray all pieces with white enamel primer. Lightly sand all surfaces when dry, then spray the bumpers with black enamel and all other pieces with yellow.

11 • Let the yellow enamel dry 48 hours. Then, using newspaper and tape, mask off all areas that will remain yellow. Press the masking tape down firmly to make a tight seal against the yellow enamel. Apply black enamel to all unmasked surfaces.

12 • Let the black enamel dry about 15 minutes, then carefully remove the tape and paper, being careful not to smear the paint. When the enamel is dry, attach the headlight carriage bolts, hood, bumpers, and wheels, and apply the press-on lettering.

BUILD THE SCHOOL BUS

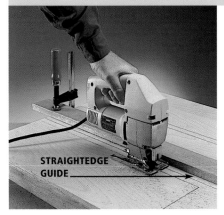

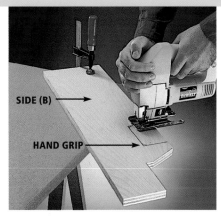

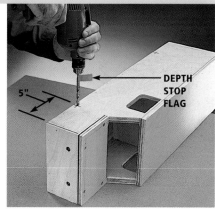

Photo 1 • Use a clamped-on straightedge to guide a saber saw for straight cuts. The distance between the guide and the cut line is equal to the distance between the saw blade and the edge of the saw base.

Photo 2 • Cut out the front-window hand grips and the windshield angles with a saber saw or band saw. Use a smooth-cutting, fine-tooth blade to reduce the amount of sanding you'll need to do later.

Photo 3 • Glue and nail the body parts together. Locate the 4d finish nails in the top at least 3/8 inch back from the edges so they won't interfere with rounding over the edges later.

Photo 4 • Drill 5/16-inch holes for the axle lag screws. Use a masking-tape flag on the drill bit as a depth-stop guide. Set the flag for a 3-inch hole depth. Align the holes properly for a smooth ride.

Famous high-flyer **airplanes**

Here are three classic aircraft toys: the famous *P-40 Flying Tiger of World War II, the modern F-16 jet fighter, and the* Spirit of St. Louis, *flown by Charles Lindbergh in his historic solo Atlantic crossing of 1927.*

These models were designed by Norman Marshall, a former U.S. Navy pilot. When he retired after 25 years as an aviator, he began making toys as a hobby. These designs and many others came out of his flying experience and his love of things mechanical. Each plane captures the essence of an aviation era and will spark the imagination of aspiring young pilots.

Getting ready

The airplanes shown here are built of clear pine, which is easy to cut and shape. You could use a harder wood, such as birch or poplar. That would require a bit more effort in cutting and sanding, but the planes would be more resistant to dents and other damage from handling in play. The planes are finished with spray lacquer. The press-on lettering and insignia shown here are available at most craft or hobby shops.

Moderate woodworking skill is involved in building these models because of the many angled parts. In addition to hand tools you'll need a table saw or radial arm saw, a drill press, and a jigsaw or saber saw.

The classic P-40 Flying Tiger fought over China in World War II. It carried honorary Chinese sun-in-circle wing markings in the early years of the war in the Far East.

This F-16 model is a composite of the F-14 through F-18 fighter jets built from 1970 to the early 1980s. Most were single-place planes with twin engines and tails.

The *Spirit of St. Louis* was built in 1926 by the Ryan Aircraft Co. Its open-cockpit fuselage and aerodynamic wheel-strut shock absorbers helped reduce fuel consumption.

Pattern Pieces — Flying Tiger

Each square = 1/2"

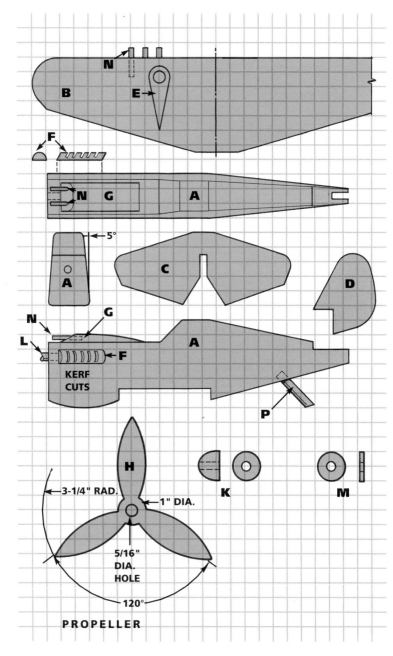

Build the Flying Tiger

1 • Make the fuselage (A) by gluing up two lengths of 1x4. Cut the notches for the wings and elevator (B, C). Tilt the saw table 5 degrees and cut bevels on the sides so the fuselage is narrower at the top than at the base. Tape the waste pieces back on, cut the fuselage side and top profiles (see patterns at left), including the notch for the tail. Round over outside edges.

2 • Cut out the wing (B), the elevator (C), and the rudder (D).

3 • Drill six 3/16-inch holes in the front edge of the wing for the guns (N). Cut the gun dowels, and glue them in place.

4 • Glue the wing (B), elevator (C), and rudder (D) onto the fuselage.

5 • Cut two blanks for the wheel fairings (E) (see gridded pattern and assembly plan detail). Drill 7/16-inch holes for the wheel struts (Q). Shape the fairings as shown in the plan detail.

6 • Make the wheels (J). First cut a 1/8-inch deep kerf in the wheel blanks with a 1-inch hole saw, then cut the wheels out with a 1-5/8 inch hole saw.

7 • Make the wheel-fairing assemblies. Cut the wheel struts (Q) and drill pilot holes for the wheel-axle screws. Attach the wheels (J). Cut off the protruding screw tips with a hacksaw and smooth the tips with a file. Glue the struts into the wheel fairings (E), aligning the wheels with the fairings. Glue the fairings to the bottoms of the wings.

8 • Cut the propeller from 1/4-inch plywood. Set a compass for a 3-1/4 inch radius and mark off a circle. Without changing the compass setting, place its point anywhere on the circle and draw an arc that crosses the circle completely.

Move the compass to one of the arc–circle intersections and draw a second arc. Repeat making arcs in this way until you have a three-blade propeller (see the pattern) at bottom left. Draw a 1-inch circle in the center and cut out the propeller.

9 • To make the propeller hub (K) and spacer (M), cut two circles from 3/4-inch stock with a 1-1/8 inch hole saw. Drill a 1/4-inch hole partway into one circle and glue in the propeller shaft (L). Chuck the shaft into a drill and use a rasp and sandpaper to shape the hub (K) as the drill turns. Cut the 1/8-inch thick propeller spacer (M) off the other circle, then glue it to the front of the fuselage (A). Drill a 1/4-inch hole through the spacer into the fuselage for the shaft, and glue on the propeller assembly.

10 • Cut out the engine exhaust stacks (F), and make angled kerfs with a thin-bladed saw. Be sure to make left and right pieces. Round over the outside edges of the exhaust stack and glue them to the fuselage.

11 • Cut out the gun cowling (G). Drill two 3/16-inch holes for the guns, cut the cowling to shape, and round the upper edges (see the patterns). Cut the guns (N), glue them into the cowling, and glue the cowling in place on the fuselage (A).

12 • Cut out the tail skid (P), drill a 5/16-inch hole 1/2 inch deep in the underside of the fuselage (A), and glue the skid in place.

13 • Sand all parts with 100-grit sandpaper. Add press-on numbers, letters, and insignia. The Chinese sun-circle wing insignia shown in the photograph (page 54) are honorary markings the P-40 Flying Tiger carried in the early years of World War II in the Far East. Finish the plane by spraying on a coat of clear lacquer.

Assembly Plan — Flying Tiger

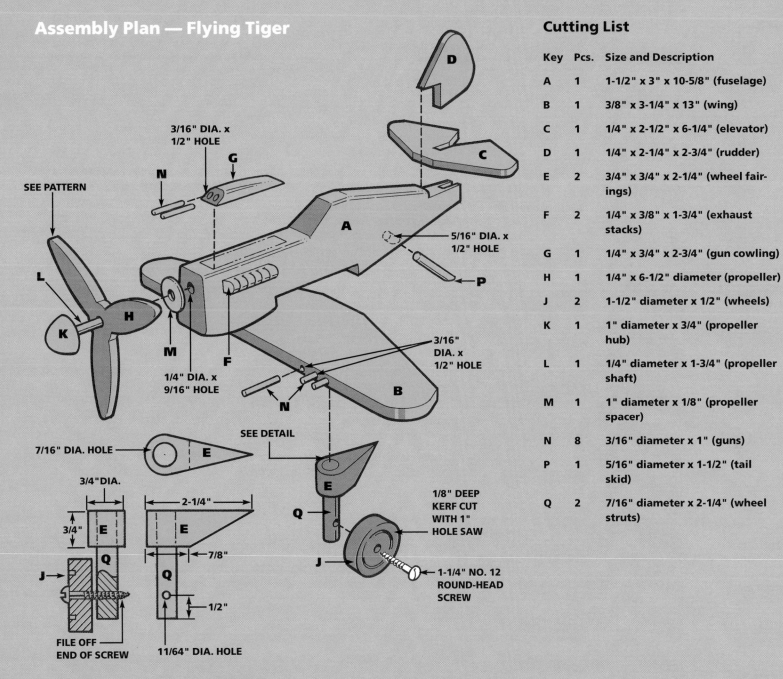

SEE PATTERN

3/16" DIA. x 1/2" HOLE

5/16" DIA. x 1/2" HOLE

3/16" DIA. x 1/2" HOLE

1/4" DIA. x 9/16" HOLE

7/16" DIA. HOLE

3/4" DIA.

3/4"

2-1/4"

7/8"

1/2"

11/64" DIA. HOLE

FILE OFF END OF SCREW

SEE DETAIL

1/8" DEEP KERF CUT WITH 1" HOLE SAW

1-1/4" NO. 12 ROUND-HEAD SCREW

DETAIL — WHEEL ASSEMBLY

Cutting List

Key	Pcs.	Size and Description
A	1	1-1/2" x 3" x 10-5/8" (fuselage)
B	1	3/8" x 3-1/4" x 13" (wing)
C	1	1/4" x 2-1/2" x 6-1/4" (elevator)
D	1	1/4" x 2-1/4" x 2-3/4" (rudder)
E	2	3/4" x 3/4" x 2-1/4" (wheel fairings)
F	2	1/4" x 3/8" x 1-3/4" (exhaust stacks)
G	1	1/4" x 3/4" x 2-3/4" (gun cowling)
H	1	1/4" x 6-1/2" diameter (propeller)
J	2	1-1/2" diameter x 1/2" (wheels)
K	1	1" diameter x 3/4" (propeller hub)
L	1	1/4" diameter x 1-3/4" (propeller shaft)
M	1	1" diameter x 1/8" (propeller spacer)
N	8	3/16" diameter x 1" (guns)
P	1	5/16" diameter x 1-1/2" (tail skid)
Q	2	7/16" diameter x 2-1/4" (wheel struts)

Pattern Pieces — F-16

Each square = 1/2"

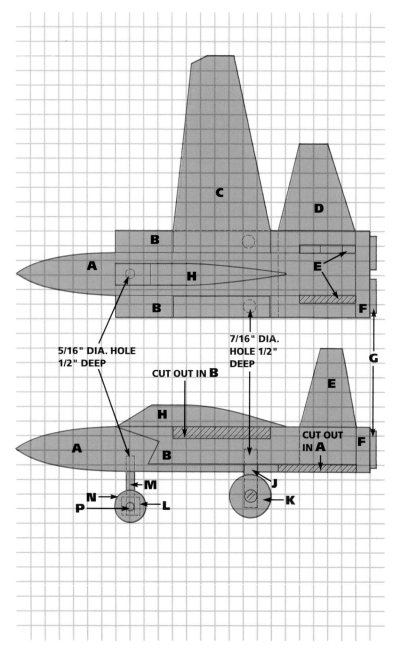

5/16" DIA. HOLE 1/2" DEEP

7/16" DIA. HOLE 1/2" DEEP

CUT OUT IN **B**

CUT OUT IN **A**

Build the F-16 fighter

1 • Glue together two pieces of 3/4-inch stock for the fuselage (A). Cut the nose profile, tape the waste pieces back on, and cut the top and bottom nose curves (see the patterns at left). Round over all edges. Cut the notch for the elevator, and drill a 5/16-inch hole for the nose wheel strut shaft (M) in the fuselage bottom.

2 • Cut out the right and left engines (B) (see detail in the plans). They are mirror images of each other, so make sure the notch for the rudder (E) in each piece is on the inside, toward the fuselage. Round over the bottom outside edges of the engines and the top outside edges from the wing notch to the tail.

3 • Cut out the wings (C), and glue them to the notches in the engines (B). When the glue is dry, glue the engines to the fuselage (A) in the positions shown in the patterns. Sand the top of the fuselage and the tops of the engine assemblies flush.

4 • Cut out the elevator (D) and the two rudders (E). The elevator is a single piece that extends on both sides of the fuselage. The pattern shows the shape on just one side of the fuselage; repeat it on the other side to make the complete shape.

5 • Glue the rudders (E) into their slots in the engines (B). Glue the elevator (D) into its notch on the underside of the fuselage.

6 • Sand the back of the fuselage (A) and the backs of the elevator (D) and the rudders (E) flush with one another. Cut out the tail cap (F). Cut out the two engine afterburners (G) with a 1-3/8 inch hole saw. Glue the afterburners to the tail cap, and glue this assembly to the back of the fuselage.

7 • Cut out and assemble the main wheels (K) and the main wheel struts (J) as for the Flying Tiger (Steps 5–6, page 56), but use 7/8-inch and 1-5/8 inch hole saws. Cut out the nose wheels (N) in the same way, using 5/8-inch and 1-1/4 inch hole saws.

8 • Cut off 2 inches of 5/8-inch dowel stock for the nose wheel strut block (L). Drill a 5/16-inch hole 1/2 inch deep in one end, and glue the nose wheel strut shaft (M) into it. Cut the strut block (L) to its final 5/8-inch length. Drill a 5/16-inch hole through the strut block for the wheel axle (P), and flatten the sides of the strut block (see detail in the plans).

9 • Glue together the nose wheels (N), axle (P), and strut assembly (L, M). Drill a 5/16-inch hole 1/2 inch deep in the bottom of the fuselage and glue the nose-wheel assembly in place.

10 • Cut out the cockpit (H), sand all surfaces except the bottom, and glue the cockpit in place on the fuselage.

11 • Sand all parts with 100-grit sandpaper. Add press-on letters, numbers, and insignia. Apply a coat of clear spray lacquer.

Assembly Plan — F-16

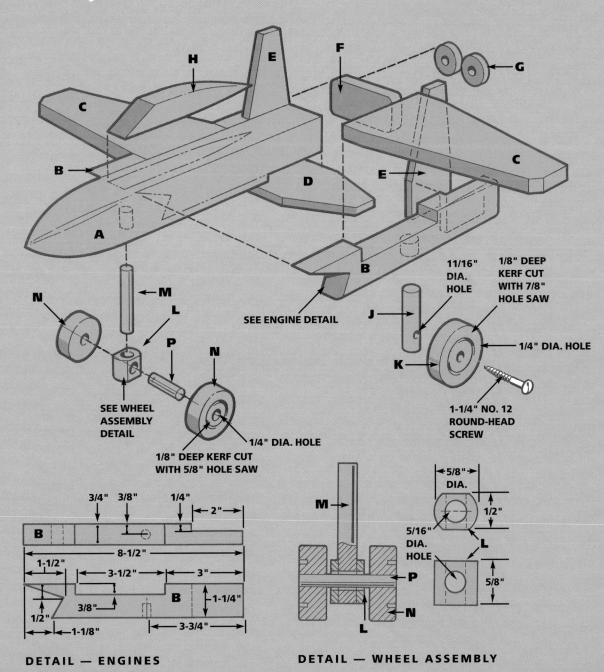

SEE ENGINE DETAIL

SEE WHEEL ASSEMBLY DETAIL

1/8" DEEP KERF CUT WITH 5/8" HOLE SAW

1/4" DIA. HOLE

11/16" DIA. HOLE

1/8" DEEP KERF CUT WITH 7/8" HOLE SAW

1/4" DIA. HOLE

1-1/4" NO. 12 ROUND-HEAD SCREW

DETAIL — ENGINES

3/4" 3/8" 1/4" 2"

8-1/2"

1-1/2" 3-1/2" 3"

3/8" B 1-1/4"

1/2" 1-1/8" 3-3/4"

DETAIL — WHEEL ASSEMBLY

M P N L

5/8" DIA.

5/16" DIA. HOLE

1/2"

5/8"

L

Cutting List

Key	Pcs.	Size and Description
A	1	1-1/2" x 1-1/2" x 12" (fuselage)
B	2	3/4" x 1-1/4" x 8-1/2" (engines)
C	2	3/8" x 3-1/2" x 6-3/4" (wings)
D	1	1/4" x 2-3/4" x 9" (elevator)
E	2	1/4" x 2" x 3-1/2" (rudders)
F	1	1/2" x 1-1/2" x 3" (fuselage tail cap)
G	2	1-1/4" diameter x 1/4" (engine afterburners)
H	1	3/4" x 3/4" x 6" (cockpit)
J	2	7/16" diameter x 1-3/4" (main wheel struts)
K	2	1-1/2" diameter x 1/2" (main wheels)
L	1	5/8" diameter x 5/8" (nose wheel strut block)
M	1	5/16" diameter x 2" (nose wheel strut shaft)
N	2	1-1/8" diameter x 1/2" (nose wheels)
P	2	1-1/8" diameter x 3/8" (nose wheels)
Q	1	1/4" diameter x 1-3/8" (nose wheel axle)

Pattern Pieces — *Spirit of St. Louis*

Each square = 1/2"

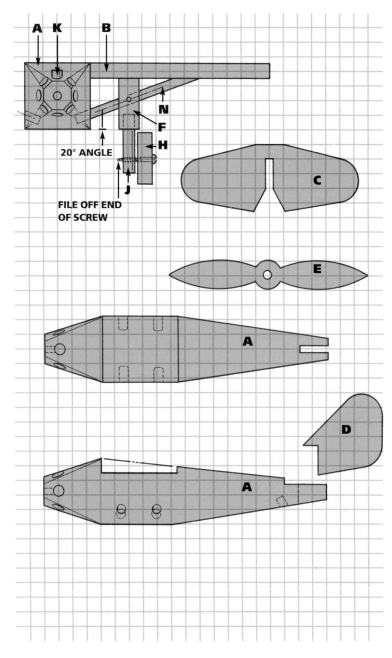

A K B

N
F
H

20° ANGLE

J

**FILE OFF END
OF SCREW**

C

E

A

D

A

Build the *Spirit of St. Louis*

1 • Glue together three pieces of 3/4-inch stock for the fuselage (A).

2 • Drill the 5/16-inch holes in the fuselage sides and 7/16-inch holes in the nose (see patterns at left and assembly plan, opposite page). You may need to cut 20- and 45-degree support blocks for the wing-strut and engine cylinder holes, respectively. Drill the holes for the engine cylinders to within 1/2 inch of the center of the fuselage.

3 • Cut a slot in the fuselage for the rudder (D), and notches for the wing and elevator (B, C).

4 • Cut out the fuselage shape. Stop just before the end of each cut and back out the blade, leaving the waste pieces attached to the fuselage block. That will give you flat surfaces to rest on the saw table when you make the remaining cuts.

5 • Draw a 1-inch diameter circle on the front of the fuselage (A), and round over the edges of the fuselage nose to meet it. Round over all other edges on the fuselage.

6 • Cut out the engine cylinders (K) and glue them to the fuselage.

7 • Resaw a length of 1x4 with the saw table tilted 5 degrees to make the wing (B). Rip it to fit the notch in the fuselage (A), and cut the wing tips to shape (see detail in the plans). Lay the wing aside.

8 • Cut out the elevator and rudder (C, D), and glue them to the fuselage (A).

9 • Make the shock absorbers (F). Drill a 7/16-inch hole 3/4 inch deep for the wheel strut (J) in each. Drill the 20-degree holes for the wing

struts (N). Note that there are right and left shock absorbers; drill these angled holes the proper direction for each one. Drill 1/8-inch holes for the lock pins (G), then cut the shock-absorber shapes.

10 • Cut out the propeller (E). Drill a 5/16-inch hole in the center, and set the propeller aside.

11 • Use a 1-1/8 inch hole saw to cut a blank for the propeller hub (L). Drill a centered 1/4-inch hole partway through one face, and glue the propeller shaft (M) into it. Chuck the shaft into a drill, then turn it against a rasp and sandpaper to make the rounded shape.

12 • Make the wheels (H). Cut 1/8-inch deep kerfs with a 1-3/8 inch hole saw, then cut the wheels out with a 1-7/8 inch hole saw. Cut the wheel struts (J), and drill 11/64-inch pilot holes in them. Screw on the wheels, cut off the protruding screw tips with a hacksaw, and smooth the cut ends with a file. Glue the wheel struts into the shock absorbers (F).

13 • Cut the wing struts (N) extra long, and fit them into the fuselage (A) without glue. Place a straightedge across the wing notch and mark the cutoff locations on the struts. Cut and glue the struts to the fuselage, then glue the shock absorbers to the struts. Again, lay a straightedge over the wing notch; position the shock absorbers where they contact the underside of the straightedge.

14 • Extend the 1/8-inch lock-pin pilot holes into the struts, and glue the lock pins (G) into the shock absorbers.

15 • Glue the wing into its notch and to the tops of the struts (N) and shock absorbers (F).

16 • Sand all parts with 100-grit sandpaper. Add press-on letters, numbers, and insignia. Apply a coat of clear spray lacquer.

Assembly Plan — *Spirit of St. Louis*

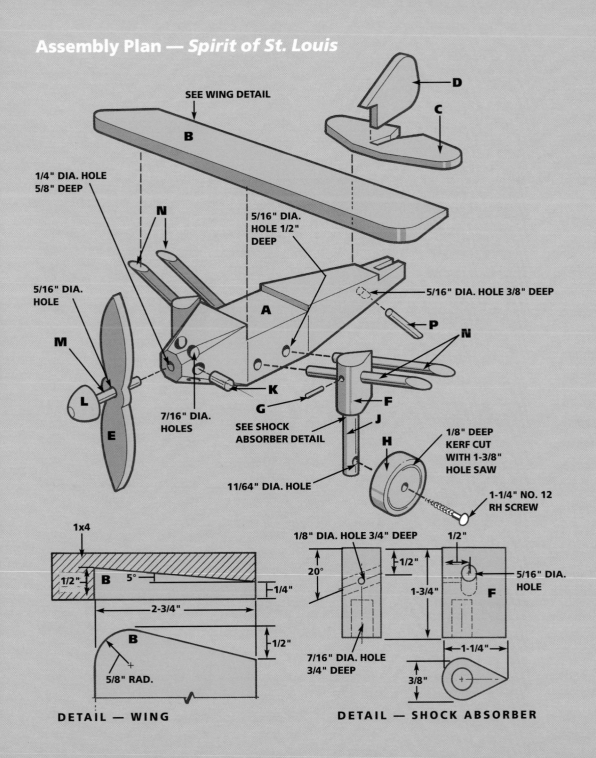

SEE WING DETAIL

1/4" DIA. HOLE 5/8" DEEP

5/16" DIA. HOLE 1/2" DEEP

5/16" DIA. HOLE

5/16" DIA. HOLE 3/8" DEEP

7/16" DIA. HOLES

SEE SHOCK ABSORBER DETAIL

11/64" DIA. HOLE

1/8" DEEP KERF CUT WITH 1-3/8" HOLE SAW

1-1/4" NO. 12 RH SCREW

DETAIL — WING

1x4

1/2"
B 5°
1/4"
2-3/4"
1/2"
B
5/8" RAD.

DETAIL — SHOCK ABSORBER

1/8" DIA. HOLE 3/4" DEEP
20°
1/2"
1-3/4"
F
5/16" DIA. HOLE
7/16" DIA. HOLE 3/4" DEEP
1-1/4"
3/8"
1/2"

Cutting List

Key	Pcs.	Size and Description
A	1	2-1/4" x 2-1/4" x 10" (fuselage)
B	1	1/2" x 2-3/4" x 15" (wing)
C	1	1/4" x 2-1/4" x 6-1/4" (elevator)
D	1	1/4" x 2-3/4" x 2-3/4" (rudder)
E	1	1/4" x 1" x 7" (propeller)
F	2	3/4" x 1-1/4" x 1-3/4" (shock absorbers)
G	2	1/8" diameter x 3/4" (lock pins)
H	2	1-3/4" diameter x 1/2" (wheels)
J	2	7/16" diameter x 2" (wheel struts)
K	8	7/16" diameter x 3/4" (engine cylinders)
L	1	1" diameter x 3/4" (propeller hub)
M	1	1/4" diameter x 1-1/2" (propeller shaft)
N	4	5/16" diameter x 5" (wing struts)
P	1	5/16" diameter x 1-1/2" (tail skid)

A *sandbox* steam shovel

This version of the classic child-powered sandbox digger is especially simple for junior earth movers to operate. It's big enough to sit on, and the pieces and hardware are sized to withstand heavy use. Best of all, this project is easy on the builder— you could have a shovel up and running this weekend.

Getting ready

Basic woodworking skills are all you'll need for this project. It requires no wood joinery or even gluing—everything goes together with screws and bolts. A saber saw and an electric drill are the only power tools called for, but a router and drill press will make some of the work go faster and easier.

Assembly Plan

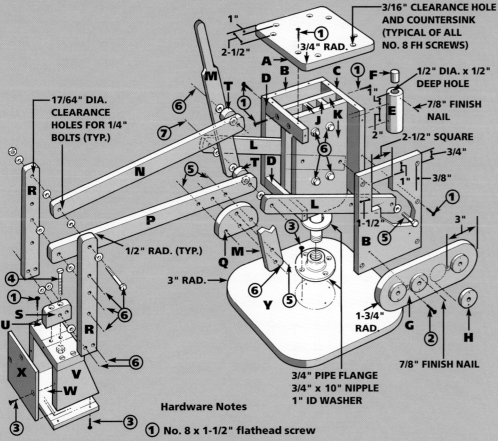

1"
2-1/2"

3/16" CLEARANCE HOLE
AND COUNTERSINK
(TYPICAL OF ALL
NO. 8 FH SCREWS)

3/4" RAD.

1/2" DIA. x 1/2"
DEEP HOLE

7/8" FINISH
NAIL

2"

2-1/2" SQUARE

3/4"

3/8"

17/64" DIA.
CLEARANCE
HOLES FOR 1/4"
BOLTS (TYP.)

1/2" RAD. (TYP.)

3" RAD.

1-3/4"
RAD.

1-1/2"

3"

1"

3/4" PIPE FLANGE
3/4" x 10" NIPPLE
1" ID WASHER

7/8" FINISH NAIL

Hardware Notes

① No. 8 x 1-1/2" flathead screw

② No. 8 x 1-1/4" flathead screw

③ No. 8 x 3/4" flathead screw

④ 1/4-20 x 2-1/2" flathead bolt and nut

⑤ 1/4-20 x 2" hex-head bolt and nut*

⑥ 1/4-20 x 3" hex-head bolt and nut*

⑦ 1/4-20 x 4-1/2" hex-head bolt and nut*

***Use 5/16" washers under all bolt heads
and nuts and between all moving parts**

Cutting List

Key	Pcs.	Size and Description
A	1	3/4" x 9" x 9" oak (cab top, seat)
B	2	3/4" x 7-3/4" x 9" oak (cab sides)
C	1	3/4" x 6-1/4" x 9" oak (cab back)
D	2	3/4" x 1-1/2" x 6-1/4" oak (cab fronts)
E	1	1-3/8" dia. x 4" pine or birch (smokestack bottom)
F	1	1/2" dia. x 1" birch (smokestack top)
G	2	3/4" x 3-1/2" x 11-3/16" oak (treads)
H	8	1/4" x 2-1/16" dia. oak plywood (tread axles)
J	2	3/4" x 1-1/8" x 10-1/4" oak (tube insides)
K	2	3/4" x 6-1/4" x 10-1/4" oak (tube outsides)
L	2	3/4" x 1-1/2" x 16" oak (primary arms)
M	2	3/4" x 1-1/2" x 16" oak (control handles)
N	1	3/4" x 1-1/2" x 20" oak (upper secondary arm)
P	1	3/4" x 1-1/2" x 21-1/2" oak (lower secondary arm)
Q	1	3/4" x 2-1/2" x 4-1/2" oak (secondary arm cleat)
R	2	3/4" x 1-1/2" x 10" oak (scoop arms)
S	1	3/4" x 1-1/2" x 2-1/2" oak (scoop cleat)
T	2	3/4" x 1-1/2" dia. oak (arm spacers)
U	1	3/4" x 2-1/2" x 5-1/2" oak (scoop top)
V	2	3/4" x 3-1/2" x 4-1/4" oak (scoop sides)
W	1	1/4" x 4-1/2" x 5-1/2" oak plywood (scoop bottom)
X	1	1/4" x 4-1/4" x 5-1/2" oak plywood (scoop back)
Y	1	3/4" x 15" x 15" fir plywood (base)

Construction Details

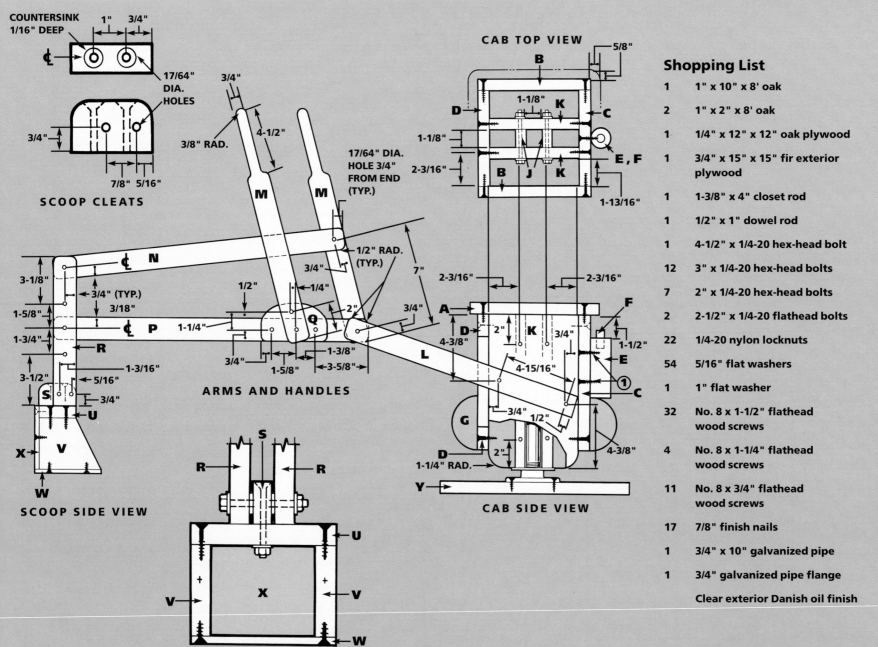

COUNTERSINK 1/16" DEEP

1" · 3/4"

¢

17/64" DIA. HOLES

3/4"

3/4" · 7/8" · 5/16"

SCOOP CLEATS

3/4"
4-1/2"
3/8" RAD.

M · M

17/64" DIA. HOLE 3/4" FROM END (TYP.)

1/2" RAD. (TYP.)

7"

3/4"

3-1/8"
¢ N
3/4" (TYP.)
3/18"
1-5/8"
¢ P
1-3/4"
R
1-3/16"
3-1/2"
5/16"
3/4"
S
U
X · V
W

SCOOP SIDE VIEW

1/2"
1/4"
3/4"
2"
Q
3/4"
1-3/8"
1-5/8"
3-5/8"
1-1/4"

ARMS AND HANDLES

S
R · R
U
V · V
X
V
W

SCOOP BACK VIEW

CAB TOP VIEW

5/8"
B
D · 1-1/8" · K · C
1-1/8"
2-3/16"
B · J · K
E, F
1-13/16"

2-3/16" · 2-3/16"

L

A
D · 2" · K · 3/4" · F
4-3/8"
1-1/2"
E
4-15/16"
C
①
G
3/4" · 1/2"
D · 2"
1-1/4" RAD.
4-3/8"
Y

CAB SIDE VIEW

Shopping List

1	1" x 10" x 8' oak
2	1" x 2" x 8' oak
1	1/4" x 12" x 12" oak plywood
1	3/4" x 15" x 15" fir exterior plywood
1	1-3/8" x 4" closet rod
1	1/2" x 1" dowel rod
1	4-1/2" x 1/4-20 hex-head bolt
12	3" x 1/4-20 hex-head bolts
7	2" x 1/4-20 hex-head bolts
2	2-1/2" x 1/4-20 flathead bolts
22	1/4-20 nylon locknuts
54	5/16" flat washers
1	1" flat washer
32	No. 8 x 1-1/2" flathead wood screws
4	No. 8 x 1-1/4" flathead wood screws
11	No. 8 x 3/4" flathead wood screws
17	7/8" finish nails
1	3/4" x 10" galvanized pipe
1	3/4" galvanized pipe flange
	Clear exterior Danish oil finish

Cut and drill the pieces

1 • Cut out the solid-oak pieces for the cab (A, B, C, D, G), the tube (J, K), the arms (L, M, N, P, Q, R), and the scoop (S, U, V) to the dimensions given in the Cutting List.

2 • Cut out the scoop bottom (W) and scoop back (X) from 1/4-inch oak plywood. Cut out the steam shovel base (Y) from 3/4-inch exterior-grade fir plywood.

3 • Mark the hole locations for all assembly screws and bolts (see Construction Details, opposite). Countersink and drill pilot holes for the No. 8 screws. Also countersink holes for the flathead machine bolts in the scoop cleat (S) so the bolts are recessed about 1/16 inch into the cleat. Use a 17/64-inch bit to drill the holes for these 1/4-inch bolts so they have ample clearance for movement.

4 • Cut out the two solid-oak arm spacers (T) with a 1-5/8 inch hole saw. For the cleanest cut, first drill a 1/16-inch pilot hole through the board. Then drill halfway into the board from each side (Photo 1), using the pilot hole to center the drill bit.

5 • Use a 2-3/16 inch hole saw to cut out the eight tread axles (H) from 1/4-inch oak plywood, using the same technique as in Step 4.

6 • Cut the smokestack bottom (E) from 1-3/8 inch closet rod. Cut the smokestack top (F) from 1/2-inch dowel stock.

7 • Drill a 1/2-inch diameter hole 1/2 inch deep in the center of one end of the smokestack. Set the smokestack top in the hole and pin it in place with a 7/8-inch finish nail.

Photo 1 • Cut the spacers that fit between the arms with a hole saw. For a clean cut, drill halfway through from opposite sides of the board.

Maintenance Tip

Encourage your young sand digger to clean the shovel frequently, in order to keep the working parts from binding and scratching. You can easily touch up worn spots by wiping on some Danish oil finish where needed.

Shape the pieces

1 • Round over the ends of the shovel arms and control handles (L, M, N, P, R) with a router or a rasp and sandpaper. For speed and accuracy, clamp the pieces together and rout them all in one pass (Photo 2). Rout both ends of the long secondary arms (N, P), but only one end of the primary arms (L), the control handles (M), and the scoop arms (R).

2 • Round the top corners of the scoop cleat (S); use a hand file, because the piece is too small to rout safely.

3 • Lay out and cut the shapes of the secondary arm cleat (Q) and the control handles (M).

4 • Lay out and cut the 1-1/4 inch radius corners of the tube outsides (K) and the 1-3/4 inch radius ends of the treads (G). Stack matching pieces to sand the curves smooth.

5 • Bolt together the tube insides (J) and the tube outsides (K) (see the notes in the plans for bolt sizes).

6 • Lay out the windows in the cab sides (B). Drill a 3/8-inch hole in each corner, and cut between the holes with a saber saw (Photo 3).

7 • Lay out and cut the 3/4-inch radius corners of the seat (A). Cut the angled ends of the scoop sides (V) and the rounded corners of the base piece (Y).

8 • Finish-sand the treads (G) and the tread axles (H). Align the axles on the treads, and nail them on with 7/8-inch finish nails.

Photo 2 • Round over the ends of all the shovel arms at once. Clamp them together and to a bench and rout them in one pass.

CAB SIDE

Photo 3 • To cut out the cab windows, drill 3/8-inch holes at each corner, then cut between the holes with a saber saw.

Assemble and finish the shovel

Make a test assembly

1 • Bolt together the shovel arms and control handles (L, M, N, P, Q, R, S, T). Place the bolt heads on the inside to avoid pinch points. Use 5/16-inch flat washers under all bolt heads and nuts and between all pivot points. Also use washers between the scoop arms (R) and the scoop cleat (S). The bolts above and below the lower secondary arm (P) where it joins the scoop arms (R) limit the travel of the scoop and help to eliminate pinch points. Locate them exactly as shown in the side view in the construction details (page 64).

2 • Bolt the primary arms (L) to the assembled tube (J, K) with 2-inch bolts.

3 • Screw together the scoop (U, V, W, X) using No. 8 flathead screws, and bolt it to the scoop cleat (S) without flat washers.

4 • Screw the smokestack (E, F) to the cab back (C), and then screw the cab back to the tube.

5 • Screw the cab fronts (D) to the tube. Now attach the cab sides (B), the seat (A), and the treads and tread axles (G, H).

6 • Screw the pipe flange to the center of the base (Y) (Photo 4). Thread the 10-inch pipe into the flange, place the 1-inch flat washer over the pipe, and slide on the body of the steam shovel. Check to see that everything operates smoothly and without binding.

Apply the Finish

1 • Take the steam shovel apart and finish-sand all parts with 100-grit sandpaper.

2 • Apply an exterior Danish oil finish. When the finish is dry, reassemble the shovel.

3 • Use a hacksaw to cut any protruding bolts flush with their nuts. Smooth the cut ends with a file to eliminate all sharp edges.

4 • Invite your young landscape engineer to climb aboard and start digging sand.

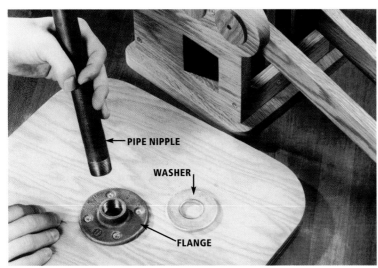

Photo 4 • Thread the pipe nipple into the pipe flange and place the 1-inch flat washer over it. Then slide the body of the steam shovel onto the pipe to rest on the washer.

Earth-moving working toys

Build a road-construction company—all it takes is a few dollar's worth of clear pine, some patience, and a pleasant weekend or two in your shop. This rugged bulldozer, road grader, and flatbed truck will keep a young person or even a team of junior engineers happily busy in a backyard sandbox.

Authentic details and accurate scale are outstanding features of these models. They were designed by Norman Marshall, the master toymaker who also contributed the airplanes on pages 54–61 and the freight train on pages 76–85.

Getting ready

You'll need a drill press to cut the wheels for these toys, but even a small portable one will do. And you'll need various sizes of hole saws: 1-1/4, 1-3/8, 1-1/2, 2-1/8, 2-1/2, and 3-1/8 inches. If you don't have a saber saw or a jigsaw, it's possible to cut all of the other parts with small fine-tooth hand saws. Be warned, though: Although the bulldozer and flatbed trailer are only moderately difficult to build, the road grader, with its many angled cuts and small engine parts, is a challenge.

The parts for all three toys are glued together, so use clamps wherever possible for best adhesion. The models shown in the photographs were left unfinished, but you might want to give the ones you make a finish of clear lacquer or polyurethane to protect the wood and make them easy to clean.

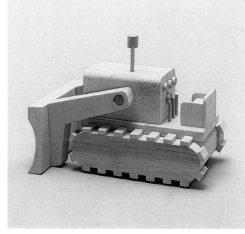

The bulldozer has realistic tracks with cleats, and a two-position blade that's held in its raised position by an interlocking movable exhaust stack.

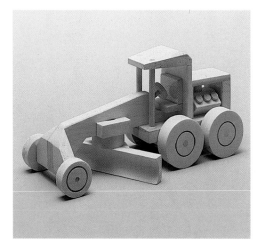

The road grader has lots of engine detail and a blade that swivels. But those features—and the angled parts—also make it a challenge to build.

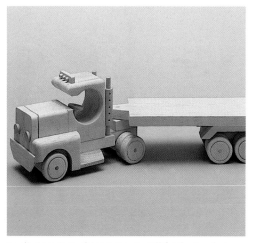

Realistic as it is, this tractor is still fairly simple to build. You also can use the flatbed trailer as a platform for a tanker, a cargo van, or stake sides.

Assembly Plan — Bulldozer

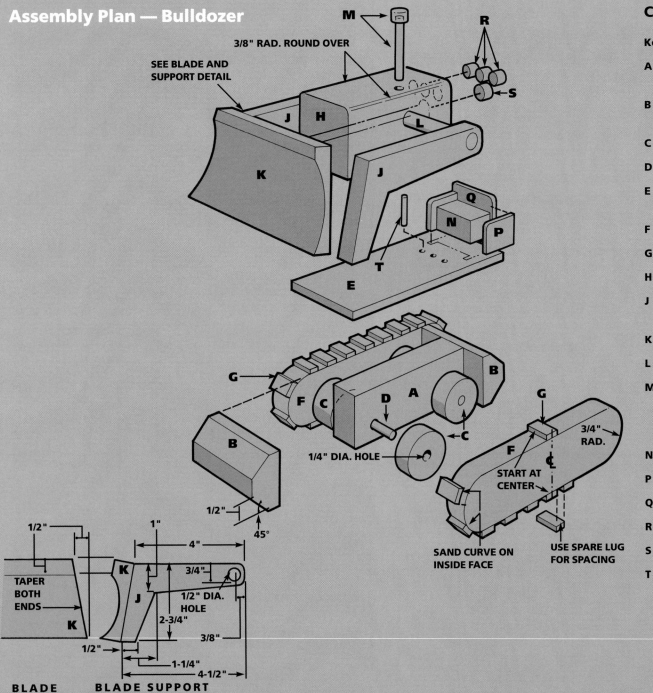

3/8" RAD. ROUND OVER

SEE BLADE AND SUPPORT DETAIL

1/4" DIA. HOLE

START AT CENTER

SAND CURVE ON INSIDE FACE

USE SPARE LUG FOR SPACING

3/4" RAD.

TAPER BOTH ENDS

1/2"

1"

4"

3/4"

1/2" DIA. HOLE

2-3/4"

3/8"

1/2"

1-1/4"

4-1/2"

45°

1/2"

BLADE **BLADE SUPPORT**

Cutting List

Key	Pcs.	Size and Description
A	1	1" x 1-1/2" x 4-1/4" (chassis center beam)
B	2	3/4" x 1-1/2" x 2-3/4" (chassis end beams)
C	4	1-1/4" diameter x 3/4" (wheels)
D	2	1/4" diameter x 2-5/8" (axles)
E	1	1/4" x 2-3/4" x 5-3/4" (chassis platform)
F	2	3/4" x 1-1/2" x 6" (track blocks)
G	36	3/8" x 3/16" x 3/4" (track lugs)
H	1	2" x 2-1/4" x 3-3/4" (engine)
J	2	3/4" x 2-3/4" 4-1/2" (blade supports)
K	1	3/4" x 2-3/4" x 6" (blade)
L	1	1/2" diameter x 4" (blade axle)
M	1	1/4" diameter x 2" (exhaust stack)
	1	1/2" diameter x 1/2" (exhaust cap)
N	1	3/4" x 3/4" 1-1/2" (seat)
P	2	1/8" x 1" x 1" (seat sides)
Q	1	1/8" x 1-1/4" x 1-3/4" (seat back)
R	3	3/8" diameter x 1/2" (gauges)
S	1	1/2" x 1/2" (gauge)
T	3	1/8" diameter x 1-1/4" (control levers)

Build the bulldozer

1 • Glue together two pieces of 5/4 clear pine for the engine (H), or glue together three pieces of 3/4-inch stock.

2 • Cut all parts to the finished sizes given in the cutting list with the assembly plan. Sand all cut edges with 100-grit sandpaper.

3 • Drill 1/4-inch axle holes in the wheels (C). Drill 5/16-inch axle holes in the chassis center beam (A) (see the Section View in the assembly details at right). Slide the axles (D) through the holes, and glue on the wheels (C).

4 • Cut 45-degree bevels on the chassis end beams (B). Glue the parts and beams to the center beam (A).

5 • Cut the 3/4-inch radius ends of the track blocks (F). Glue the track lugs (G) to the track blocks, starting at the top and bottom centers and working toward the ends. Use a spare lug as a spacer for consistent placement. Sand a concave surface on the inside face of lugs that must fit against the rounded ends, using a dowel wrapped with sandpaper. Glue the track block assemblies to the chassis end beams (B).

6 • Round the corners of the seat parts (P, Q) with a saber saw. Make 3/8-inch round overs on the top edges of the engine block (H) with a belt sander or a file.

7 • Drill a 9/16-inch hole for the blade axle (L) through the engine block. Center the axle in the hole, and drill a 1/4-inch hole in the top of the engine for the exhaust stack (M); this hole passes through the blade axle. Remove the blade axle, and redrill the exhaust-stack hole to 5/16-inch diameter to let the stack slide in and out easily.

8 • The blade (K) has a concave face (see detail in the plans). Shape this face with a belt sander or drum sander. Cut the tapered blade ends as shown in the detail.

9 • Cut the angles on the blade supports (J). Locate and drill 1/2-inch holes in the supports for the blade axle (L) (see blade support detail in the plans). Reinsert the blade axle in the engine (H), and glue the blade supports to the axle. See the Section View in the Assembly Details to correctly align the exhaust-stack axle hole with the supports. When the glue is dry, glue the blade to the supports.

10 • Drill the 3/8- and 1/2-inch holes on the rear of the engine (H) for the gauges (R, S), and glue the gauges in place. Drill 1/8-inch holes in the chassis platform (E) for the levers (T) and glue them in place.

11 • Glue the seat sides (P) and back (Q) to the seat (N) with all bottom surfaces flush. Sand the edges of the seat back flush with the surfaces of the sides. Glue the seat assembly to the chassis platform (E).

12 • Glue the chassis platform assembly to the chassis center beam (A) and end beams (B).

13 • Glue the engine assembly to the chassis platform (E).

14 • Finish-sand all parts with 150-grit sandpaper, then apply a clear lacquer or polyurethane finish.

Assembly Details — Bulldozer

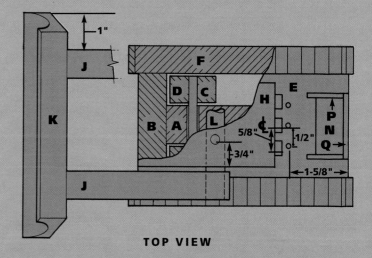

TOP VIEW

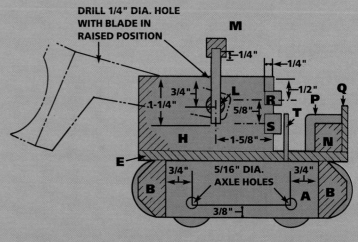

SECTION VIEW

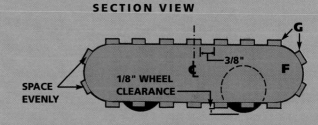

TRACK DETAIL

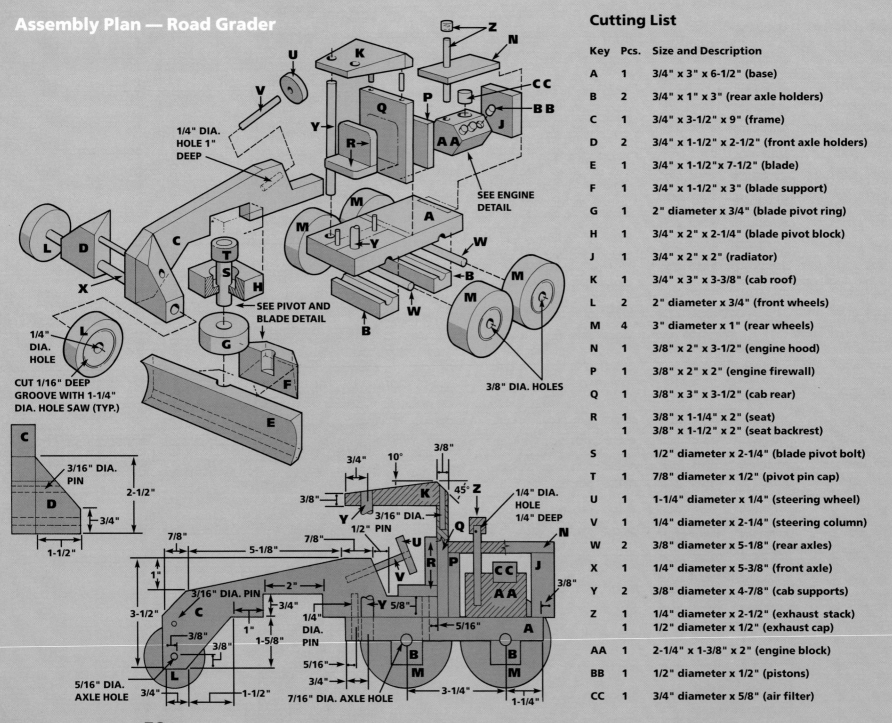

Assembly Plan — Road Grader

Cutting List

Key	Pcs.	Size and Description
A	1	3/4" x 3" x 6-1/2" (base)
B	2	3/4" x 1" x 3" (rear axle holders)
C	1	3/4" x 3-1/2" x 9" (frame)
D	2	3/4" x 1-1/2" x 2-1/2" (front axle holders)
E	1	3/4" x 1-1/2" x 7-1/2" (blade)
F	1	3/4" x 1-1/2" x 3" (blade support)
G	1	2" diameter x 3/4" (blade pivot ring)
H	1	3/4" x 2" x 2-1/4" (blade pivot block)
J	1	3/4" x 2" x 2" (radiator)
K	1	3/4" x 3" x 3-3/8" (cab roof)
L	2	2" diameter x 3/4" (front wheels)
M	4	3" diameter x 1" (rear wheels)
N	1	3/8" x 2" x 3-1/2" (engine hood)
P	1	3/8" x 2" x 2" (engine firewall)
Q	1	3/8" x 3" x 3-1/2" (cab rear)
R	1	3/8" x 1-1/4" x 2" (seat)
	1	3/8" x 1-1/2" x 2" (seat backrest)
S	1	1/2" diameter x 2-1/4" (blade pivot bolt)
T	1	7/8" diameter x 1/2" (pivot pin cap)
U	1	1-1/4" diameter x 1/4" (steering wheel)
V	1	1/4" diameter x 2-1/4" (steering column)
W	2	3/8" diameter x 5-1/8" (rear axles)
X	1	1/4" diameter x 5-3/8" (front axle)
Y	2	3/8" diameter x 4-7/8" (cab supports)
Z	1	1/4" diameter x 2-1/2" (exhaust stack)
	1	1/2" diameter x 1/2" (exhaust cap)
AA	1	2-1/4" x 1-3/8" x 2" (engine block)
BB	1	1/2" diameter x 1/2" (pistons)
CC	1	3/4" diameter x 5/8" (air filter)

1/4" DIA. HOLE 1" DEEP

SEE ENGINE DETAIL

SEE PIVOT AND BLADE DETAIL

1/4" DIA. HOLE

CUT 1/16" DEEP GROOVE WITH 1-1/4" DIA. HOLE SAW (TYP.)

3/8" DIA. HOLES

3/16" DIA. PIN

2-1/2"

3/4"

1-1/2"

7/8"

5-1/8"

7/8"

1"

2"

3-1/2"

3/16" DIA. PIN

3/4"

3/4"

1"

1-5/8"

5/16"

3/8"

5/16"

3/8"

3/4"

1-1/2"

5/16" DIA. AXLE HOLE

7/16" DIA. AXLE HOLE

1/4" DIA. PIN

5/8"

3/4"

10°

3/8"

45°

3/16" DIA.

1/2" PIN

1/4" DIA. HOLE 1/4" DEEP

3/8"

5/16"

3-1/4"

1-1/4"

Build the road grader

1 • Cut all parts to size except the wheels (L, M), blade pivot ring (G), and steering wheel (U).

2 • Make the angled cuts on the blade (E), blade support (F), cab roof (K), and engine block (AA) (see details at right). Then make the angled cuts on the sides of the front axle holders (D); you'll make the front angled cuts later. Cut the profile of the frame (C), again leaving the front angle cut for later.

3 • Cut 3/8-inch rounded outside corners on the seat pieces (R).

4 • Cut the concave face of the blade (E) with a belt or drum sander.

5 • Glue and clamp the rear axle holders (B) to the base (A); when the glue is dry, drill 7/16-inch axle holes in the assembly. Glue and clamp the front axle holders (D) to the frame (C); then drill a 5/16-inch axle hole and a 3/16-inch pin hole through this assembly.

6 • Make the 45-degree angle cut on the fronts of the frame and front axle holders (C, D). Glue the 3/16-inch pin in the assembly, and file its ends flush with the front axle holders.

7 • Make the wheels: Cut 1/16-inch deep kerfs for the front and rear wheels (L, M) with a 1-3/8 inch hole saw. Cut out the front wheels with a 2-1/8 inch hole saw, and drill 1/4-inch holes for the front axle (X). Cut out the rear wheels with a 3-1/8 inch hole saw, and drill 3/8-inch holes for the rear axles (W). Cut out the steering wheel (U) with a 1-3/8 inch hole saw, and drill a 1/4-inch center hole for the steering column (V). Round over all of the wheel edges with sandpaper.

8 • Cut the blade pivot ring (G) with a 1-3/8 inch hole saw. Counterbore a 1-inch hole in the blade pivot block (H). Drill 1/2-inch holes in the pivot pin cap (T), the blade pivot block, and the blade pivot ring. Test-fit the moving blade parts, then glue the pivot pin cap (T) to the pivot pin (S).

9 • Drill 3/8-inch holes for the cab supports (Y) in the base and roof. Drill a 1/4- x 1 inch hole for the steering column (V) in the frame (C). Drill holes for the 1/4-inch pins in the base and the frame. Pin and glue the frame to the base.

10 • Sand the bevel on the roof (K). Drill 3/16-inch holes for the pins in the roof and cab rear (Q). Glue the cab parts (Q, Y) to the base, the seat components (R) to the frame and cab rear, and the roof to the cab supports and cab rear.

11 • Cut the angled sides of the engine block (AA), and drill 1/4-, 1/2-, and 3/4-inch holes in the top and sides (see detail at right). Locate and drill a corresponding 1/4-inch hole in the engine hood (N) for the exhaust stack (Z).

12 • Glue the pistons (BB) and air filter (CC) to the engine block. Assemble the engine compartment (P, J, N). Glue the exhaust cap to the exhaust stack (Z); insert the stack into the engine block through the engine hood, and glue it in place. Glue the steering wheel (U) to the steering column (V) and the column to the frame (C).

13 • Glue and clamp the blade support (F) to the blade (E); then drill a 1/2-inch hole for the blade pivot pin (S). Insert the blade pivot pin through the blade pivot block (H); glue the block into the frame notch, but keep glue off the pivot pin cap (T). Thread the blade pivot ring (G) onto the pin, and glue the pin to the blade assembly so the lower edge of the blade is raised about 1/8 inch when the grader is on a flat surface. Trim the blade a bit if necessary.

14 • Insert the axles into their holders, and glue the wheels to the axle ends.

15 • Finish-sand all parts with 120-grit paper. Seal the wood with a clear lacquer or polyurethane finish.

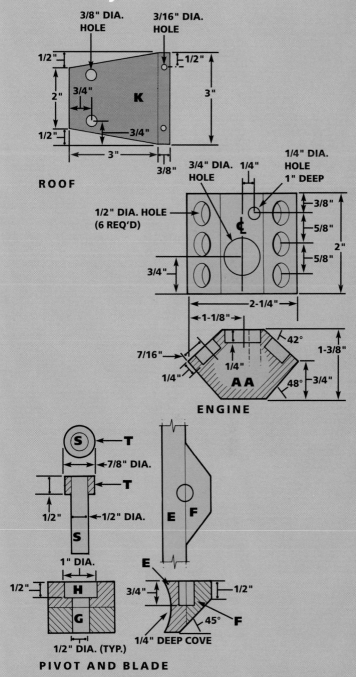

Assembly Details — Road Grader

ROOF

ENGINE

PIVOT AND BLADE

Assembly Plan — Tractor-Trailer

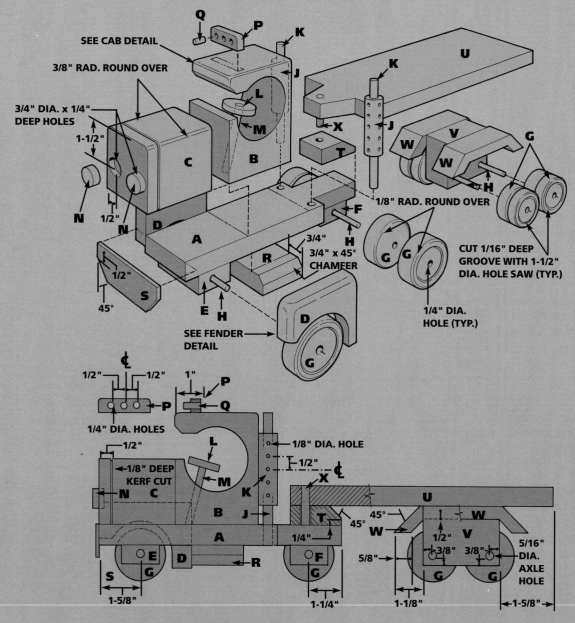

SEE CAB DETAIL

3/8" RAD. ROUND OVER

Q

P

K

J

K

U

3/4" DIA. x 1/4" DEEP HOLES

1-1/2"

L

M

C

B

T

X

J

V

W

W

G

H

N

1/2"

N

D

A

1/8" RAD. ROUND OVER

F

3/4"

3/4" x 45° CHAMFER

H

R

CUT 1/16" DEEP GROOVE WITH 1-1/2" DIA. HOLE SAW (TYP.)

G

G

1/2"

S

E

H

D

45°

SEE FENDER DETAIL

G

1/4" DIA. HOLE (TYP.)

Cutting List

Key	Pcs.	Size and Description
A	1	3/4" x 3" x 9-1/2" (base)
B	1	3" x 3-1/4" x 4-1/4" (cab)
C	1	3" x 2-1/2" x 3" (engine)
D	2	3/4" x 2-1/2" x 3-5/8" (tractor fenders)
E	1	3/4" x 1-1/2" x 3" (front axle holder)
F	1	3/4" x 1-1/2" x 1-1/2" (rear axle holder)
G	14	2" diameter x 3/4" (wheels)
H	4	1/4" diameter x 4-5/8" (axles)
J	2	3/4" diameter x 2-3/4" (mufflers)
K	2	3/8" diameter x 5" (exhaust pipes)
L	1	1-1/4" diameter x 1/4" (steering wheel)
M	1	1/4" diameter x 3" (steering shaft)
N	2	3/4" diameter x 1/2" (headlights)
P	1	3/8" x 1/2" x 2" (cab light holder)
Q	3	1/4" diameter x 5/8" (cab lights)
R	1	3/4" x 2" x 4-1/2" (step)
S	1	1/8" x 1-1/4" x 4-1/2" (front bumper)
T	1	3/4" x 1-1/2" x 2" (trailer hitch)
U	1	3/4" x 5" x 12-1/2" (trailer bed)
V	1	1-1/2" x 2-1/4" x 3" (axle holder)
W	2	1-1/2" x 1" x 5-1/4" (trailer fenders)
X	1	3/8" diameter x 1-3/8" (coupling pin)

C̸

1/2"

1/2"

1"

P

1/4" DIA. HOLES

P

Q

1/8" DIA. HOLE

1/2"

1/2"

L

1/8" DEEP KERF CUT

M

K

X

C̸

N

C

U

B

J

T

45°

45°

W

W

A

1/4"

V

E

D

R

G

F

G

S

G

5/8"

1/2"

3/8"

3/8"

V

5/16" DIA. AXLE HOLE

G

G

1-5/8"

1-1/4"

1-1/8"

1-5/8"

Build the tractor-trailer

1 • Glue together four lengths of 3/4-inch stock for the larger pieces—the cab (B) and engine (C)—and two pieces of 3/4-inch stock for the axle holder (V). Use 5/4 or 3/4-inch clear pine for all other pieces.

2 • Cut out all parts to the sizes in the Cutting List, except for the wheels (G) and the steering wheel (L).

3 • Make the cutouts in the tractor Base (A) and trailer bed (U) with a jigsaw (see Base and Bed details at right).

4 • Round over the top edges of the engine (C), the top edges of the cab (B), the outside edges of the fenders (D), and the corners of the cab light holder (P).

5 • Cut a 1/8-inch kerf on the sides and top of the engine to represent the radiator. Use a table saw or jigsaw, or make the cut by hand with a dovetail saw.

6 • Make the angled cuts and chamfers on the step (R), bumper (S), trailer hitch (T), and fenders (W) with a radial arm saw or jigsaw.

7 • Locate, mark, and drill all holes, as shown in the plans: A 7/16-inch hole in the trailer hitch (T); 3/8-inch holes in the base (A), trailer bed (U), and mufflers (J); 5/16-inch holes in the front axle holder (E), rear axle holder (F), and trailer axle holder (V); a 1/4-inch hole in the cab (B); 1/4-inch holes in the cab light holder (P); 3/4-inch holes in the engine (C); and 1/8-inch holes in the mufflers (J). Test-fit dowels in their respective holes.

8 • Make the cutouts in the cab (B) and the fenders (D) with a 2-1/2 inch hole saw in a drill press (see details at right). For the cab cutout, use a 1/4-inch bit to drill a pilot hole all the way through the piece; then, with the hole saw, cut halfway through the piece, turn it over, and complete the hole from the other side.

9 • To make the wheels, cut shallow 1/16-inch kerfs with a 1-1/2 inch hole saw, then cut out the wheels with a 2-1/8 inch hole saw. Drill 1/4-inch axle holes, and round over the tire edges with sandpaper.

10 • Cut out the steering wheel (L) with a 1-1/4 inch hole saw and drill a 1/4-inch center hole for the shaft (M).

11 • Glue and clamp the parts together as shown in the plans, using small scraps of wood or cardboard to protect the wood.

12 • Finish-sand all parts with 150-grit sandpaper, then apply a clear lacquer or polyurethane finish.

Assembly Details — Tractor-Trailer

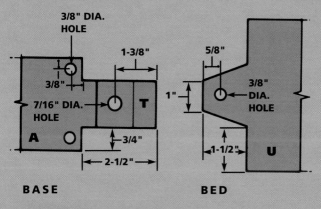

BASE

BED

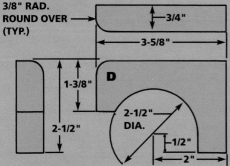

FENDER

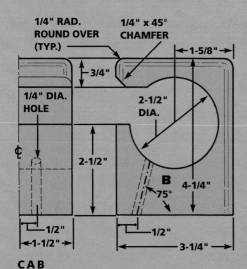

CAB

A realistic model freight train

More than just a toy, this freight train is for everyone: It delights children, it stands up to hard play, and it has enough realism to appeal to train buffs of all ages. Its modular design lets you mass-produce many of the parts, so the authentic-looking cars go together quickly.

The train is built from clear pine and finished with a clear lacquer. You could make it from maple or birch and give it an oil or polyurethane finish. Or you could paint the cars and decorate them with transfer lettering from an art-supply store.

This outstanding design was the work of Norman Marshall. Other toys created by this well-known toymaker appear on pages 54–61 and 68–75.

Safety Tip

Like many other toys with small parts that could break off and be swallowed, this train is recommended only for children age six and older.

Getting ready

You'll need intermediate woodworking skills to build this project. In addition to hand tools you'll need the following power tools: a planer—or the services of a cabinet shop—for the 3/8-inch stock for the bases of the cars, a table saw or radial arm saw, a jigsaw or saber saw, a band saw, and a belt sander or a sanding drum to chuck in your electric drill.

Assembly Plan — Locomotive

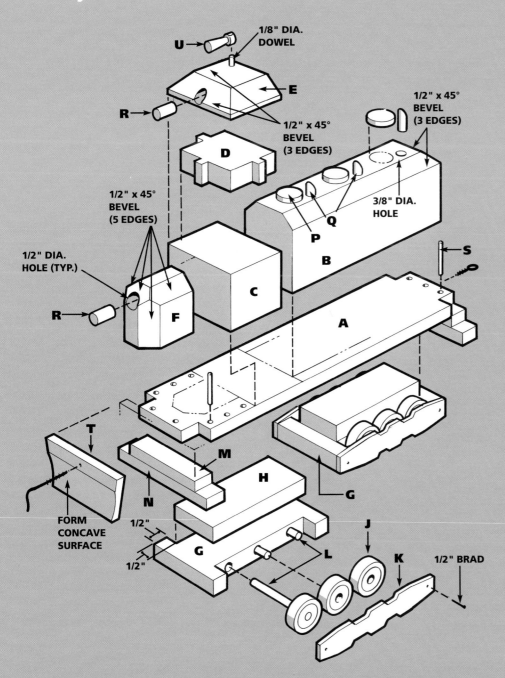

1/8" DIA. DOWEL

1/2" x 45° BEVEL (3 EDGES)

1/2" x 45° BEVEL (3 EDGES)

1/2" x 45° BEVEL (5 EDGES)

1/2" DIA. HOLE (TYP.)

3/8" DIA. HOLE

FORM CONCAVE SURFACE

1/2"

1/2"

1/2" BRAD

Cutting List

Key	Pcs.	Size and Description
A	1	3/8" x 3" x 13" pine (base)
B	1	2-1/4" x 2-1/2" x 7-1/4" pine (engine)
C	1	1-1/2" x 2-1/4" x 3" pine (compartment base)
D	1	3/4" x 2-1/4" x 3" pine (window area)
E	1	3/4" x 2-1/4" x 3" pine (roof)
F	1	1-1/2" x 1-3/4" x 2" pine (nose section)
G	2	1/2" x 2-3/4" x 5-1/4" pine (axle holders)
H	2	1/2" x 1-3/4" x 4-1/4" pine (axle spacers)
J	12	1-1/4" diameter x 3/8" pine (wheels)
K	4	1/8" x 3/4" x 5-1/4" pine (wheel covers)
L	6	1/4" diameter x 2-1/2" birch (axles)
M	2	3/8" x 3/4" x 3" pine (upper steps)
N	2	3/8" x 3/4" x 4" pine (lower steps)
P	3	1" diameter x 3/16" pine (fan covers)
Q	3	3/8" diameter x 1" birch (exhaust pipes)
R	2	1/2" diameter x 1" birch (headlamps)
S	11	3/16" diameter x 1-3/8" birch (stanchions)
T	1	3/8" x 1-1/2" x 3-1/4" pine (pilot)
U	1	3/8" x 1-1/8" birch (air horn)

Assembly Details — Locomotive

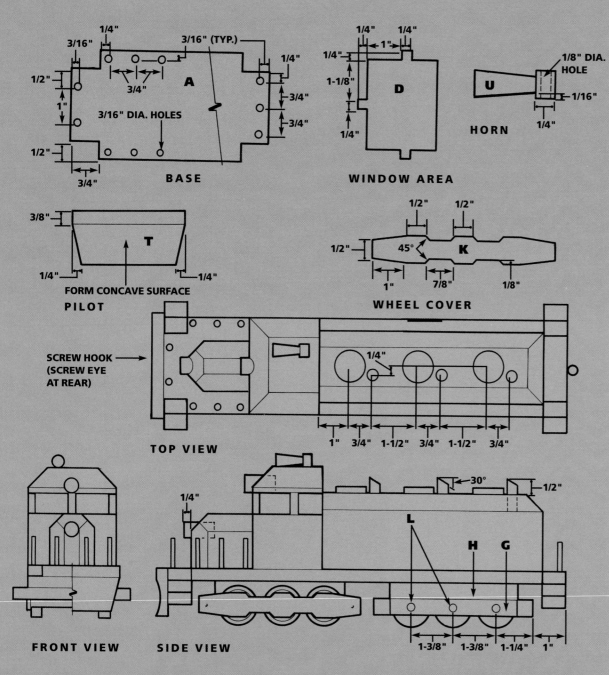

BASE

WINDOW AREA

HORN

PILOT

FORM CONCAVE SURFACE

WHEEL COVER

SCREW HOOK
(SCREW EYE
AT REAR)

TOP VIEW

FRONT VIEW   **SIDE VIEW**

Build the locomotive

1 • Plane or resaw a board for the 3/8-inch stock you need for the base (A). Cut it to 3 x 13 inches, and cut out the 1/2 x 3/4-inch corner notches (see base detail in the Assembly Details at left).

2 • Glue and clamp together three pieces of 3/4-inch stock for the engine (B). Cut the glued-up blank to 2-1/4 x 2-1/2 x 7-1/4 inches, making sure the side that will attach to the base (A) is flat. Cut a 1/2-inch bevel around the three edges of the top of the engine. Drill three 3/8-inch holes in the engine top for the exhaust pipes (Q).

3 • Cut out the dowel exhaust pipes (Q), bevel one end of each pipe at about 30 degrees, and glue them in place on the engine.

4 • Cut the fan covers (P) from 3/16-inch pine with a 1-1/8 inch hole saw, and glue them to the top of the engine (B).

5 • Make the engineer's compartment. First glue and clamp together four pieces of 3/4-inch stock. Cut a block 3 x 2-1/4 x 3 inches, and sand it smooth. This will be cut apart for pieces C, D, and E. Drill a 1/2-inch hole centered near one 3-inch edge for a headlamp (R) (see part E in the Assembly Plan, page 77). Cut a 1/2-inch bevel on that edge and the two adjoining side edges of the same end with a band saw or a sander. Cut off this beveled end in a piece 3/4 inch thick for the roof (E).

6 • From the same block, cut off another 3/4-inch piece for the window area (D), and cut out the notches for the windows (see detail at left). The remaining piece of the block is the compartment base (C). Glue the three pieces (C, D, E) together again to make the finished compartment. Cut one headlamp (R), glue it in the hole in the beveled roof edge, and set the compartment assembly aside.

7 • For the nose section (F), glue and clamp together two pieces of 3/4-inch stock. Cut out a piece 1-1/2 x 1-3/4 x 2 inches. Drill a 1/2-inch hole centered near one 1-3/4 inch edge for the headlamp (R). Using a band saw or sander, bevel the three top and two front edges as shown in the plan. Cut out the headlamp, glue it to the nose section, and then set the assembly aside.

8 • Cut the two axle holders (G) to 2-3/4 x 5-1/4 inches, and drill three 5/16-inch holes through each one (see side view at left). These will let the 1/2-inch diameter axles (L) turn freely. Then make the rectangular cutouts (wheel wells) in the axle holders with a coping saw or a jigsaw. Finally, cut out the axle spacers (H), center them on top of the axle holders, and glue them in place.

9 • To make each wheel (J), cut a 1/8-inch kerf in 3/8-inch stock with a 1-inch hole saw. Then cut out the wheel with a 1-1/4 inch hole saw and drill a 1/4-inch center hole. (All train cars use the same size wheels, so make 52 wheels now and sand their edges smooth.) Cut the locomotive axles (L) 2-1/2 inches long, insert them through the axle holders (G), and glue on the wheels. Make sure each wheel–axle assembly turns freely.

10 • Cut the wheel covers (K) one at a time from 1/8-inch stock with a coping saw or jig-saw. Or cut a piece of 3/4-inch stock to the shape of the cover, and resaw it into 1/8-inch thick sections to make the four covers. Attach the covers to the axle holders (G) with glue and 1/2-inch brass brads. Do not glue them to the wheels.

11 • Cut the steps (M, N) to size. Center M on N, and glue them together. Glue and clamp the completed step assemblies to the underside of the base (A) at each end.

12 • Shape the air horn (U) from a 2-inch length of 3/8-inch dowel (chuck the dowel in a drill and turn it with a file). Drill a shallow hole in the air horn for a 1/8-inch dowel and glue in a short length of dowel as a mounting pin.

13 • Cut the stock extra long for the pilot (T) on the front of the locomotive; this is the diesel equivalent of the old cow catcher. Shape the concave front surface of the pilot with a belt sander or a sanding drum (see plan and detail at left). Cut the pilot to length, cut the side angles, and glue the pilot to the base and front step assembly with its top edge flush with the surface of the base.

14 • Mark the locations of the engineer's compartment (C, D, E), nose assembly (F), and engine assembly (B) on the base (A). Glue on the compartment first, then the other two assemblies.

15 • Locate and drill 3/16-inch holes in the base (A) for the stanchions (S), and glue the stanchions to the base.

16 • Drill a 1/8-inch hole at one side in the top of the roof for the mounting pin of the air horn and glue the horn in place.

17 • Drill a 3/32-inch hole at each end of the engine and attach the screw eye and hook.

18 • Glue the wheel assemblies to the underside of the base (A) (see Side View detail at left for location).

19 • Finish-sand all parts with 150-grit sandpaper, and spray on a clear finish.

Locomotive

Assembly Plan — Wheel Trucks

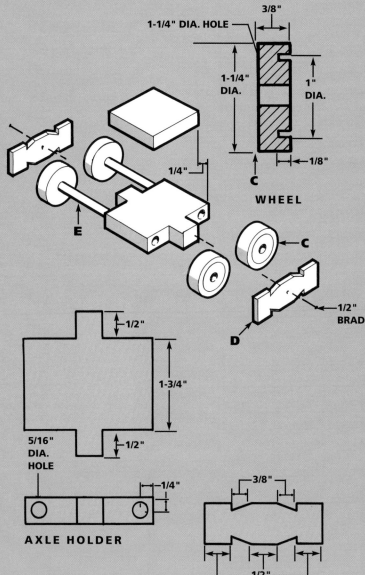

1-1/4" DIA. HOLE

3/8"

1-1/4" DIA.

1" DIA.

1/8"

1/4"

WHEEL

C

C

D

1/2" BRAD

E

1/2"

1-3/4"

5/16" DIA. HOLE

1/2"

1/4"

3/8"

AXLE HOLDER

1/2"

WHEEL COVER

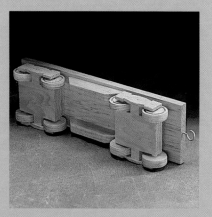

Wheel truck assemblies

Cutting List

For each wheel truck

Key	Pcs.	Size and Description
A	1	1/2" x 2-3/4" x 2-1/2" pine (axle holder)
B	1	1/2" x 1-3/4" x 2" pine (axle spacer)
C	4	1-1/4" diameter x 3/8" pine (wheels)
D	2	1/8" x 3/4" x 2-1/4" pine (wheel covers)
E	2	1/4" diameter x 2-5/8" birch (axles)

Build the wheel trucks

1 ● Each car rolls on wheel assemblies called trucks. The locomotive instructions explain how to cut the wheels (see Step 9, page 79). Use them here to make 10 truck assemblies—two for each car—at one time. Plane or resaw boards for the 1/2-inch stock they require.

2 ● Cut axle holders (A) to 2-3/4 x 2-1/2 inches, and axle spacers (B) to 1-3/4 x 2 inches. Drill 5/16-inch holes for the axles in the axle holders. Cut 1 x 1/2-inch notches (wheel wells) in the axle holders.

3 ● Cut out wheel covers (D) one at a time with a coping saw or jigsaw. Or cut the profile on a piece of 3/4-inch stock at least 3-1/2 inches wide and resaw it into 1/8-inch thick strips for individual wheel covers.

4 ● Glue the axle spacers (B) to the axle holders (A). Cut and install the axles (E), then glue a wheel to each axle end. Check that each wheel-axle assembly spins freely.

5 ● Attach the wheel covers (D) to the axle holders with glue and 1/2-inch brass brads. Do not glue them to the wheels.

6 ● Finish-sand all parts with 150-grit sandpaper and spray on a clear finish. Turn the wheels a few times as the finish is drying to make sure they will spin freely.

Assembly Plan — Flatcar and Stake Car

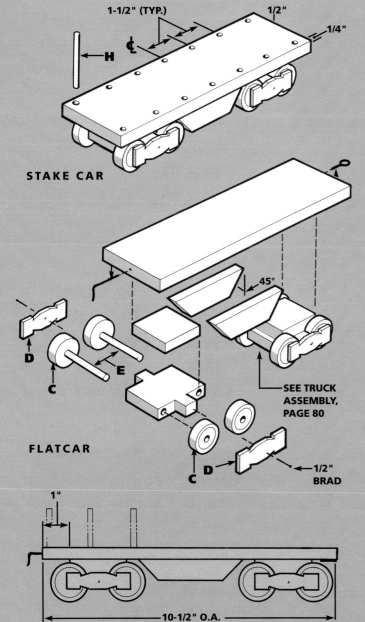

1-1/2" (TYP.)

1/2"

1/4"

H

STAKE CAR

45°

D

C

E

SEE TRUCK ASSEMBLY, PAGE 80

D

C

1/2" BRAD

FLATCAR

1"

10-1/2" O.A.

SIDE VIEW

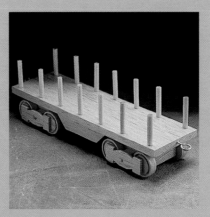

Stake car

Cutting List

For each car

Key	Pcs.	Size and Description
A–E	2	Truck assemblies; see opposite page
F	1	3/8" x 3" x 10-1/2" pine (base)
G	2	3/8" x 3/4" x 3-3/4" pine (base supports)
H	14	1/4" diameter x 1-3/4" birch (stakes; stake car only)

Build the flatcar and stake car

1 • These two cars are identical except that the stake car has dowels along two sides. Plane or resaw thicker stock to 3/8-inch thickness for the base (F), and cut it to 3 x 10-1/2 inches. For the stake car, drill 1/4-inch holes along the sides; hole location is shown in the Side View detail in the plans at left.

2 • For each car, outline the base support (G) on 3/4-inch stock. Cut out the shape, then resaw it to make two pieces about 3/8-inch thick. (Note: The gondola car and boxcar use the same size bases, F, and base supports, G. To simplify cutting, make all four bases and all eight supports at the same time.)

3 • For each car, glue two completed truck assemblies (A–E) to the base (F), locating the axle spacer blocks on the trucks 1 inch from each end of the base (see Side View at right). Glue on the base supports (G), centering them between the wheel trucks and lining them up with the wheels.

4 • For the stake car, cut the stakes (H), round their ends, and glue them into the predrilled holes along the sides of the base (F).

5 • For each car, drill 3/32-inch pilot holes centered in the edges of the base at each end. Install a screw eye at one end and a screw hook at the other end.

6 • Finish-sand all parts with 150-grit sandpaper and spray on a clear finish.

Assembly Plan — Gondola Car

2-3/4"

2-1/8"

3-1/2"

3"

END VIEW

10-1/2" OVERALL

2" — **1-1/2"** — **1-1/2"** — **1-1/2"** — **1-1/2"** — **2"**

SIDE VIEW

Cutting List

Key	Pcs.	Size and Description
A–E	2	Truck assemblies (see page 80)
F	1	3/8" x 3" x 10-1/2" pine (base)
G	2	3/8" x 3/4" x 3-3/4" pine (base supports)
H	2	3/8" x 1-3/4" x 10" pine (sides)
J	2	3/8" x 1-3/4" x 2" pine (ends)
K	14	1/8" x 3/8" x 1-3/4" pine (side reinforcements)

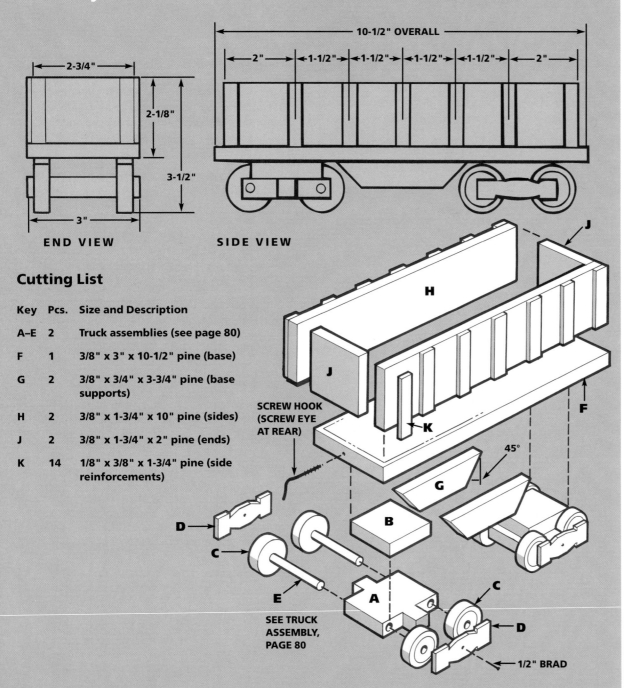

J

H

J

SCREW HOOK
(SCREW EYE
AT REAR)

K

F

45°

G

D

C

B

E

A

C

D

SEE TRUCK
ASSEMBLY,
PAGE 80

1/2" BRAD

Build the gondola car

1 Glue two completed truck assemblies (A–E; see page 80) to one of the bases (F) you cut out previously (Step 2, opposite page). Position the axle spacer blocks of the trucks 1 inch from each end of the base. Glue the base supports (G) in place, centered between the trucks and lined up with the wheels.

2 Cut 3/8-inch thick stock for the sides (H) to 1-3/4 x 10 inches, and for the ends (J) to 1-3/4 x 2 inches. Sand them smooth.

3 Cut long 3/8-inch wide strips of 1/8-inch stock for the side reinforcements (K), and cut off 14 pieces 1-3/4 inches long. Glue seven reinforcements to each side (H), following the spacing in the side view in the plans at left.

4 Glue the sides to the ends (J). Plane and sand the bottom edges of this assembly smooth, then glue it to the base assembly.

5 Drill a 3/32-inch pilot hole in the center of the front and back edges of the base. Screw a hook in one hole and a screw eye at the opposite end of the car.

6 Finish-sand all parts with 150-grit sandpaper and spray on a clear finish.

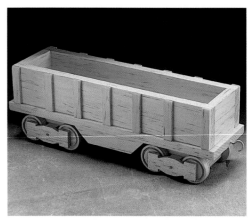

Gondola car

Build the boxcar

1 • Make a flatcar as described on page 81. Then cut two 1/8-inch thick strips for the bottom door rails (N) and glue them along the side edges of the base (F).

2 • Cut the sides (K) and the ends (L). Cut 1-3/4 x 2-1/2 inch openings in the sides and glue the sides to the ends. Sand all edges flush. Center the assembly on the base and glue it in place.

3 • Cut a piece of 3/4-inch stock for the roof (H). (The caboose roof has the same profile, so make it now, too.) Bevel the sides, leaving a 3/4-inch flat area on the top. Resaw the piece to 3/8-inch thickness and cut it to length.

4 • Cut the vent strip (J) and glue it to the top of the roof. Then cut out the top door rails (M) and glue them to the underside of the roof. Sand the ends of the roof assembly flush and glue it to the car assembly.

5 • Make the ladders. (Also make the caboose ladder now; it has one extra rung.) Drill holes at the rung locations in 1/4-inch stock, then resaw the piece in half for rails (T) 1/8 inch thick. Cut the rungs (U) a bit long, glue them in the rails, and sand the ends flush. Cut the ladder supports (V) and glue them to the ends of the car. Glue a ladder to each support.

6 • Resaw stock to 1/8 inch thick for the doors (P), and cut them out. Sand the edges until the doors slide freely between the top and bottom rails on each side of the car.

7 • Cut the top and bottom door braces (Q) and glue them to the doors. Cut the diagonal braces (R) to fit, and glue them in place. Fit the doors into the rails, and cut out and glue on the doorstops (S) at the rail ends.

8 • Drill pilot holes in the front and back edges, and screw in a hook and eye. Finish-sand all parts and spray on a clear finish.

Assembly Plan — Boxcar

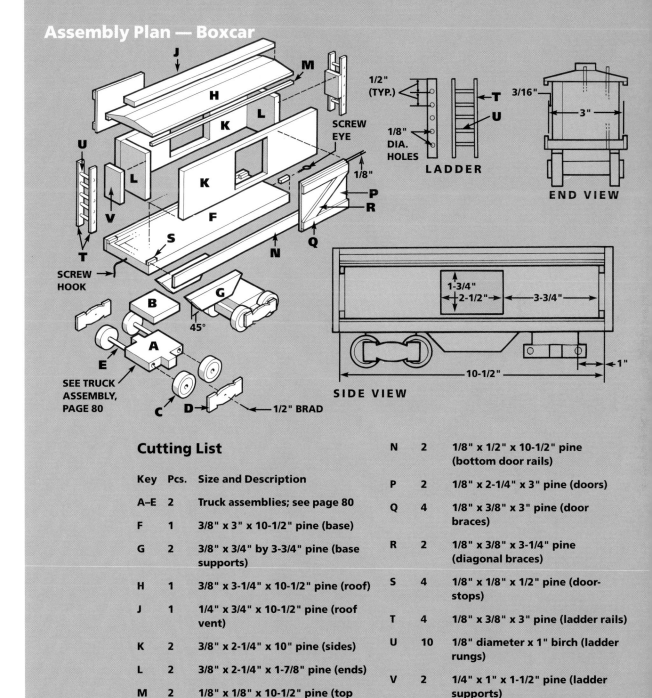

Cutting List

Key	Pcs.	Size and Description
A–E	2	Truck assemblies; see page 80
F	1	3/8" x 3" x 10-1/2" pine (base)
G	2	3/8" x 3/4" by 3-3/4" pine (base supports)
H	1	3/8" x 3-1/4" x 10-1/2" pine (roof)
J	1	1/4" x 3/4" x 10-1/2" pine (roof vent)
K	2	3/8" x 2-1/4" x 10" pine (sides)
L	2	3/8" x 2-1/4" x 1-7/8" pine (ends)
M	2	1/8" x 1/8" x 10-1/2" pine (top door rails)
N	2	1/8" x 1/2" x 10-1/2" pine (bottom door rails)
P	2	1/8" x 2-1/4" x 3" pine (doors)
Q	4	1/8" x 3/8" x 3" pine (door braces)
R	2	1/8" x 3/8" x 3-1/4" pine (diagonal braces)
S	4	1/8" x 1/8" x 1/2" pine (door-stops)
T	4	1/8" x 3/8" x 3" pine (ladder rails)
U	10	1/8" diameter x 1" birch (ladder rungs)
V	2	1/4" x 1" x 1-1/2" pine (ladder supports)

Assembly Plan — Caboose

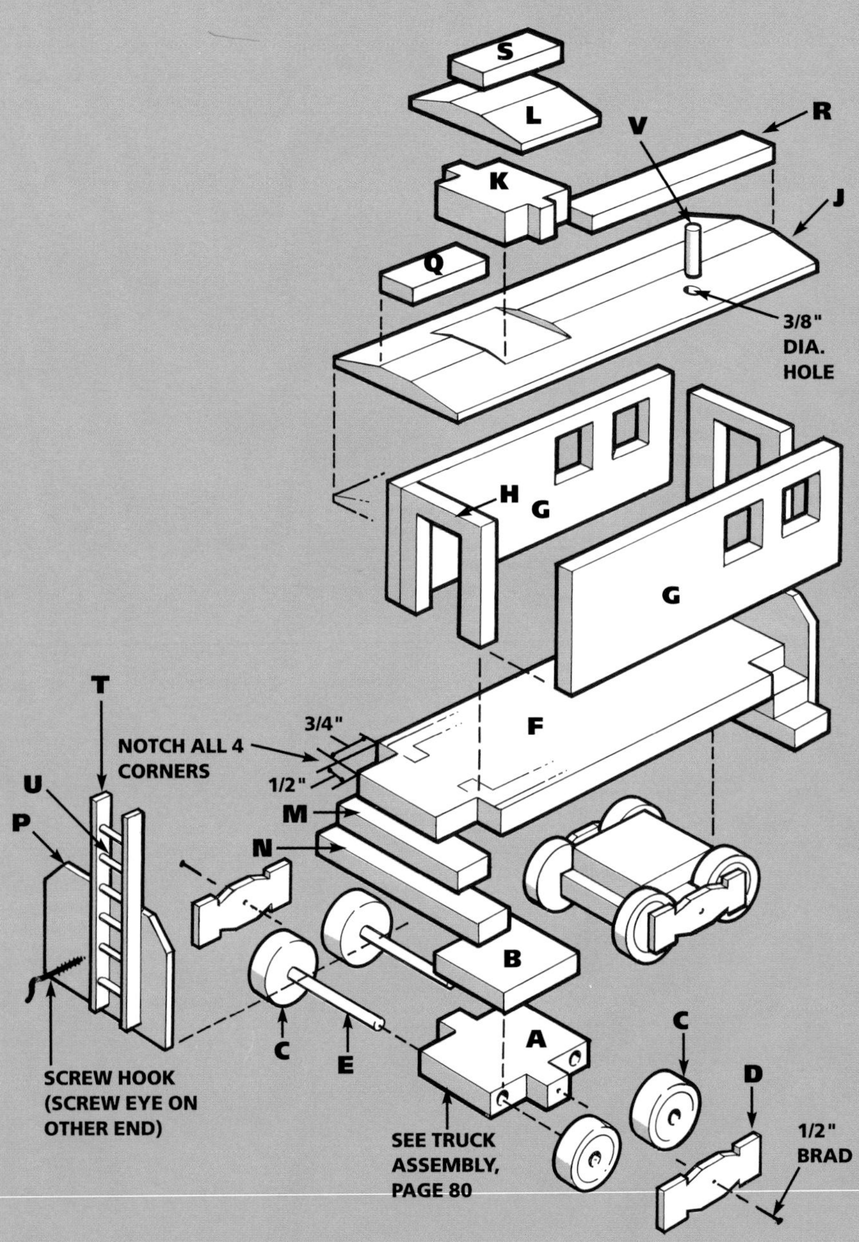

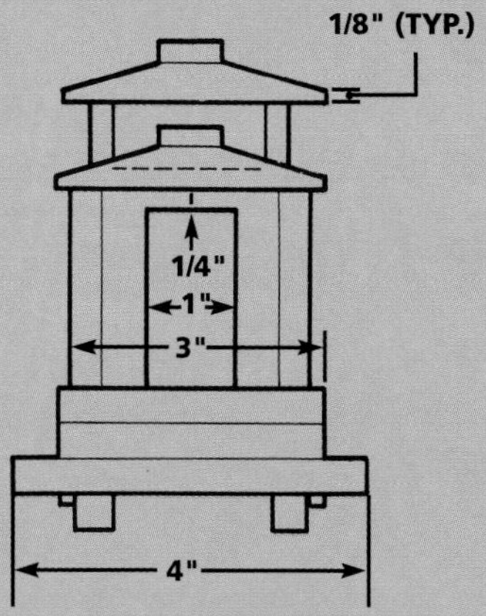

S

L

K

V

R

Q

J

3/8" DIA. HOLE

H

G

G

F

NOTCH ALL 4 CORNERS

3/4"

1/2"

T

U

P

M

N

B

C

E

A

C

D

1/2" BRAD

SCREW HOOK (SCREW EYE ON OTHER END)

SEE TRUCK ASSEMBLY, PAGE 80

END VIEW

1/8" (TYP.)

1/4"

1"

3"

4"

Caboose

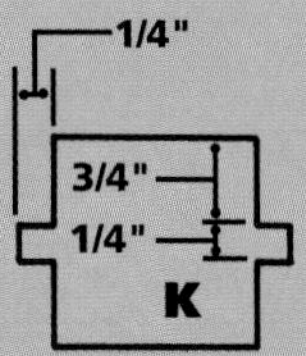

CUPOLA

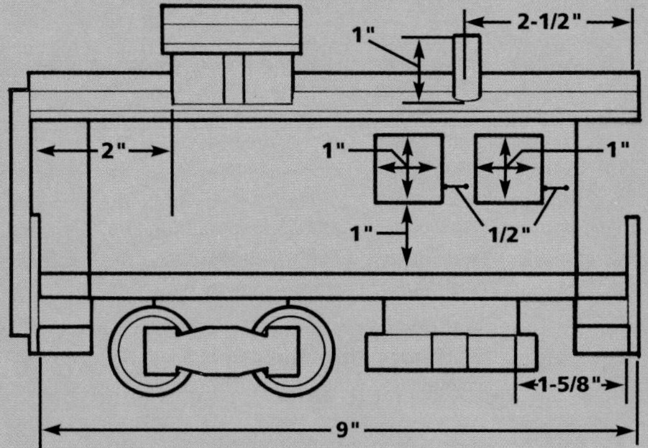

1/4"

3/4"

1/4"

K

SIDE VIEW

1"

2-1/2"

2"

1"

1"

1"

1/2"

1-5/8"

9"

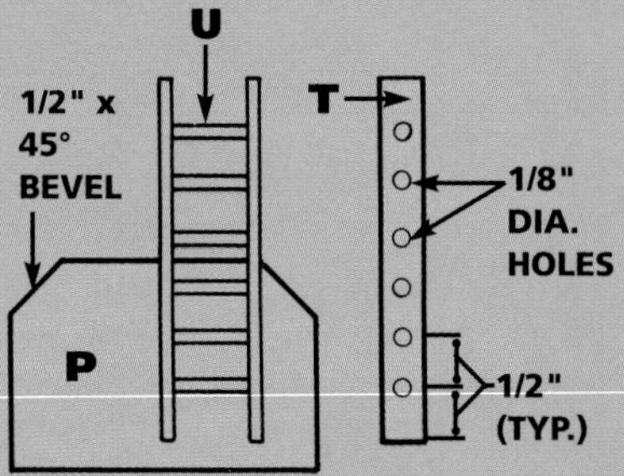

END RAIL/LADDER

U

1/2" x 45° BEVEL

T

P

1/8" DIA. HOLES

1/2" (TYP.)

Cutting List

Key	Pcs.	Size and Description
A–E	2	Truck assemblies; see page 80
F	1	3/8" x 3" x 8-3/4" pine (base)
G	2	3/8" x 2-1/4" x 7-1/4" pine (sides)
H	2	3/8" x 2-1/4" x 2" pine (ends)
J	1	3/8" x 3" x 9" pine (main roof)
K	1	3/4" x 2-1/4" x 1-3/4" pine (cupola)
L	1	3/8" x 2" x 2-3/4" pine (cupola roof)
M	2	3/8" x 3/4" x 3" pine (upper steps)
N	2	3/8" x 3/4" x 4" pine (lower steps)
P	2	1/8" x 3" x 2" pine (end rails)
Q	1	1/4" x 3/4" x 2" pine (small vent)
R	1	1/4" x 3/4" x 5-1/4" pine (large vent)
S	1	1/4" x 3/4" x 2" pine (cupola roof vent)
T	2	1/8" x 3/8" x 3-1/2" pine (ladder rails)
U	6	1/8" diameter x 1" birch (ladder rungs)
V	1	3/8" diameter x 1-1/4" birch (smokestack)

Build the caboose

1 • Cut 3/8-inch thick stock for the base (F) to 3 x 8-3/4 inches, then cut a notch 1/2 x 3/4 inches in each corner. Glue two truck assemblies (see page 80) to the base, placing the axle spacer blocks 1 inch from the ends.

2 • Cut the upper and lower steps (M, N) to size, then clamp and glue them to the base (F).

3 • Cut the sides (G) and ends (H) to size, and use a jigsaw or a coping saw to cut the window and door openings (see Side View and End View in the plans, opposite page). Glue the sides to the ends, sand the edges flush, and glue the assembly to the base.

4 • Lay out the end rails (P) so the wood grain runs vertically. Cut out the rails, bevel the upper corners (see detail in plans). Glue them to the steps and edge of the base at each end of the caboose.

5 • Cut the cupola (K) to 2-1/4 x 1-3/4 inches, then use a jigsaw or a coping saw to cut away the sides to simulate windows. Then set the cupola aside.

6 • For the roof (J), cut a 9-inch length of the stock you shaped for the boxcar. Drill a 3/8-inch hole for the smokestack (V), and chisel or saw the flat area where the cupola (K) attaches. File the area smooth so the cupola sits flat.

7 • Make the cupola roof (L) as you did the boxcar and caboose roofs, but use 2-inch wide stock. Cut the shaped and resawed piece to 2-3/4 inches long.

8 • Glue the cupola roof (L) and cupola roof vent (S) to the top of the cupola (K), and glue the cupola assembly to the caboose roof (J).

9 • Cut out the small and large vents (Q, R), and glue them to the roof (J). Sand the ends of the roof flush and glue it to the caboose, lining up the rear edge of the roof with the end rail (P) (see the Side View detail in the plans).

10 • Glue the ladder (T, U) that you made earlier (see Step 5, page 83) to the end of the caboose nearest the cupola. It is offset to the right side of the rail (P) on the end (see detail in the plans).

11 • Drill a 3/32-inch pilot hole centered in the front and back rails, at a height to match the other cars. Screw in a hook at one end and an eye at the other end.

12 • Finish-sand all parts with 150-grit sandpaper and finish in the same way as all the other train cars. Hook them all together and: All aboard! You're ready to roll.

Games

Chinese Checkers Game

This beautiful hardwood board and box invite everybody to play this age-old game of strategy.

92

Marble Hockey Game

Building this playroom classic won't require much skill, but you'll need *lots* of skill to block those fast-moving goal shots.

88

Ring Toss Game

A fun game for anyone, anywhere. Clever built-in storage makes this set easy to transport, too.

96

Jigsaw Puzzles

All you need is the right saw, a little cutting practice, and a favorite picture to make a custom puzzle anyone would love to piece together.

100

Tabletop Soccer Game

Here's some off-the-field fun for soccer and hockey fans. Rugged construction holds up to plenty of hard play.

106

An exciting **marble hockey game**

Drop a marble on the face-off square in the middle of the board, then flip the paddles to shoot it toward your opponent's goal. But watch your own goal— that marble is going to come whistling right back!

A slight hump in the middle of the playing surface keeps the marble always in play. And the paddles have a superfast action to keep the game exciting.

Getting ready

This is a perfect project for a beginning woodworker. It requires only basic skills and minimal power tools—an electric drill, portable saber saw, and circular saw are enough. However, a table saw or radial arm saw and a jigsaw will give you cleaner cuts.

The only part of the project that's at all time-consuming is sanding the curved parts. You can do the work by hand with a file and sandpaper wrapped around a curved block, but a sanding drum in your electric drill will be quicker and easier, and a power sander will make finishing go faster, too.

Assembly Plan

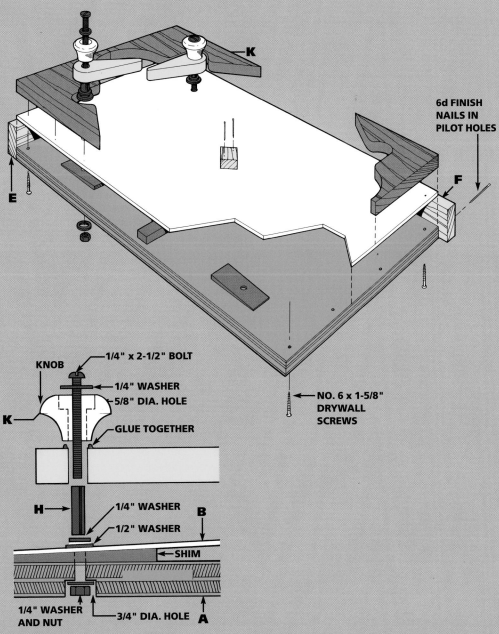

6d FINISH NAILS IN PILOT HOLES

K

F

E

NO. 6 x 1-5/8" DRYWALL SCREWS

KNOB DETAIL

- 1/4" x 2-1/2" BOLT
- KNOB
- 1/4" WASHER
- 5/8" DIA. HOLE
- **K**
- GLUE TOGETHER
- **H**
- 1/4" WASHER
- 1/2" WASHER
- **B**
- SHIM
- 1/4" WASHER AND NUT
- 3/4" DIA. HOLE
- **A**

Cutting List

Key	Pcs.	Size and Description
A	1	3/4" x 14" x 28" plywood (base)
B	1	1/8" x 14" x 28" tileboard (playing surface)
C	1	1/2" x 3/4" x 13" pine (center strip)
D	4	3/4" x 7" x 9" oak (corners)
E	2	3/4" x 2-1/4" x 14" oak (frame ends)
F	2	3/4" x 2-1/4" x 29-1/2" oak (frame sides)
G	4	3/4" x 1-3/4" x 5-1/4" oak (paddles)
H	4	3/8" diameter water supply tube (spacers)
J	1	3/4" x 1-1/2" x 1-1/2" oak (face-off square)
K	4	1-1/2" diameter cabinet knobs
L	4	6" x 1-1/2" shims, tapered 1/4" to 1/16"

Materials List

3 feet	1x8 oak
10 feet	1x3 oak
2 feet	1x1 pine
	3/4" plywood (see Cutting List)
	1/8" tileboard (see Cutting List)
	6d finish nails
	No. 6 x 1-5/8" drywall screws
4	1/4" x 2-1/2" slotted round-head bolts and nuts
8	1/4" washers
4	1/2" washers
	Oil finish
	Wood putty

Pattern Pieces

Each square = 1"

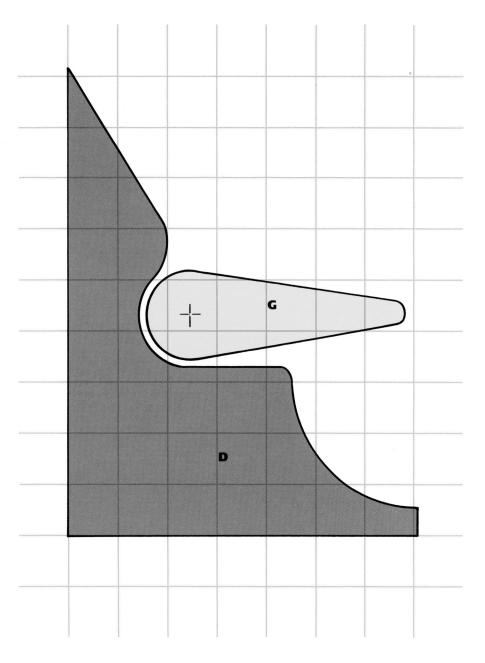

Build the marble hockey game

1 · Cut out the base (A), playing surface (B), center strip (C), and face-off square (J) to the sizes in the Cutting List.

2 · Drill and countersink holes for No. 6 drywall screws in the back of the base (A)—four holes evenly spaced across each short end as shown in the Assembly Plans.

3 · For tapered shims (L), use stock door shims or cedar shingles, available from lumberyards and home centers. Or cut shims from scrap 1x2 pine. Make them about 6 x 1-1/2 inches long, tapering from 1/4 inch to 1/16 inch thick.

4 · Dry-fit the shims and the center strip (C). Adjust the shims so the playing surface (B) is in tight contact with them and with the base (A) at the ends and is smoothly curved. Trim the shims if necessary, but don't locate them more than 3 inches from the ends of the base. Glue on the center strip and the shims (Photo 1).

5 · Draw a grid of 1-inch squares on a piece of 1x8 oak long enough for one corner piece (D) and one paddle (G). Copy the shapes from the pattern plan onto this grid and cut out each piece. Sand the cut edges smooth (Photo 2). Trace the outlines of the remaining three corners and paddles from these pieces, cut them out, and sand them.

6 • Drill a small hole all the way through each knob (K) from the bottom to mark the center of the knob top.

7 • Secure each knob with a wooden clamp or with V-shaped blocks in a vise and drill a 5/8-inch counterbore hole in the top.

8 • Glue the knobs (K) to the paddles (G), centering them over the points where the paddle holes will be located.

9 • Drill 7/16-inch holes through the knobs (K) and paddles (G).

10 • Clamp the playing surface (B) and the corner pieces (D) to the base at one end, with all edges aligned. Drill up through the four holes in the base to make 1/8-inch screw holes in the pieces above. Drive No. 6 x 1-5/8 inch

drywall screws into these holes to fasten the playing surface and corner pieces. Remove the clamps and repeat the procedure at the other end of the base.

11 • Use a small bit to predrill holes for the paddle bolts through the playing surface (B), shims (C), and base (A). This will locate the holes on the base bottom.

12 • Drill 3/4-inch counterbore holes in the bottom, and then 1/4-inch holes for the bolts that are the paddle pivots.

13 • Cut lengths of 3/8-inch diameter sink or toilet water supply tubing with a hacksaw to make spacers (H). Be sure the ends are square and that they extend 1/16 inch below the bottom of the paddle when inserted fully into

the paddle. Assemble and test the paddles for good action (see Knob Detail in the Assembly Plans and Photo 3).

14 • Sand the sides of the corners and playing surface flush with the edges of the base.

15 • Cut the frame pieces (E, F), sand them smooth, and drill pilot holes for the finish nails in the frame pieces and the base.

16 • Disassemble, finish-sand all parts with 100-grit sandpaper, and apply an oil finish. Reassemble, nail on the sides and ends, set the nailheads, and putty all nail holes.

Working Tip

The best playing surface (piece B) is smooth tileboard, a plastic-surfaced paneling sold in 4- x 8-foot sheets. You need only a small piece, so check the damaged-goods bin at your home center for a small piece of scrap. If you can't locate tileboard, substitute tempered hardboard spray-painted white, or a piece of white plastic laminate.

BUILD THE MARBLE HOCKEY GAME

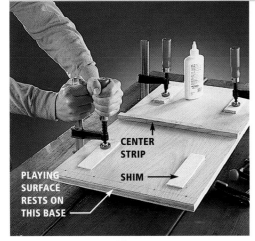

Photo 1 • Glue the shims and center strip to a plywood base so the playing surface will bend over them and gently slope toward each end.

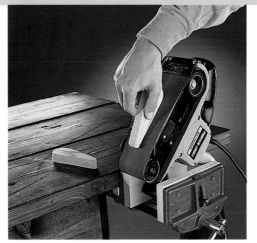

Photo 2 • Smooth the curved parts with a clamped belt sander or a sanding drum in an electric drill, or by hand with a file and sandpaper.

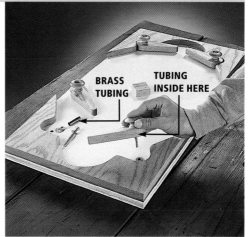

Photo 3 • Each paddle assembly contains a spacer made from a short length of plumbing tubing for a free-swinging action.

An *easy-to-build* Chinese checkers game

Chinese checkers is a classic family game. The rules are simple—although they involve plenty of strategy—and two to six people can play.

This version has a classy hard-wood playing board that lifts out of a cherry-edged box for access to storage space for the marble playing pieces. To simplify the project, you could build just the playing board.

Getting ready

This is another project that's ideal for beginning woodworkers. You'll need just an electric drill with a countersink bit and a table saw or a radial arm saw. For the wide playing board, you may be able to buy already glued-up stock at a local home center. If not, glue and clamp hardwood boards edge to edge.

The most exacting part of building this game is laying out the holes on the playing board. The method explained on pages 94–95 simplifies the process.

Assembly Plan

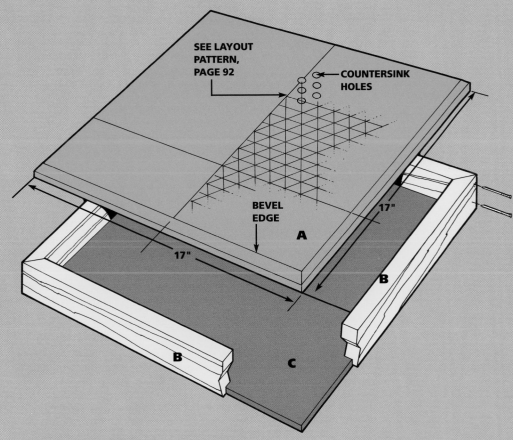

SEE LAYOUT PATTERN, PAGE 92

COUNTERSINK HOLES

BEVEL EDGE

17"

17"

A

B

B

C

SECTION VIEW

A

1/4" x 1/2" RABBET

B

1/4" HARDBOARD

C

CONSTRUCTION TIP

Instead of laying out the hole pattern directly on the playing board (see pages 94–95), lay it out on a piece of heavy paper, so you can make any corrections easily. Mark a colored dot at each hole position on the pattern. Tape the pattern onto the playing board and use an awl of nail to indent the board at each dot. Then remove the pattern and drill the holes.

Cutting List

Key	Pcs.	Size and Description
A	1	3/4" x 17" x 20" cherry (playing board)
B	4	3/4" x 1-1/4" x 17-3/4" cherry (box sides)
C	1	1/4" x 17" x 17" hardboard (box bottom)

Materials List

Ruler

1-inch brads

Wood putty

Stain (optional)

Danish oil finish or equivalent

2–6 sets marbles, 10 of each color or pattern

Pattern for Hole Layout

Method of drawing pattern is explained in text, steps 2–5.

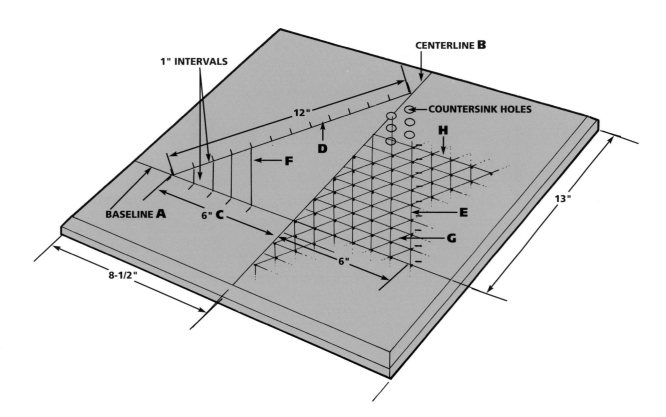

CENTERLINE **B**

1" INTERVALS

CENTERSINK HOLES

12"

D

F

H

BASELINE **A**

6" **C**

E

G

6"

13"

8-1/2"

Build the Chinese checkers game

1 • Glue-up and clamp two or three lengths of 3/4-inch cherry for the playing board, if necessary. Cut it about 3 inches oversize each way.

2 • Draw a baseline, A, and a centerline, B, as shown in the Pattern for Hole Layout. The measurements for locating these lines are taken from the final 17- x 17-inch trim size of the board; remember this when laying out the lines on the oversize board. Use a sharp pencil throughout the marking process.

3 • With a ruler, mark off six 1-inch intervals, C, on the baseline, to the left of the centerline. Do the same thing to the right of the centerline. Then use the ruler to draw lines D and E, and mark off 1-inch intervals on them. This gives you an equilateral triangle with each side 12 inches long.

4 • Draw parallel diagonal lines, F, from the marks along side D to the marks on the baseline. Then draw diagonal lines, G, from side E to each mark on the baseline.

5 • Draw horizontal lines, H, from each mark on side D to the corresponding mark on side E. Extend these lines and the diagonals to form a symmetrical six-pointed star (Photo 1).

6 • Mark each marble hole with an awl or a finish nail and hammer. Make an indentation that will keep the countersink bit from straying. Holes are located at every point where three layout lines cross, and at the tip of each point of the star.

7 • Drill the marble holes with a countersink bit. Use a new four- or six-flute bit for a clean cut. Set the tip of the bit in the indentation for each hole before starting the drill. If you use a hand drill (Photo 2), you can either judge hole depth by eye or mark the bit with a felt-tip pen. If you have a drill press, set it for the desired depth; it will give you greater control and will speed the work.

8 • Trim the playing board to its final size of 17 x 17 inches, making sure the playing area is centered in the board.

9 • Cut a 1/4- x 1/2-inch rabbet around the back of the playing board with several passes of your table saw or radial arm saw. Then cut the bevel around the top edges of the board.

10 • Cut the sides (B) and bottom (C) of the storage box. Rabbet the sides so the bottom will fit flush, and miter the ends for the corner joints. Assemble the box with glue and 1-inch brads; drill pilot holes for the brads.

11 • Finish-sand the sides (B) and playing board (A). Sandpaper wrapped into a cone shape will help you smooth the edges of the marble holes. Darken each hole with stain if you wish. Apply an oil finish to all parts, and fill all nail holes with wood putty.

BUILD THE CHINESE CHECKERS GAME

Photo 1 • Lay out marble holes by drawing a triangle 12 inches on a side and marking 1-inch intervals on each leg. Connect and extend the marks to plot the hole locations.

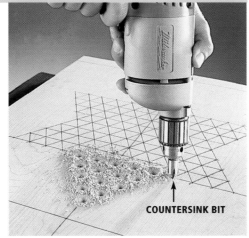

Photo 2 • Drill marble holes with a countersink bit in a portable drill. For greater precision, use a portable drill guide or a drill press to control hole depth and placement.

Playing Chinese Checkers

Each player starts with a set of ten marbles in one point of the star and, taking turns, tries to move them all into the opposite point directly across the board.

You can move a marble in any direction, either into an adjacent empty hole (Figure A) or by jumping a line of your own or other players' marbles to reach an empty hole (Figure B). You can make continuous multiple jumps that go forward, sideways, or until you reach a spot where there are no more marbles to jump over (Figure C,D).

A move or jump is only to change position. You do not remove marbles that are jumped. Also, you are not allowed to keep marbles in your point simply to block your opponent from getting there.

The first player to move all his or her marbles across the board and into the opposite point of the star wins the game.

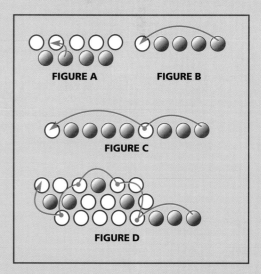

FIGURE A   **FIGURE B**

FIGURE C

FIGURE D

A *self-storing* ring-toss game

This take-anywhere game is simple to play—just position the bases to suit your skill level, insert the posts, and start tossing rings. As a bonus, the whole game stores compactly within the two base pieces so nothing can get lost.

Getting ready

The only power tools you'll need to make this game are a saber saw, a router, and an electric drill. Large clamps are handy for holding the parts of the base together while the glue dries. If you don't have clamps—or if they're not deep enough—you can put heavy weights on the parts. Use spray enamel to make the finish work simple.

Assembly Plan

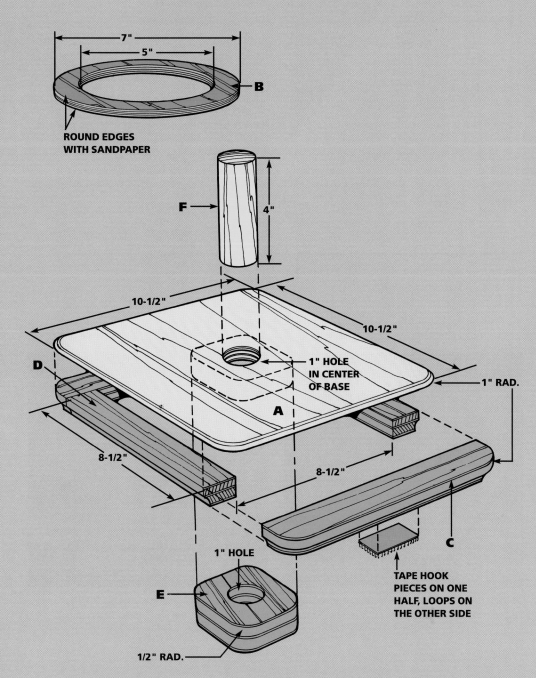

7"

5"

B

ROUND EDGES WITH SANDPAPER

F

4"

10-1/2"

10-1/2"

1" HOLE IN CENTER OF BASE

1" RAD.

D

A

8-1/2"

8-1/2"

C

1" HOLE

E

1/2" RAD.

TAPE HOOK PIECES ON ONE HALF, LOOPS ON THE OTHER SIDE

Cutting List

Key	Pcs.	Size and Description
A	2	1/4" x 10-1/2" x 10-1/2" plywood (bases)
B	4	1/4" x 9" x 9" plywood (rings)
C	4	1/2" x 1" x 10-1/2" plywood (edges)
D	4	1/2" x 1" x 8-1/2" plywood (edges)
E	2	1/2" x 2" x 2" plywood (post supports)
F	2	1" diameter x 4" dowel (posts)

Materials List

1	1/4" x 24" x 36" plywood
1	1/2" x 12" x 24" plywood
1	1" diameter x 10" dowel
12 inches	3/4" adhesive-backed hook-and-loop tape
	White spray enamel primer
	Orange, yellow, blue, pink spray enamel

Build the ring-toss game

1 • Cut the bases (A), the rings (B), the base edges (C, D), the post supports (E), and the posts (F) to the sizes given in the Cutting List. The cutting size for the rings is intentionally large, to provide support for your saber saw when you cut out the circles.

2 • Round over the corners of the post supports (E) to a 1/2-inch radius.

3 • Locate and mark the center point on the faces of both bases (A). Do the same on the undersides of the bases, mark centered locations for the post supports (E), and glue them in place on the underside.

4 • When the glue is dry, drill holes for the posts with a 1-inch spade bit (Photo 1). For smooth edges, drill from the top until the

point of the bit just penetrates the post support. Then turn over the base and drill from the bottom to complete the hole.

5 • Glue and clamp the long edges (C) to the undersides of the bases (A), then glue and clamp the short edges (D) between them. Butt the pieces together tightly and keep their outside edges flush with the edges of the bases.

6 • Cut 1-inch radius corners on the bases (A), including the edge pieces (C, D). Shape the top edges of the bases with a router and a 3/16-inch round-over bit. Then use a 1/4-inch cove bit to rout finger grips along the bottom edges of the bases (Photo 2).

7 • Mark the center of each 1/4-inch plywood ring piece (B). Use a compass to draw the 5- and 7-inch diameter concentric circles. Drill a 3/8-inch hole anywhere inside each 5-inch circle. Start your saber saw's blade in the hole

and cut out the inside circle (Photo 3). Then cut along the outer circle. Use a fine-tooth blade for the smoothest cut.

8 • Round over the edges of the posts (F) and the inside and outside edges of the rings (B) with 80-grit sandpaper. Finish-sand all parts with 100-grit paper.

9 • Spray all parts with white enamel primer. Lightly sand the primer coat after it's dry, and spray-paint the parts distinctive colors. For example, paint two rings blue and the other two pink. Paint the bases orange, and the posts yellow. Let the enamel dry for 48 hours.

10 • Cut the hook-and-loop tapes into four pairs of equal length. Center them on the base edges and press them in place.

BUILD THE RING-TOSS GAME

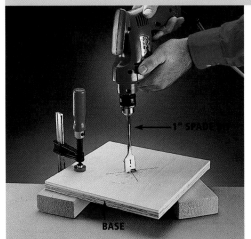

Photo 1 • Drill holes for the posts with a 1-in. spade bit, going through the center of the base and the post support. Drill from the top, then from the bottom.

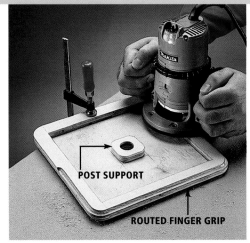

Photo 2 • Rout finger grips on the bottom edges of both bases. They make it easy to separate the bases when they are held by the Velcro closures.

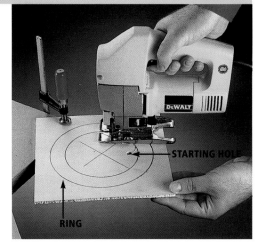

Photo 3 • Cut the inside ring shape first, using a starting hole for the saw blade. Then cut the outer circle. Trace additional rings from the first.

Storing the ring-toss game

1 Four pairs of hook-and-loop tape strips hold the bases together with the posts and rings stored in between. Use adhesive-backed hook-and-loop tape, available at fabric stores and home centers. Finger grips around the edges make it easy to separate the bases.

2 Place the bottom edges of the bases together to create storage space. If you cut six rings instead of four, use thicker edge pieces for additional space between the bases.

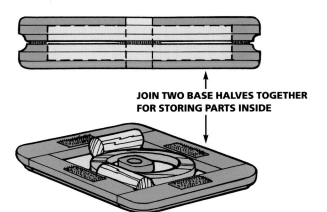

JOIN TWO BASE HALVES TOGETHER FOR STORING PARTS INSIDE

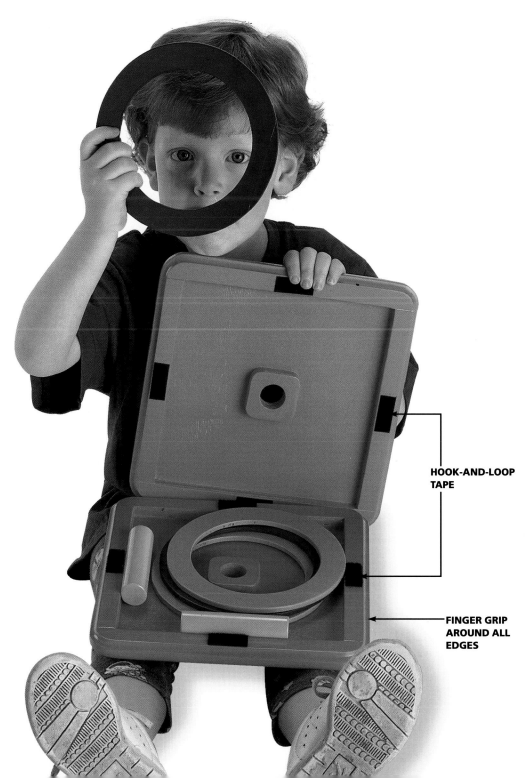

HOOK-AND-LOOP TAPE

FINGER GRIP AROUND ALL EDGES

Personalized photo **jigsaw puzzles**

Here's a great gift for jigsaw-puzzle fans: a "custom" puzzle made from a favorite photo, a child's drawing, or even a heavy-weight page from a magazine. Once you master the cutting technique, it takes only a few hours to turn out a professional-looking puzzle._

Getting ready

You'll need a scroll saw or jigsaw to make smooth cuts on the intricate puzzle shapes—the thicker, wider blades of a saber saw won't work well. Fortunately, even the least-expensive scroll saws are fine for cutting out picture-puzzle pieces.

You can make a puzzle from almost anything that's printed on good-quality, heavy paper; enlargements of photographs work especially well. Pictures printed on thin paper or newsprint are not suitable because they wrinkle easily when glued to the plywood.

Cutting Plans

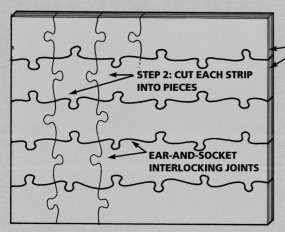

STEP 1. CUT INTO HORIZONTAL STRIPS

STEP 2: CUT EACH STRIP INTO PIECES

EAR-AND-SOCKET INTERLOCKING JOINTS

STRIP CUTTING

Glue pictures with white glue to 1/4" no-void plywood.

Average piece size = photo size ÷ no. of pieces (30 to 50). Do not cut smaller than two pieces per square inch.

Cut at least one interlocking joint on each side of each piece, except outside edges.

STEP 1: DIVIDE INTO FOUR SECTIONS

STEP 2: CUT EACH SECTION INTO RANDOM-SHAPE PIECES

FIRST CUT

SECOND CUT

EAR-AND-SOCKET INTERLOCKING JOINTS

RANDOM CUTTING

CONSTRUCTION TIP

For the smoothest results and best bond, use a stiff, smooth plastic blade to press the picture into the glue on the plywood base. The kind of squeegee blade used for spreading auto body putty is ideal; get one at an auto-parts or hardware store.

Shopping List

Quantity	Item
As needed	1/4" no-void plywood, smooth both sides
As needed	180-grit sandpaper
1 can	Spray-on lacquer or wood finish
1 bottle	Liquid white glue
1	2 or 3" wide paintbrush
1	Stiff plastic squeegee blade
8–10	Binder clips
1 can	Clear acrylic floor wax
10 or more	Scroll saw blades; see text

Scroll Saw

A scroll saw or jigsaw may be a freestanding unit mounted on legs, with moving arms, as shown below. Or it may be a tabletop model with a rigid arm as shown in Photo 6, page 105.

The critical dimension in a scroll saw is the throat depth, which determines the maximum size of the workpiece that can be sawed.

The saw blade passes through a hole in the saw table and moves up and down to cut wood, plastic, or metal. The ends of the blade are secured in chucks or clamps on the upper and lower arms. The table can be tilted for angled cuts through the thickness of the material. An adjustable hold-down prevents the workpiece from being pulled off the table surface on the saw blade's upward stroke. A blade guard (removed for clarity in the photo) is an important safety feature.

Most saws can be operated at different speeds to accommodate various materials. The handiest accessories include a blower tube that keeps the cutting area free of sawdust, and a small adjustable worklight that clamps to the upper arm.

Prepare tools and materials

Saw and blades

1 • Any scroll saw or jigsaw is suitable for cutting puzzles. However, the throat depth—the distance from the blade to the support arm at the rear—will limit how large the puzzle can be. You can easily cut an 11 x 14-inch photo into 300 pieces using a saw with a 15-inch throat. A 16 x 20-inch photo can yield up to 600 pieces, but the scroll saw must have a throat depth of about 20 inches.

2 • Decide the size and number of pieces according to who will be doing the puzzle, then choose appropriate blades. Preschool children can assemble puzzles of up to 25 large-size pieces. Adults can master a puzzle of 250 to 400 pieces in an evening's time; the maximum number of pieces depends only on the dedication of the puzzle fan. In any case, don't try to squeeze in more than two pieces per square inch; such tiny pieces are hard to cut, hard to handle, and easy to lose.

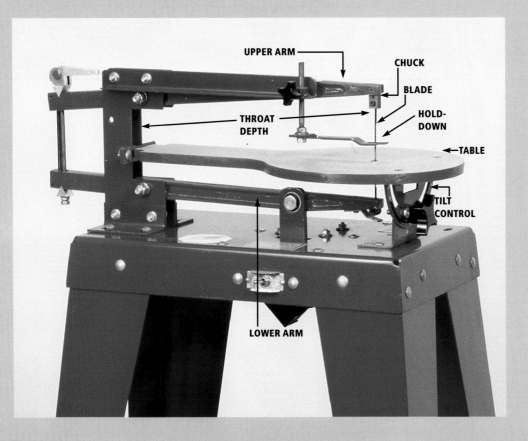

UPPER ARM

CHUCK

BLADE

THROAT DEPTH

HOLD-DOWN

TABLE

TILT CONTROL

LOWER ARM

3 • For most puzzle work, common 5-inch plain-end blades work best. Use blades that are less than .030 inch wide and .011 inch thick, with 25 to 30 teeth per inch. Blade width determines how tight a curve you can cut; blade thickness determines how tightly the puzzle pieces will fit together; the number of teeth per inch determines how smooth the cut edges will be.

4 • Expect to use at least 10 thin, fine-tooth blades in the course of making each puzzle. The blades break frequently as they get dull or pinched; the sound of a breaking blade may startle you at first, but you'll get used to it. If a blade breaks in the middle of a cut, replace the blade and start cutting from another edge until you meet the precise point where the break in the cut occurred.

5 • Set the correct blade tension. Too much will cause your blades to break prematurely; too little will produce sloppy cuts. Also make sure the blade is exactly perpendicular to the saw table. Turning a very tight curve with a tilted table will snap a blade almost instantly. Make practice cuts to find the blade tension and alignment that give you smooth, easy cuts without edge burning or blade breakage.

Plywood

1 • Choose 1/4-inch or 5 mm plywood as a mount for your picture. The wood should be flat and smooth on both sides. Basswood and birch are both good choices for surface woods. The core should be a soft wood like lauan, and should be free of voids. Unless the manufacturer specifically states that the core is "no void," you'll probably find gaps that will weaken the edges of the puzzle pieces. Don't use hardboard—it's weak and hard to cut, and quickly dulls saw blades.

2 • Look for special offers of small panels in various sizes from mail-order suppliers and at lumberyards and home centers. It doesn't make sense to invest in a 4x8-foot sheet of plywood just to make two or three puzzles.

3 • Measure the length and width of the picture, and cut a piece of plywood backing about 1 inch larger in each dimension; you'll trim the excess later. Sand both sides smooth with 180-grit sandpaper and wipe them clean with a tack cloth. Choose the best side as the back of the puzzle, and seal it with three coats of clear spray lacquer or wood finish (Photo 1). This prevents warping and splinters, and helps protect the pieces when handled.

4 • Assemble the other materials you need—white glue, paintbrush, squeegee blade, binder clips—and construct the puzzle.

1/4" PLYWOOD

Photo 1 • Apply three coats of finish to the best side of a piece of thin plywood. This will be the back of the puzzle.

Working Tip

Don't let the ease of using a scroll saw make you careless; keep safety in mind. Always wear safety glasses, remove rings and watches, and roll up long shirt sleeves.

Mount the picture

1 • Before mounting the actual picture you want to use, practice with scrap plywood and a piece of paper that's about the same weight as the one you plan to mount.

2 • Wipe the unfinished (front) side of the plywood and the back of the picture with a clean rag to remove any dust. For pictures other than photographs, lightly moisten the back of the paper with a sponge to reduce wrinkling. Run a bead of white glue in continuous loops over the surface of the plywood, then smooth it out into a thin, even coat, using a 2- or 3-inch wide fine-bristle paintbrush (Photo 2).

3 • Align one end of the picture a bit inside and parallel to an edge of the plywood backing. Gradually lower or unroll the rest of the picture onto the glue. Then use a plastic squeegee blade to lightly press the picture into the glue and remove any air bubbles and wrinkles (Photo 3). Work from the center of the picture toward the edges; be careful at the edges not to pick up glue on the squeegee. If you accidentally get glue on the face of the picture, dab it off with a damp paper towel; don't use a rubbing or wiping motion.

4 • Thick paper may tend to curl up at the edges; prevent that by clamping the edges with binder clips. Place the clips as close to the edges of the picture as possible, and leave them on for 10 to 15 minutes (Photo 4). The binder clips can dent the paper, so you may have to trim away the damaged edges when you cut the puzzle.

5 • When the glue is dry, apply two coats of non-yellowing acrylic floor wax with a paper towel (Photo 5). Let the wax dry overnight; it will protect the picture while you cut the puzzle pieces, as well as later when the pieces are handled repeatedly.

MOUNT THE PICTURE

WHITE GLUE

Photo 2 • Spread a thin, even coat of white glue over the face of the plywood with a fine-bristle paintbrush.

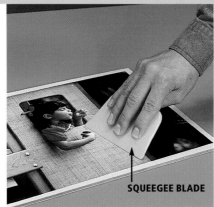
SQUEEGEE BLADE

Photo 3 • Press the picture into the glue with a squeegee. Use light pressure to work out air bubbles under the paper.

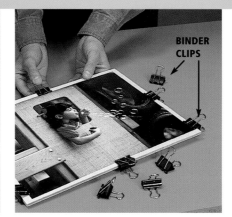
BINDER CLIPS

Photo 4 • Use binder clips around the picture border if the edges start to curl. Trim off the border later.

PAPER TOWEL — FUTURE — FLOOR WAX

Photo 5 • Before cutting, apply two coats of acrylic floor wax. Wet a paper towel with wax and apply in straight, light strokes.

Cut the puzzle

1 • You must cut the mounted picture into pieces with interlocking ear-and-socket joints, no more than two pieces per square inch. Layout and cutting methods are described in the following steps. It's easy to make the actual cuts, but the technique takes some practice. Use the test picture you mounted on scrap plywood to cut out various shapes and sizes until you're comfortable with the procedure. Make cuts with the picture side facing up.

2 • Determine the average size of the puzzle pieces by dividing the area of the picture by the number of pieces you plan to cut. When you make the cut, try to include at least one ear or socket on each side of every piece. A piece with four sides, for instance, should have ears on at least two sides, and sockets on the other sides. Long or irregularly shaped pieces can have an ear and a socket on a single side.

3 • There are two different ways to cut the pictures into a jigsaw puzzle: strip cutting and random cutting (see Cutting Plans, page 101). With either method, start by cutting away the excess plywood and picture border, and any areas along the edges that were damaged by the binder clips.

4 • To strip cut, first saw the picture into horizontal strips with alternating sockets and ears. Then cut each strip crosswise into individual pieces. If a piece has ears on the top and bottom, cut sockets in both sides; it if has sockets

top and bottom, cut ears in the sides. Strip cutting produces a simple gridlike pattern of puzzle pieces, with almost all of them four-sided and square. This is fine for making children's puzzles, but doesn't pose much of a challenge for adults.

5 • Random cutting does not follow a set pattern; instead, you determine the pattern as you cut. Begin by dividing the picture into four large sections (Photo 6). First make an irregular cut across the center of the entire picture from top to bottom. Then make a similar cut from side to side. Now cut each section into individual pieces along meandering lines with sockets

and ears wherever you like (Photo 7). This lets you give each piece a unique shape. Random cutting is slower but more fun to do, and produces puzzles that are a good deal more challenging to assemble.

6 • As you cut out the pieces, reassemble them on a piece of cardboard or plywood so none gets misplaced. When the entire puzzle is cut, place a piece of cardboard or plywood on top and turn it face down. Check for any rough saw cuts on the back and sand them smooth with 180-grit sandpaper. Store the pieces in a sturdy box. If you wish, paste a duplicate picture on the cover.

Safety Tip

Puzzle pieces smaller than 2 x 2 inches pose a choking hazard to children under three years of age. Cut large puzzle pieces for young children, and warn the recipients of your other puzzles to keep pieces out of reach of very young children.

CUT THE PUZZLE

QUARTER SECTION

BLADE GUARD REMOVED FOR CLARITY — USE YOURS

REASSEMBLE PIECES AFTER CUTTING

BLADE GUARD REMOVED FOR CLARITY — USE YOURS

Photo 6 • For random cutting, first cut the picture into four large pieces with an irregular series of ears and sockets.

Photo 7 • Random-cut the individual puzzle pieces by eye, creating at least one ball-and-socket joint on each side of each piece.

A *fast-action* tabletop soccer game

If you like soccer or hockey, this tabletop game is for you. Its hardwood construction is tough enough for lots of overtime play. When the game is over, everything quickly disassembles and stores right inside the box.

Getting ready

Building this game requires intermediate woodworking skills and some power tools: a table saw with a dado blade, a router with a 1/4-inch straight bit, a belt sander with a 60-grit or coarser sanding belt, a portable saber saw, and an electric drill with a 13/16-inch spade bit and a 3/8-inch plug cutter. You'll also need 4-foot bar clamps, two 6-inch clamps, and a hot-glue gun.

You first make a routing jig to cut grooves in the player and goalie rods. Then you build and assemble the game box. A plunge router is helpful for cutting grooves in the dowels, but not really essential.

Assembly Plan

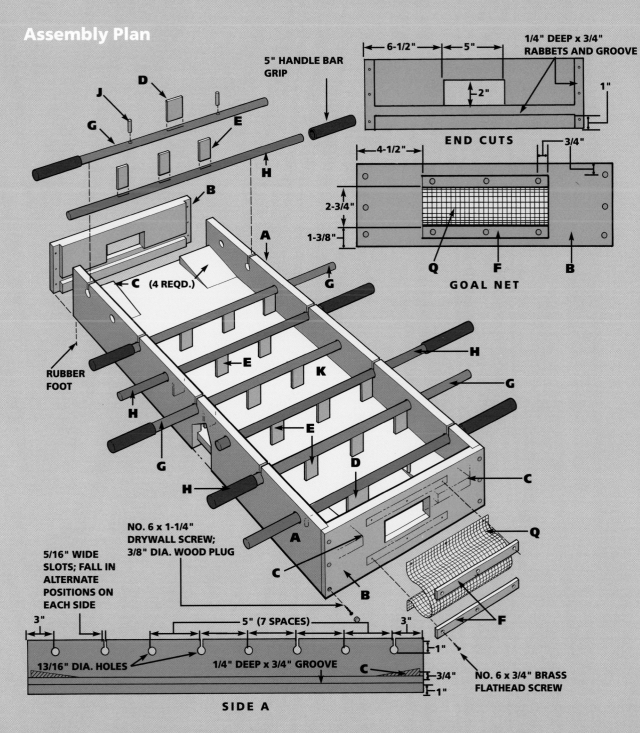

5" HANDLE BAR GRIP

D

J

G

E

H

B

A

G

C (4 REQD.)

RUBBER FOOT

E

K

H

E

G

D

H

A

C

B

C

H

Q

F

NO. 6 x 1-1/4" DRYWALL SCREW; 3/8" DIA. WOOD PLUG

5/16" WIDE SLOTS; FALL IN ALTERNATE POSITIONS ON EACH SIDE

3"

5" (7 SPACES)

3"

1"

13/16" DIA. HOLES

1/4" DEEP x 3/4" GROOVE

C

3/4"

1"

NO. 6 x 3/4" BRASS FLATHEAD SCREW

SIDE A

END CUTS

6-1/2"

5"

1/4" DEEP x 3/4" RABBETS AND GROOVE

2"

1"

GOAL NET

4-1/2"

3/4"

2-3/4"

1-3/8"

Q

F

B

Cutting List

Key	Pcs.	Size and Description
A	2	3/4" x 5-1/2" x 41" oak (sides)
B	2	3/4" x 5-1/2" x 18" oak (ends)
C	4	3/4" x 4" x 5" oak (ramps)
D	2	1/4" x 2" x 2-1/2" oak (goalies)
E	18	1/4" x 1-1/4" x 2-1/2" oak (players)
F	4	1/4" x 3/4" x 9" oak (net supports)
G	4	3/4" dia. x 29" birch dowels (player/goalie rods)
H	4	3/4" dia. x 29" walnut dowels (player/goalie rods)
J	4	1/4" diameter x 1" birch dowels (goalie rod stops)
K	1	3/4" x 17" x 41" oak plywood (playing field)
L	1	3/4" x 7" x 20" scrap plywood (routing jig base)
M	1	3/4" x 4-5/16" x 20" scrap plywood (routing jig rear support)
N	1	3/4" x 2-1/8" x 20" scrap plywood (routing jig front support)
P	1	3/4" x 1-1/2" x 20" scrap plywood (routing jig fence)
Q	2	7" x 9" cloth mesh (goal nets)

Materials Tip

Walnut dowels are available at wood-worker's stores and from mail-order suppliers. Check hobby, crafts, and toy stores for the rubber handgrips and nylon mesh netting.

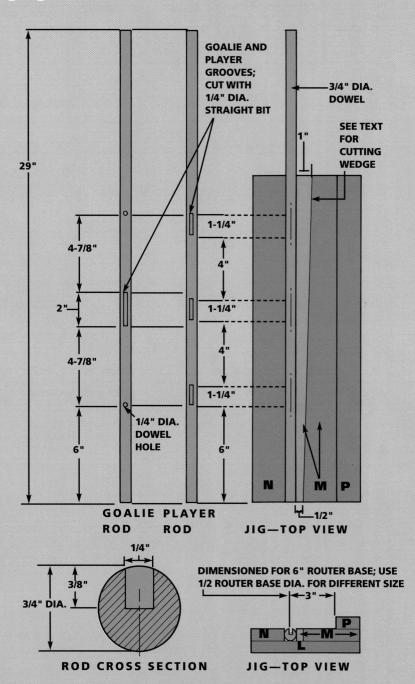

GOALIE AND PLAYER GROOVES; CUT WITH 1/4" DIA. STRAIGHT BIT

3/4" DIA. DOWEL

SEE TEXT FOR CUTTING WEDGE

29"

4-7/8"

2"

4-7/8"

6"

1-1/4"

4"

1-1/4"

4"

1-1/4"

6"

1"

1/4" DIA. DOWEL HOLE

GOALIE ROD **PLAYER ROD**

JIG—TOP VIEW

1/2"

N M P

1/4"

3/8"

3/4" DIA.

ROD CROSS SECTION

DIMENSIONED FOR 6" ROUTER BASE; USE 1/2 ROUTER BASE DIA. FOR DIFFERENT SIZE

3"

N M P
L

JIG—TOP VIEW

Shopping List

2	1x6 x 8' oak
1	3/4" x 24" x 48" oak plywood
4	3/4" diameter x 36" birch dowels
4	3/4" diameter x 36" walnut dowels
1	1/4" diameter x 9-1/2" birch dowel
1	1-1/4" diameter birch ball
12	No. 6 x 1-1/4" drywall screws
12	No. 6 x 3/4" brass flathead screws
6	Nonskid rubber feet with screws
8	Rubber handgrips
	Nylon mesh netting
	Danish oil finish or equivalent

Make the player/goalie rods

1 • Cut pieces L–P to make a jig for routing the grooves in the player/goalie rods (G, H); sizes are given in the Cutting List. Then cut a sliding wedge off piece M as follows: Clamp a 50-inch auxiliary fence to the table saw fence. Use a blade that cuts a 1/8-inch kerf and set the fence 3-11/16 inches from the blade. Tape a riser or spacer block measuring 1/2 x 3/4 x 2 to piece M so it holds the long edge at one corner 1/2 inch away from the auxiliary fence. Then use push sticks to cut the tapered wedge off the opposite side (Photo 1).

2 • Glue and clamp the jig pieces together as shown in the plans (opposite page). Glue the wide section of piece M to the base (L), but not the tapered piece; it must slide to provide a wedging action. The jig is designed for a router with a 6-inch diameter base. If your router has a different size base, glue the jig fence (P) to the rear support (M) so the router bit will be centered over a rod in cutting position. The distance from the fence is half the diameter of the router base.

3 • Draw routing guidelines onto the top of the front support (N) of the jig (Photo 2). The spacing is shown in the jig plans.

4 • To use the jig, clamp it to your workbench. Set a player rod (G) in place with its right end flush with the right end of the jig (Photo 3). Tap in the wedge with a hammer to hold the rod securely. With a combination square, transfer the routing guidelines from the jig to the player rod.

5 • Rout three grooves in each player rod with a 1/4-inch straight router bit. Cut the grooves just slightly past the marks drawn on the rod.

Rout three birch rods (G) and three walnut rods (H) in this way.

6 • Make goalie rods by routing a single groove in the center of one birch and one walnut rod. Because the goalies (D) are wider than the players (E), mark and cut the groove 3/8 inch longer at each end than the size of the player groove. While each rod is in the jig, also drill 1/4-inch holes for the rod stops (J), as shown in the rod plans.

7 • Use a table saw and a regular rip blade to cut 1/4-inch oak for two goalies (D), each 2 x 2-1/2 inches, and for 18 players (E), each 1-1/4 x 2-1/2 inches. Check that they fit tightly in the routed rod grooves.

MAKE THE PLAYER/GOALIE RODS

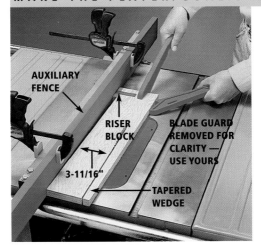

Photo 1 • Clamp a 50-in. auxiliary fence to the table saw's fence. Set the auxiliary fence 3-11/16 in. away from the saw blade. Use a blade that cuts a kerf 1/8-in. wide.

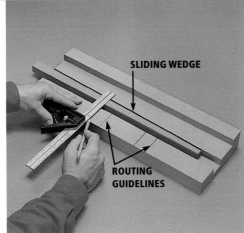

Photo 2 • Measure and mark the jig routing guidelines relative to the right end of the jig. Use a combination square to draw the lines on the front piece of the jig.

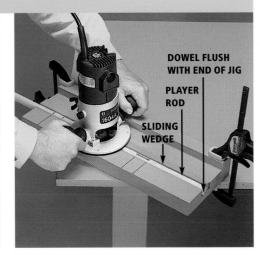

Photo 3 • Clamp down the routing jig and wedge each dowel firmly in place, flush at the right end. Keep the router base against the rear fence when cutting grooves.

Cut and drill the pieces

• •

1 • Cut pieces A–C, F, J, K, and Q to the dimensions in the Cutting List. When you cut the goal nets (Q), follow the weave of the cloth so you get straight sides and square corners.

2 • Lay out and drill the 13/16-inch rod holes in the sides (A). Drill screw holes in the ends (B) and counterbore them for 3/8-inch diameter. Also drill pilot holes in the net supports (F). Hole locations are shown in the side and end details in the plans.

3 • Using a table saw with a dado blade, cut rabbets for the playing field in the sides and ends (A, B). Make the rabbets 3/4 inch wide and 1/4 inch deep. Cut the same size rabbets on the inside edges of the ends (Photo 4).

4 • Dry-assemble the sides (A), playing field (K), and ends (B). Drill through the screw holes in (B) to make matched pilot holes in the ends of the sides. Lay out the 5/16-inch player/goalie slots above the rod holes in the sides (A). These permit sliding the player and goalie rods into place during final assembly. Note that the slots are at every other hole, starting at opposite

ends of the two sides. After marking the positions, disassemble the parts and cut the slots with a saber saw.

5 • Lay out and cut the goal holes in the ends (B), as shown in the End View detail in the plans (Photo 5).

CUT AND DRILL THE PIECES

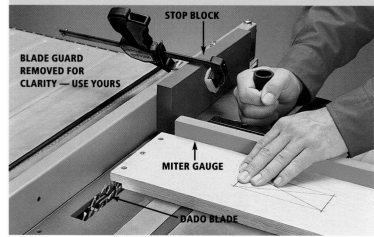

Photo 4 • Use a dado blade on your table saw to cut 3/4-in. rabbets and grooves in the end pieces and sides. Clamp a stop block to the fence to prevent binding when cutting.

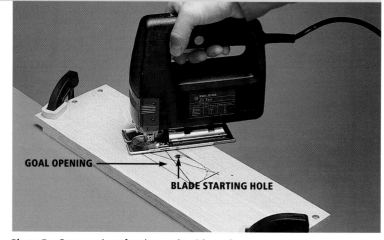

Photo 5 • Cut openings for the goals with a saber saw. Drill a 3/8-in. hole inside the cutout to insert the blade. Smooth the cut edges with a file or sandpaper wrapped around a dowel.

Finish the game

1 • Taper the ramps (C) with a belt sander and a 60-grit or coarser sanding belt (Photo 6). Spot-glue the ramps to a support surface for sanding.

2 • Sand the inside surfaces of all parts smooth; wait to sand the outsides of the sides (A) and ends (B). Start with 120-grit sandpaper and finish with 180-grit paper.

3 • Glue and clamp one side (A) to the playing field (K). Let the glue dry, then glue and clamp the other side to the playing field. Before the glue dries, glue and screw the ends (B) to the sides. You may need to loosen the clamps on the sides to get the ends to fit.

4 • Cut 12 oak cover plugs with a 3/8-inch plug cutter. Glue and hammer the plugs into the counterbored holes in the ends (B). Now finish-sand the outsides of the sides and ends.

5 • Glue the players (E), goalies (D), and goalie rod stops (J) into their rod slots and holes. Also glue the ramps (C) to the corners of the playing field (K). Sand all sharp edges smooth.

6 • Attach the net supports (F) and goal nets (Q) over the goals with No. 6 x 3/4-inch flat-head screws, to establish their holes (Photo 7). Then remove the supports and nets.

7 • Apply two coats of Danish oil finish to all wood pieces except the ball. Spray the ball with red enamel, painting one half at a time.

8 • Screw the rubber feet into the bottom edges of box—one at each corner and one the midway between on each long side. Reattach the goal nets and net supports.

9 • Hammer the handgrips onto the player/goalie rods, then slide the rods in place. Turn each rod so the player or goalie pieces point straight upward, so they can slide through the slots above the holes. Push the rod into the holes and turn it to bring the players/goalies down into playing position.

Working Tip

The rubber handgrips must be absolutely tight on the player and goalie rods for fast, accurate action. If they fit loosely at first, wrap the ends of the rods with electrician's tape, then force the handgrips over the tape.

FINISH THE GAME

Photo 6 • To taper the ramps, temporarily attach them to a scrap board with spots of hot glue for sanding. Pop the ramps free with a putty knife when finished.

RAMP

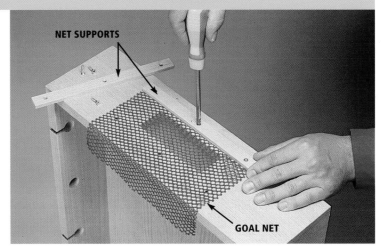

NET SUPPORTS

GOAL NET

Photo 7 • Align the nets and net supports over the goals. Drill pilot holes and insert the screws through the supports and net mesh before driving them into the holes.

Wagons and Rocking Toys

Rocking Dinosaur

Let your favorite youngster sit back and rock through the ages with this friendly and colorful dinosaur.

118

Running, Jumping Rocking Horse

It may *look* like it's flying, but this little pony is built low for safe and stable—yet spirited—rocking.

114

Stake-Side Wagon

Cut-away front corners and side stakes update this traditional design for a wagon kids will love today.

128

Thoroughbred Rocking Horse

Here's a mount that's as gentle as it is strong. Stops on the rockers ensure that it won't throw even the most enthusiastic rider.

122

Little Red Wagon

Solid, durable construction combines with modern hardware and materials to make this enduring classic even easier to build and enjoy.

136

A running, jumping **rocking horse**

With its legs extended in front and behind, this rocking horse looks like it's flying through the air—just what a child longs to do.

The horse is designed to be safe and stable, but it retains a lively rocking action that will satisfy even the most energetic rider.

Getting started

The only trick to building this rocking horse is to follow the sequence of the construction steps exactly—that will save you a lot of time. The horse is built from standard-size lumber. Lumberyard pine may be your most economical choice, but you also can use oak or birch if you can find them in standard sizes.

In addition to your regular hand tools you'll need a saber saw, jigsaw, or band saw to cut the curves. A router is handy for rounding over the edges but isn't essential.

Assembly Plan

Materials List

16d casing nails

No. 6 x 1-5/8" drywall screws

1" brads

Carpenter's glue

Wood stain and polyurethane finish

Cutting List

Key	Pcs.	Size and Description
A	2	3/4" x 11" x 30-1/4" pine (rocker sides)
B	2	3/4" x 13" x 6" pine (rear legs)
C	2	3/4" x 5-1/2" x 8-1/2" pine (horse sides)
D	2	3/4" x 6-1/4" x 13-1/2" pine (front legs)
E	1	3/4" x 5" x 17-3/4" pine (seat)
F	1	3/4" x 2-1/2" x 4" pine (rear pommel)
G	1	3/4" x 1-3/4" x 2-1/4" pine (rear pommel support)
H	1	3/4" x 2-1/2" x 4" pine (front pommel)
J	2	3/4" x 3-3/4" x 6-1/2" pine (horse head)
K	2	1-1/2" x 7-3/4" x 9-1/2" pine (braces)
L	2	3/4" diameter x 7-1/2" birch dowel (footrests)
M	4	1-1/2" diameter birch balls (footrest and handhold trim)
N	1	3/4" diameter x 8-3/4" birch dowel (handhold)
P	1	3/4" x 7-3/4" x 10-3/8" pine (horse neck and head)

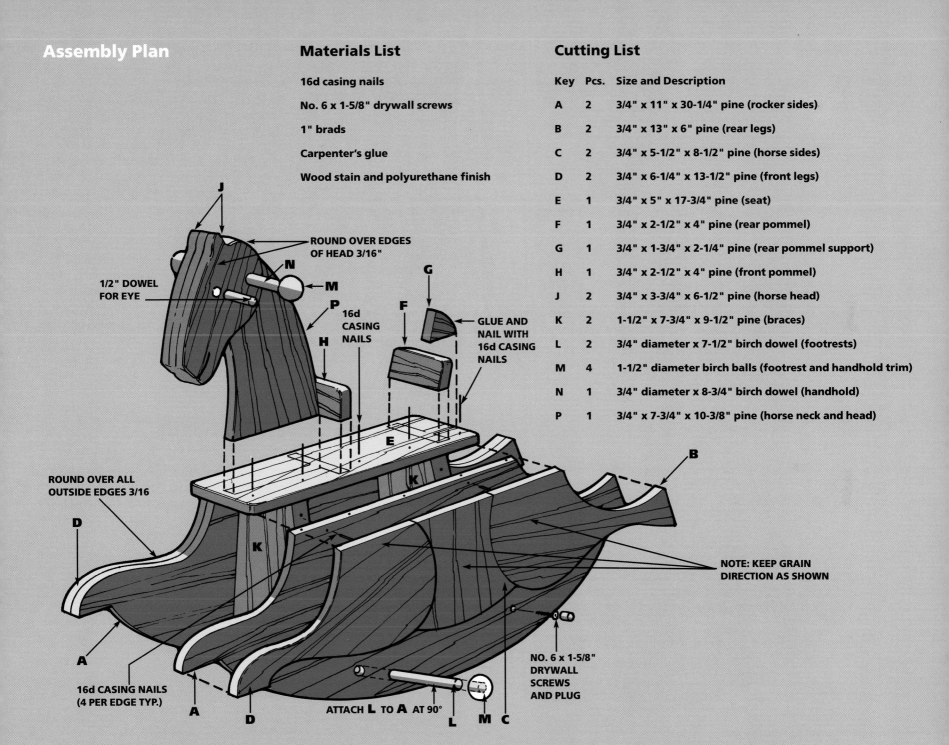

ROUND OVER EDGES OF HEAD 3/16"

1/2" DOWEL FOR EYE

16d CASING NAILS

GLUE AND NAIL WITH 16d CASING NAILS

ROUND OVER ALL OUTSIDE EDGES 3/16

NOTE: KEEP GRAIN DIRECTION AS SHOWN

16d CASING NAILS (4 PER EDGE TYP.)

ATTACH L TO A AT 90°

NO. 6 x 1-5/8" DRYWALL SCREWS AND PLUG

Pattern Pieces

Each square = 1"

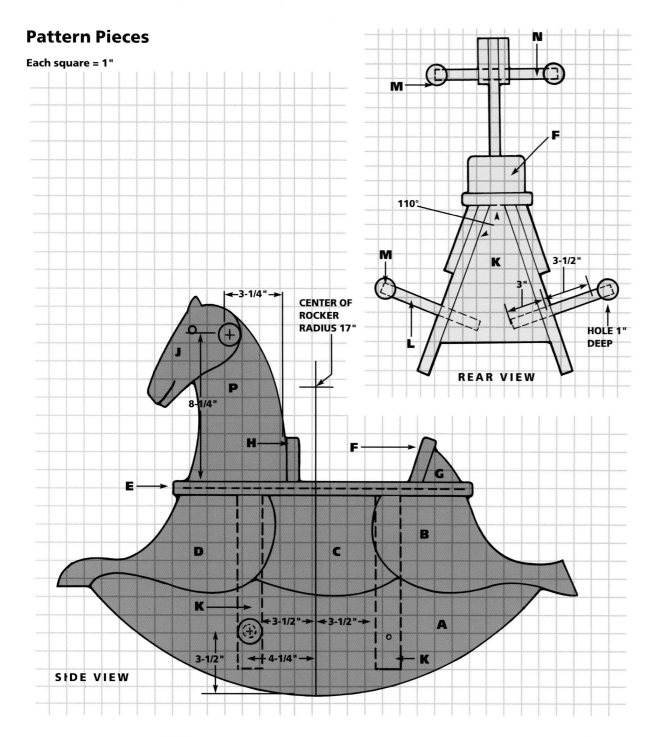

CENTER OF ROCKER RADIUS 17"

3-1/4"

8-1/4"

J

P

H

E

F

G

B

D

C

A

K

K

K

3-1/2"

3-1/2"

3-1/2"

4-1/4"

SIDE VIEW

N

M

F

110°

M

K

L

3-1/2"

3"

HOLE 1" DEEP

REAR VIEW

Build the rocking horse

1 • Mark a grid of 1-inch squares on pieces of 1x8 pine and copy the pattern outlines of parts B, C, and D. Note the grain directions shown in the Assembly Plan. Cut the pieces out in pairs. Sand the good outer face of each piece—one goes on the left side of the horse, the other on the right side—and round over all but the top edges on that face.

2 • Mark a 1-inch grid on a piece of 1x12 for a side (A) and copy just the rocker curve from the bottom of the pattern. (You'll do the upper curves in Step 3.) To draw a smooth curve, tack a thin strip of wood along the outline to help you trace. Clamp or spot-glue this piece to a second 1x12 and cut out two matching rockers at the same time.

3 • Separate the two sides (A). Position the proper B, C, and D pieces on each side and drill pilot holes. Glue and nail those pieces to the sides. Now you can cut the front and back leg and hoof curves on A, following those on parts B and D. Sand the cut edges flush, and round over the edges and the tips of the hooves.

4 • Plane or cut a 20-degree bevel on the top of each side-rocker assembly (Photo 1). This will provide level support for the seat (E) when it is spread at an angle (see pattern rear view).

5 • Transfer the outline of a brace (K) to 1x8 pine, using the gridded pattern. Cut it out, trace its shape onto another 1x8, and cut out the second brace.

6 • Locate and drill pilot holes, and nail the sides (A) to the braces (K) with 16d casing nails (see pattern side view).

7 • Drill a 3/4-inch hole 3 inches deep through each side for the footrests (L). Drill perpendicular to each side, into the front brace (see pattern rear and side views). Then drill and counterbore a screw hole above the footrest hole on each side. Drive in No. 6 x 1-5/8 drywall screws, cover the heads with glued-in wood plugs, and sand the plugs flush.

8 • Transfer the outlines of parts J and P onto 1x10 pine, using the gridded pattern, and cut the pieces a bit oversize.

9 • Tack the blanks for the head (J) in position on each side of the neck (P) with dabs of hot-melt glue. Cut the common edges of the head in this stack (Photo 2).

10 • Pop off the two head pieces (J) and complete cutting their shapes. Then glue and nail them back onto the neck (P), and round over all outside edges.

11 • In the head cut a saw kerf for the mouth and drill a 1/2-inch diameter hole on each side for the eyes. Glue in pieces of dowel and sand them flush. Finally, drill a 3/4-inch hole completely through the head for the handhold (N).

12 • Cut the dowels for the handhold (N) and footrest (L), and glue them into their respective holes. Drill 3/4-inch holes in the wooden balls (M) (Photo 3), and glue them onto the dowel ends. Drive a brad through each ball and dowel for extra strength.

13 • Lay out and cut parts E, F, G, and H. Glue and nail part H to the neck (P) and part F to part G, then screw both assemblies to the seat (E). Round over all edges.

14 • Position the seat and head assembly on the rockers, drill pilot holes, and fasten it in place with glue and 16d casing nails.

15 • Apply the stain and finish of your choice. Polyurethane gives a finish that will stand up to a lot of rough riding.

BUILD THE ROCKING HORSE

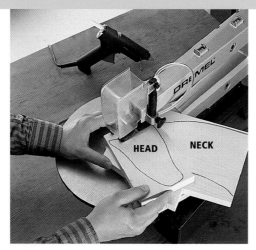

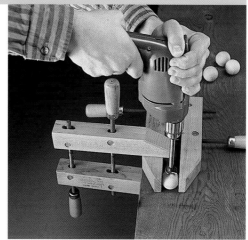

Photo 1 • Plane a 20-degree bevel on the top edges of the rocker sides, or tack on a straight piece of scrap as a support and cut the bevel with a jigsaw or table saw.

Photo 2 • As with the legs, sides, and rockers, spot-glue the head and neck pieces together to cut matching edges. A couple of dabs of hot glue will be sufficient to hold the pieces.

Photo 3 • Clamp the wooden balls to your bench with hand screws to secure them for drilling. The balls fit on the ends of the handhold and footrests, to prevent injury.

An *easy-to-build* rocking dinosaur

Dinosaurs are perennial favorites with children, and this colorful rocking stegosaurus is no exception. It can provide lots of imaginative adventure, time and time again.

Getting started

Building this stegosaurus is a simple project, even for beginning woodworkers. You can do it with just a circular saw, an electric drill with a 3/8-inch plug-cutting bit, a router with a 1/8-inch round-over bit, and a saber saw. An oscillating block sander will speed the finishing work but isn't essential. And you can lay all the parts flat for easy painting before making the final assembly.

Baltic or all-birch plywood is the best material to use for this project. If you can't locate it, use ordinary birch plywood instead.

Assembly Plan

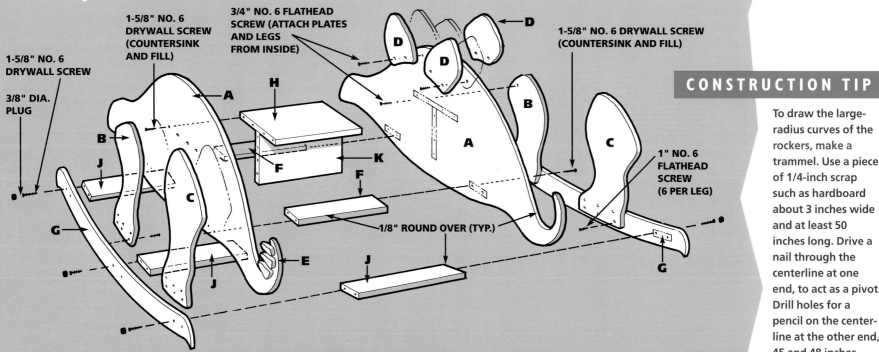

1-5/8" NO. 6 DRYWALL SCREW (COUNTERSINK AND FILL)

3/4" NO. 6 FLATHEAD SCREW (ATTACH PLATES AND LEGS FROM INSIDE)

1-5/8" NO. 6 DRYWALL SCREW

3/8" DIA. PLUG

1-5/8" NO. 6 DRYWALL SCREW (COUNTERSINK AND FILL)

1" NO. 6 FLATHEAD SCREW (6 PER LEG)

1/8" ROUND OVER (TYP.)

CONSTRUCTION TIP

To draw the large-radius curves of the rockers, make a trammel. Use a piece of 1/4-inch scrap such as hardboard about 3 inches wide and at least 50 inches long. Drive a nail through the centerline at one end, to act as a pivot. Drill holes for a pencil on the center-line at the other end, 45 and 48 inches from the nail. To use the trammel, see Step 6, page 120.

Cutting List

Key	Pcs.	Size and Description
A	2	1/2" x 17-3/4" x 40-1/4" birch plywood (body)
B	2	1/2" x 7" x 16-1/4" birch plywood (front legs)
C	2	1/2" x 9-3/4" x 19-1/4 birch plywood (back legs)
D	26	1/2" x (various sizes) birch plywood (plates)

Key	Pcs.	Size and Description
E	6	1/2" x (various sizes) birch plywood (tail spikes)
F	2	3/4" x 3" x 12" oak (footrests)
G	2	3/4" x 5-1/2" x 36" oak (rockers)
H	1	3/4" x 7" x 12" oak (seat)
J	3	3/4" x 3" x 14" oak (rocker rungs)
K	1	3/4" x 7" x 12" oak (seat brace)

Shopping List

1 sheet	4' x 8' x 1/2" Baltic birch plywood
13 feet	1x8 oak
1 box	No. 6 x 3/4" flathead screws
24	No. 6 x 1" flathead screws
36	No. 6 x 1-5/8" drywall screws
	Double-sided carpet tape
	Wood filler
	Enamel primer
	Green, yellow, gray enamel
	Danish oil finish

Build the rocking dinosaur

Working Tip

At several points in this project, parts must be clamped together. Because the parts are painted before drilling and assembly, be sure to use cardboard shims under the clamp faces to protect the painted surfaces.

1 • Draw a grid of 2-inch squares on the plywood. Transfer and enlarge the outlines of the pattern pieces, beginning with the body sides (A). Fill in the remaining space on the plywood with the smaller pieces—the front legs (B), the back legs (C), the plates (D), and the tail spikes (E).

2 • Cut out all plywood pieces with a saber saw. Or rough-cut them with the saber saw and finish cutting with a jigsaw or a band saw to minimize sanding of the cut edges. Since all elements on both sides of the rocker are identical, you can stack two blanks and cut both shapes at the same time (Photo 1). Sand the edges by hand or with an oscillating sander.

3 • Rout 1/8-inch round overs on the edges of as many pieces as you can. Fasten the smaller pieces to a piece of scrap wood with double-sided carpet tape to hold them for routing. Round over the edges of the smallest plates and the spikes by hand with a file.

4 • Fill any imperfections in the edges of the plywood with wood filler and sand smooth. Sand all surfaces with 180-grit sandpaper, and prime all plywood pieces on both sides. When the primer is dry, paint both sides of the body (A) and the legs (B, C) green. Paint plates (D) and tail spikes (E) yellow. For the smoothest results, use a roller or sprayer to paint the flat surfaces. Apply at least two coats to all surfaces and let the paint dry.

5 • Paint the edges of all pieces gray, using a small foam brush to apply two coats. Paint the eye, nostril, and toenail outlines and the detail lines on the plates and body gray with a small artist's brush (Photo 2). Fill in the eyes, nostrils, and toenails with yellow.

6 • Use a trammel (see Construction Tip with the plans) to enlarge and transfer the outline of the rockers (G) to pieces of 1x8 oak. Center the bottom end of the trammel in the middle of one board, perpendicular to the bottom long edge. Tap the trammel pivot nail into the supporting work surface. Insert a pencil in one of the trammel holes and swing it right and left to draw the first rocker arc. Move the pencil to the other hole and draw the second arc (Photo 3). Use a compass to lay out the small curves at the ends of the rockers (see the pattern side view).

7 • Cut out each rocker with a saber saw, jigsaw, or band saw. Then clamp the two rockers together to sand and file their edges smooth at the same time. Use a sanding drum in an electric drill on the large curves, and a file on the ends. Finish-sand by hand.

8 • Cut out the rectangular oak pieces for the seat (H), the seat brace (K), the footrests (F), and rocker rungs (J). Sand them smooth and rout 1/8-inch round overs on all exposed edges. Glue the brace to the underside of the seat. Center it and make sure the ends are flush. Apply Danish oil to the seat assembly now, before final assembly.

9 • Lay out and drill holes for attaching the outer plates (D) and the tail spikes (E) to each body piece (A); see the pattern side view for screw locations. Countersink the holes on the outer surfaces of the plates. Glue and screw the outer set of plates and the spikes to each of the body pieces, using No. 6 x 3/4-inch flathead screws. Attach the inner set of plates in the same way.

BUILD THE ROCKING DINOSAUR

Photo 1 • Cut pairs of matching parts at one time by joining blanks with double-sided carpet tape. Sand the edges before separating them.

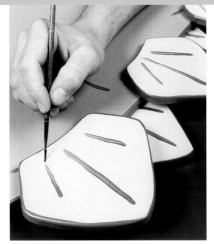

Photo 2 • Add details to the painted body parts with a small artist's brush. Lift the brush gently at the end of each line to avoid getting a blob or teardrop of paint.

Photo 3 • Lay out the long rocker curves with a trammel—a piece of hardboard with a pivot nail in one end and pencil holes at the required radius distances.

10 • Lay out the position of the seat assembly (H, K) and the footrests (F) on the inside surfaces of the body pieces (A) (see pattern side view). Drill countersunk pilot holes in the body pieces. Clamp the two sides of the rocker together with the seat assembly and footrests in place between them. Drill matching pilot holes in the edges of the oak pieces, then screw the body pieces to the seat assembly and the footrests with No. 6 x 1-5/8 inch drywall screws. Fill the screw holes with wood filler, sand, and touch up with green enamel.

11 • Mark the locations of the rocker rungs (J) on the rockers (G)—see the pattern side view—and drill the 3/8-inch plug holes in the outside faces of the rockers. Clamp the rockers and rungs together and drill pilot holes through the plug holes into the ends of the rocker rungs. Drive No. 6 x 1-5/8 inch drywall screws into all the holes. Cut 12 3/8-inch diameter walnut plugs and glue them in place over the screw heads. Cut the plugs, sand them flush with the rocker surfaces, and apply Danish oil to the rocker assembly.

12 • Lay out and drill countersunk pilot holes in the body (A) where the legs (B, C) attach, and in the legs where the rockers (G) attach. Clamp the legs to the body and to the rocker assembly. Drill additional pilot holes where necessary. Then screw the body to the legs with No. 6 x 3/4-inch flathead screws. Finally, screw the legs to the rockers with No. 6 x 1-inch flathead screws. Now you can invite a youngster to take a prehistoric ride.

Pattern Pieces

Each square = 2"

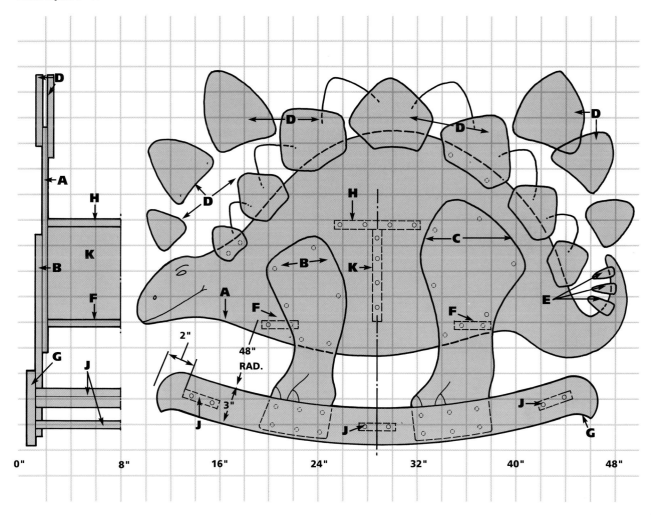

A thoroughbred rocking horse

This classic rocking horse combines a graceful design with the durability of hardwood. For safety, it has stops on the rockers to keep enthusiastic riders from tipping over.

Getting started

The only power tools you'll need to build this horse are a saber saw or band saw and an electric drill with standard bits, a 3/4-inch spade bit, a 3/8-inch plug-cutting bit, and a sanding drum. It's helpful, but not essential, to have a router to round over the edges, and a belt sander to speed finishing. This horse is made from cherry, a durable hardwood that becomes richer looking with age. The oil finish makes it easy to touch up nicks or scratches. If you substitute pine, choose the lumber carefully to avoid knots in the leg pieces.

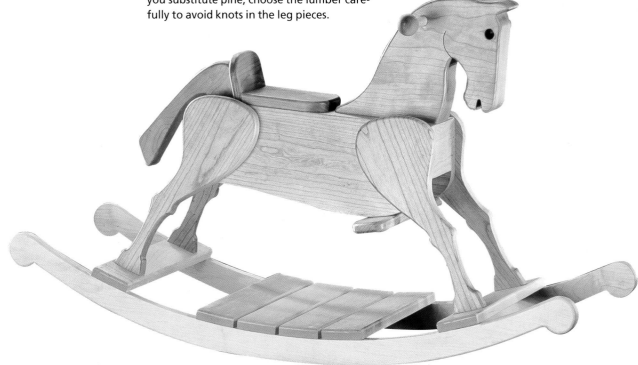

Assembly Plan

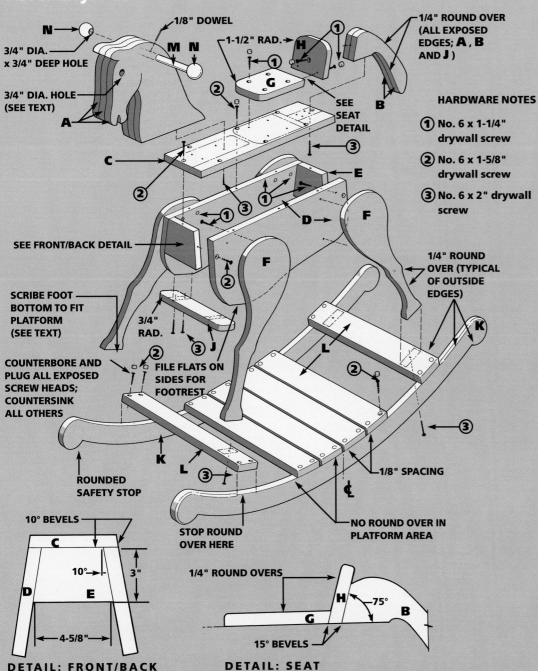

N → 3/4" DIA. x 3/4" DEEP HOLE

1/8" DOWEL

M N

3/4" DIA. HOLE (SEE TEXT)

A

1-1/2" RAD.

H

1/4" ROUND OVER (ALL EXPOSED EDGES; **A**, **B** AND **J**)

① **G**

SEE SEAT DETAIL

B

C

②

②

③

③

①

D

E

F

SEE FRONT/BACK DETAIL

F

②

1/4" ROUND OVER (TYPICAL OF OUTSIDE EDGES)

F

K

SCRIBE FOOT BOTTOM TO FIT PLATFORM (SEE TEXT)

3/4" RAD.

③ **J**

②

COUNTERBORE AND PLUG ALL EXPOSED SCREW HEADS; COUNTERSINK ALL OTHERS

②

FILE FLATS ON SIDES FOR FOOTREST

L

②

③

K

L

③

ROUNDED SAFETY STOP

STOP ROUND OVER HERE

1/8" SPACING

¢

NO ROUND OVER IN PLATFORM AREA

③

HARDWARE NOTES

① No. 6 x 1-1/4" drywall screw

② No. 6 x 1-5/8" drywall screw

③ No. 6 x 2" drywall screw

Cutting List

Key	Pcs.	Size and Description
A	3	3/4" x 9" x 14" cherry (head)
B	2	3/4" x 4" x 11" cherry (tail)
C	1	3/4" x 5" x 18-1/2" cherry (body top)
D	2	3/4" x 6" x 18-1/2" cherry (body sides)
E	2	3/4" x 3" x 4-5/8" cherry (body front and back)
F	4	3/4" x 6" x 16" cherry (legs)
G	1	3/4" x 4-1/2" x 6-1/2" cherry (seat)
H	1	3/4" x 3-1/2" x 4-1/2" cherry (seat back)
J	1	3/4" x 2-1/2" x 12" cherry (footrest)
K	2	3/4" x 7" x 44" maple (rockers)
L	6	3/4" x 3" x 15" maple (platform)
M	1	3/4" diameter x 7-1/2" birch dowel (handle)
N	2	1-1/2" diameter birch balls (handle ends)

Shopping List

1	1x10 x 4' cherry
2	1x8 x 8' cherry
1	1x8 x 8' maple
1	1x4 x 8' maple
19	No. 6 x 1-1/4" drywall screws
36	No. 6 x 1-5/8" drywall screws
16	No. 6 x 2" drywall screws
1	1/8" x 3" dowel
2	1-1/2" diameter birch balls
1	3/4" diameter x 7" birch dowel rod
	Danish oil finish

DETAIL: FRONT/BACK

10° BEVELS

C

10°

3"

D **E**

4-5/8"

DETAIL: SEAT

1/4" ROUND OVERS

H 75°

G

B

15° BEVELS

Pattern Pieces

Each square = 1"

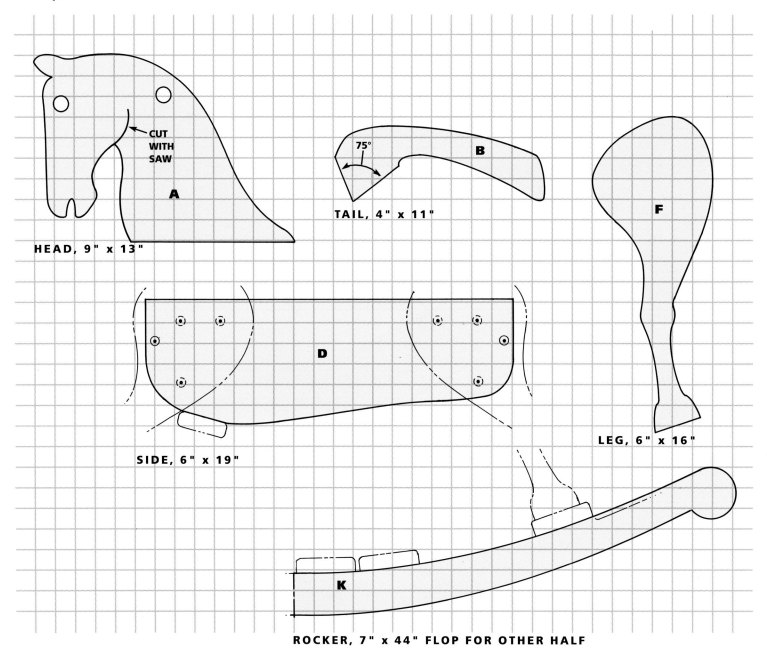

CUT WITH SAW

A

HEAD, 9" x 13"

75°

B

TAIL, 4" x 11"

F

LEG, 6" x 16"

D

SIDE, 6" x 19"

K

ROCKER, 7" x 44" FLOP FOR OTHER HALF

Cut and shape the pieces

1 • Cut all cherry and maple pieces (A–L) to the dimensions in the Cutting List. These are all blanks that will be cut to final shape.

2 • Glue and clamp together the three head pieces (A) and the two tail pieces (B) (Photo 1). Let the glue cure overnight.

3 • Draw grids or 1-inch squares on the blanks for the head (A), tail (B), one body side (D), one leg (F), and one rocker (K). Transfer the outlines of the shapes from the patterns to the grids on the wood. Then draw the radiused corners of the seat (G), seat back (H), and footrest (J).

4 • Cut 10-degree bevels on the long edges of the body top (C) and body sides (D) (see front/back detail in the Assembly Plans). Also cut 15-degree bevels on the adjoining edges of the seat (G) and seat back (H) (see Seat Detail in the plans).

5 • Cut out the head (A), tail (B), body side (D), leg (F), and rocker (K), and sand the cut edges smooth (Photo 2). Use a sanding drum in an electric drill to smooth the concave curves; sand other areas with a stationary belt sander or a belt sander held in a vise.

6 • Use the cut-out body side (D), leg (F), and rocker (K) as templates to draw the outlines of the matching pieces. Cut out the pieces and sand their edges smooth.

7 • Locate and drill screw holes in all pieces except those in the footrest (J), and those for attaching the legs to the front and rear platform pieces (L). Counterbore all the rocker screw holes in the platform pieces (L) to receive 3/8-inch wood plugs.

8 • Drill 3/4-inch holes for the eye dowel and the handle (M) in the head (A) (see the head pattern, and the construction tip with the plans). Use a drill press or a guide to hold your electric drill vertical for straight, true holes.

9 • Cut approximately 40 cherry plugs with a 3/8-inch plug-cutting bit.

10 • Round over the exposed edges of the head (A), tail (B), footrest (J), seat (G), and seat back (H) with a router and a 1/4-inch round-over bit for best results.

11 • Round over the outside edges of the legs (F) and the top edges of the platform pieces (L). Also round over the outside edges of the rockers (K) that extend beyond the front and rear platform pieces (see the plans).

Working Tip

The rocking horse handle must fit tightly in its hole. If the dowel rod is too loose in a 3/4-inch hole and too tight in an 11/16-inch hole, grind or file the sides of a 3/4-inch spade bit until it makes a hole that the dowel fits perfectly. Remove metal equally from both sides of the bit, and drill test holes often in a scrap piece of hardwood to avoid removing too much.

CUT AND SHAPE THE PIECES

CARPENTER'S GLUE

Photo 1 • Glue and clamp the three head blanks together. Make sure the edges remain aligned while you install the clamps.

GRID

Photo 2 • Cut out the curved pieces. If you use a saber saw the blade must be long enough to cut through the glued-up head.

Assemble the body and rockers

. . . .

1 • Glue and screw the body top (C) to the body sides (D) with No. 6 x 2-inch drywall screws. The sides will flare out at the bottom because of the bevel on their top edges (see front/back detail in the plans).

2 • The front and back body pieces (E) should taper about 10 degrees to the top on each side. For a proper fit, hold the blanks for these pieces at each end of the body assembly and trace the exact angles. Cut the marked angles, then use glue and No. 6 x 1-5/8 inch drywall screws to fasten them in place.

3 • Glue cherry plugs into the counterbored screw holes in the body top (C) (Photo 3). Cut the plugs flush with the surface, and finish-sand the body and unassembled parts.

4 • Attach the platform pieces (L) to one of the rockers (K). Clamp the rocker on its side to your workbench and stand each platform piece on end to drive No. 6 x 1-5/8 inch drywall screws in the predrilled holes (Photo 4). This method avoids any rocking movement and makes it easy to get the platform pieces square to the rocker and flush at the outside edge.

5 • When the first rocker is done, clamp the second rocker in its place. Turn the first assembly over, position the free ends of the platform pieces against the second rocker, and attach them with screws.

6 • Finish the rocker-platform assembly by gluing 3/8-inch cherry plugs into the counterbored screw holes. Cut the plugs flush with the surface and sand them smooth.

7 • Individually clamp—don't screw—each leg (F) to the body and set this assembly on the rocker platform (Photo 5). Working one leg at a time, loosen the clamp and adjust the leg so the foot rests on its front or rear platform piece and the shoulder or haunch is correctly positioned with the side of the body (see side pattern). Then tighten the clamp. When everything is correctly aligned, turn the assembly over and drive No. 6 x 1-1/4 inch drywall screws from the inside to fasten the legs in position.

Working Tip

Proper size pilot holes are very important in hardwood, to avoid scarring the head or breaking the shaft when driving a screw. For the No. 6 screws used in this project, drill 3/32 in. and 1/8 in. holes in a scrap piece of hardwood and see which is better with the screws you intend to use. It's a good idea to first rub wax on the screw threads, to reduce friction. Do not use soap; it absorbs moisture from the air, causing discoloration or rusting.

ASSEMBLE THE BODY AND ROCKERS

PLUGS

Photo 3 • Cherry plugs cover the screws that hold the body together. Make them with a plug-cutting bit and a drill. Drive them in with glue, trim, and sand flush.

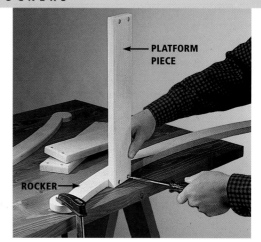

PLATFORM PIECE

ROCKER

Photo 4 • Screw the platform pieces to one rocker while it's clamped flat to your work table. This will help keep the edges flush and platform square. Do the other rocker in the same way.

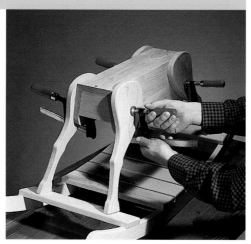

Photo 5 • Clamp the legs to the body and set the horse on the rocker. Adjust the leg positions, then turn the assembly over to screw the legs to the body from the inside.

Finish the rocking horse

1 • Set the body–leg assembly upright on the rocker platform. Hold a pencil flat on the platform and mark the angle of the platform piece on each foot (Photo 6). File or sand the bottom of the feet so they sit flush on the platform. Check carefully to make sure that no leg is short and that all the feet are in full contact with the platform.

2 • Reposition the horse on the rocker assembly and trace the location of each foot on the platform pieces. Drill pilot holes in the platform pieces and feet for the No. 6 x 2-inch drywall screws. Drill these holes at a slight angle so the screws will run straight up the centers of the legs and not protrude from the angled sides. Screw the legs to the platform.

3 • Position the head (A) and tail (B) on the body, and attach them with No. 6 x 2-inch drywall screws.

4 • Screw the seat back (H) to the seat (G), glue plugs in the screw holes, and trim and sand the plug ends. Position the seat assembly on the body and attach it to the body top and the tail (B) with No. 6 x 1-5/8 inch drywall screws. Plug the screw holes like the others.

5 • File flats on the bottom edges of the body sides (D) at the front, where the footrest (J) will attach. Locate and drill pilot holes, then screw the footrest to the body with No. 6 x 2-inch drywall screws.

6 • Using the same bit as for the eye and handle holes, drill a hole 3/4 inch deep in each of the birch balls (N) that cap the ends of the handle (M). Hold the balls in a hand screw clamped to your work table or the bed of your drill press (Photo 7).

7 • Insert the handle (M) to the head. Locate and drill a 1/8-inch hole through the back of the head, at the upper center, into the handle. Glue a 1/8-inch dowel in the hole to pin the handle in place (Photo 8). File and sand the dowel end flush with the head. Now glue the balls onto the ends of the handle.

8 • Finish-sand any unsanded surfaces, and sand all sharp edges and corners smooth.

9 • Apply at least three coats of Danish oil, sanding with 220-grit sandpaper between coats. When the final coat is dry, let your little equestrian mount up and put this thoroughbred through its paces.

FINISH THE ROCKING HORSE

HOLD PENCIL FLAT

Photo 6 • Mark the angle of the platform on the bottom of each leg. File or sand the angle so each leg sits squarely on the platform. Drive screws up through the platform into the legs.

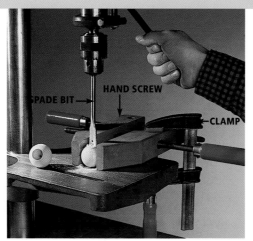

SPADE BIT → | HAND SCREW | ←CLAMP

Photo 7 • Drill holes partway into the birch balls that finish the ends of the handle. Use a hand screw to hold them; clamp the hand screw to your drill press bed or work surface.

1/8" DOWEL

Photo 8 • Use a short length of 1/8-in. diameter dowel to pin the handle in place. Drive the pin with glue into a pilot hole. File and sand the pin flush with the horse's head.

An *updated* stake-side wagon

Here's an up-to-date version of the stake-side design, which has a long tradition in wagon building. The raised sides and back are removable for hauling an oversize load, and the front corners are cut away to make it easy for youngsters to climb in and out. Pinstriping adds a special decorative touch.

Getting ready

The wagon shown here is built from light-colored ash to show off the red pinstriping. Oak, maple, or another hardwood would be just as suitable.

Building the wagon requires only moderate skill. The parts fit together without exacting joinery. Because many parts are less than 3/4 inch thick, you'll need a band saw or planer—or you can ask a local carpenter or cabinet shop to resaw thicker stock for you. Other tools you'll need are a table saw, a saber saw or handsaw, and a table-mounted router with a core box bit. Specialized hardware is available; see the Construction Tip with the Assembly Plan at right.

Assembly Plan

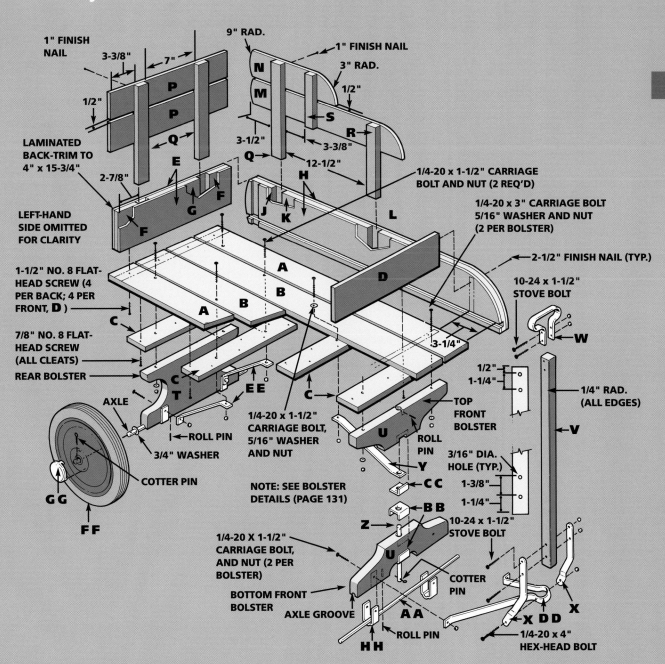

1" FINISH NAIL

3-3/8"

7"

9" RAD.

1" FINISH NAIL

3" RAD.

1/2"

N

P

P

Q

1/2"

M

S

R

LAMINATED BACK-TRIM TO 4" x 15-3/4"

3-1/2"

3-3/8"

12-1/2"

Q

2-7/8"

E

H

1/4-20 x 1-1/2" CARRIAGE BOLT AND NUT (2 REQ'D)

F

G

F

LEFT-HAND SIDE OMITTED FOR CLARITY

F

J

K

L

1/4-20 x 3" CARRIAGE BOLT 5/16" WASHER AND NUT (2 PER BOLSTER)

1-1/2" NO. 8 FLAT-HEAD SCREW (4 PER BACK; 4 PER FRONT, **D**)

A

B

D

2-1/2" FINISH NAIL (TYP.)

10-24 x 1-1/2" STOVE BOLT

B

A

7/8" NO. 8 FLAT-HEAD SCREW (ALL CLEATS)

C

3-1/4"

W

REAR BOLSTER

A

C

1/2"

1-1/4"

AXLE

C

C

U

TOP FRONT BOLSTER

1/4" RAD. (ALL EDGES)

T

EE

ROLL PIN

C

ROLL PIN

V

ROLL PIN

3/4" WASHER

1/4-20 x 1-1/2" CARRIAGE BOLT, 5/16" WASHER AND NUT

Y

3/16" DIA. HOLE (TYP.)

COTTER PIN

NOTE: SEE BOLSTER DETAILS (PAGE 131)

CC

1-3/8"

1-1/4"

GG

10-24 x 1-1/2" STOVE BOLT

FF

BB

Z

U

1/4-20 X 1-1/2" CARRIAGE BOLT, AND NUT (2 PER BOLSTER)

COTTER PIN

BOTTOM FRONT BOLSTER

AXLE GROOVE

AA

X DD X

HH

ROLL PIN

1/4-20 x 4" HEX-HEAD BOLT

CONSTRUCTION TIP

For best results, invest in commercial wagon hardware for this project. Wheels and axles, pivots and braces, yokes, handle fittings, and related hardware for the wagon shown are available in sets from the Wisconsin Wagon Company, Inc. Call this supplier at 608-754-0026 for information about availability and ordering instructions.

Cutting List

Key	Pcs.	Size and Description
A	2	1/2" x 2-3/4" x 36" ash (outer floorboards)
B	2	1/2" x 4" x 36" ash (inner floorboards)
C	4	1/2" x 2-1/2" x 15-1/4" ash (floorboard cleats)
D	1	3/4" x 3-1/2" x 15-1/4" ash (bed front end)
E	2	1/4" x 4-1/4" x 16-1/4" ash (faces of laminated back)
F	2	3/4" x 4-1/4" x 3-1/8" ash (end cores of laminated back)
G	1	3/4" x 4-1/4" x 7" ash (middle core of laminated back)
H	4	1/4" x 5-1/4" x 36-1/2" ash (faces of laminated sides)
J	2	3/4" x 5-1/4" x 3-1/2" ash (rear cores of laminated sides)
K	2	3/4" x 5-1/4" x 12-1/2" ash (middle cores of laminated sides)
L	2	3/4" x 5-1/4" x 17" ash (front cores of laminated sides)
M	2	1/4" x 3" x 22" ash (lower slats of stake sides)
N	2	1/4" x 3" x 12-3/4" ash (upper slats of stake sides)

Key	Pcs.	Size and Description
P	2	1/4" x 3" x 17-1/4" ash (slats of stake back)
Q	4	11/16" x 1-7/16" x 11" ash (stakes)
R	2	11/16" x 1-7/16" x 7-1/2" ash (stakes)
S	2	11/16" x 1-7/16" x 6-1/2" ash (side cleats)
T	1	1-1/16" x 5-3/4" x 12-3/4" ash (rear bolster)
U	2	1-1/16" x 3-5/8" x 12-3/4" ash (top and bottom front bolsters)
V	1	1-1/16" x 1-1/16" x 23" ash (handlebar)
W	1	Zinc-plated steel handle
X	2	Zinc-plated steel handlebar brackets
Y	1	Zinc-plated steel front bolster brace
Z	1	5-1/2" x 1/2" diameter steel vertical axle (front pivot)
AA	2	5-1/2" x 1/2" diameter steel wheel axles
BB	2	Zinc-plated steel axle pivot plates (bottom front bolster)
CC	1	Zinc-plated steel axle pivot plate (top front bolster)
DD	1	Zinc-plated steel yoke
EE	2	Zinc-plated steel braces (rear bolster)
FF	4	10" diameter ball-bearing wheels
GG	4	2" diameter chrome-plated hubcaps
HH	4	Zinc-plated steel axle clips

Shopping List

20 board feet	4/4 ash
5 board feet	6/4 ash
24	No. 8 x 7/8" flathead wood screws
8	No. 8 x 1-1/4" flathead wood screws
4	1/4-20 x 3" carriage bolts
7	1/4-20 x 1-1/2" carriage bolts
1	1/4-20 x 4" hex-head machine bolt
4	10-24 x 1-1/2" stove bolts
12	1/4-20 nylon locknuts
4	10-24 nylon locknuts
4	1/4" flat washers
1	5/16" flat washer
4	3/4" flat washers
2	2-1/2" finish nails
28	1" finish nails
	Semigloss clear exterior polyurethane
	Automotive pinstriping tool
	Red gloss enamel
	Resorcinol glue

Front and Rear Bolster Details

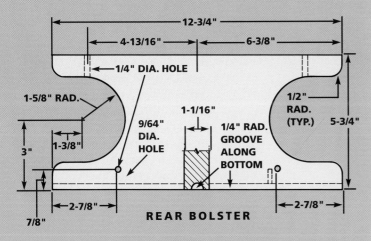

1/4" DIA. HOLE

12-3/4"

4-13/16"   **6-3/8"**

1-5/8" RAD.

9/64" DIA. HOLE

1-1/16"

1/4" RAD. GROOVE ALONG BOTTOM

1/2" RAD. (TYP.)

5-3/4"

3"

1-3/8"

2-7/8"

2-7/8"

7/8"

REAR BOLSTER

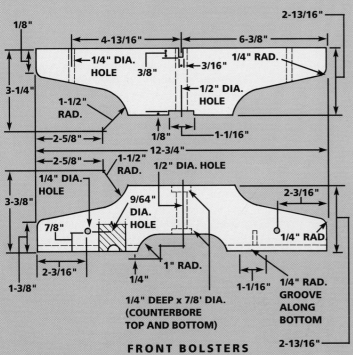

1/8"

2-13/16"

4-13/16"   **6-3/8"**

1/4" DIA. HOLE

3/8"

3/16"

1/4" RAD.

3-1/4"

1-1/2" RAD.

1/2" DIA. HOLE

2-5/8"

1/8"

1-1/16"

12-3/4"

2-5/8"

1-1/2" RAD.

1/2" DIA. HOLE

1/4" DIA. HOLE

3-3/8"

9/64" DIA. HOLE

2-3/16"

7/8"

1/4" RAD

2-3/16"

1" RAD.

1/4"

1-1/16"

1/4" RAD. GROOVE ALONG BOTTOM

1-3/8"

1/4" DEEP x 7/8' DIA. (COUNTERBORE TOP AND BOTTOM)

FRONT BOLSTERS

2-13/16"

Resaw and plane the stock

1 • Mark the lumber for the parts to be cut from each piece. Cut all the 3/4-inch thick pieces to the widths and lengths in the Cutting List. Rough-cut the pieces you need to plane or resaw 1 inch longer and 1/4 inch wider than the dimensions in the Cutting List. For safety, thickness-plane the wood for short pieces (see Step 3) before cutting the parts to length.

2 • Resaw the sides (H), back (E), stake sides (M, N), and stake backs (P) from 3/4-inch material, using a band saw with a wide, coarse blade. First plane one long edge of the boards flat and square, then cut each board to half thickness with the band saw, using a coarse blade and a fingerboard for safety (Photo 1).

3 • Run each half-thick piece through a thickness planer to smooth the band-sawn surface and reduce the piece to final 1/4-inch thickness (Photo 2). Plane both sides of each piece.

4 • Rip the pieces to width, square one end of all boards, and cut them to the lengths in the Cutting List. These will be the outside layers of the laminated sides and back of the wagon.

RESAW AND PLANE THE STOCK

FINGERBOARD

Photo 1 • Resaw lumber for thin parts using a wide, coarse blade in a band saw. Use a fingerboard to hold the material against the fence.

Photo 2 • Plane boards to finished thickness, taking material off both sides. This relieves internal board stress and prevents cupping.

Side and Back Jigs

The jigs are frames that hold core blocks in position while outside laminating layers are glued to them. Each jig consists of vertical separators and end pieces permanently screwed to a bottom rail. The top of the jig is a head rail secured by removable screws. You can use either slotted round-head screws for removal with a screwdriver, or hex-head screws for removal with a socket wrench. The jigs also have cauls—separate flat side plates that are placed over the outside layers to distribute clamping pressure evenly over the surfaces.

Core blocks are cut to fit inside the spaces in the jig. They must fill the spaces but not bind, so the jig can be removed during lamination. The outside layers of the laminated assembly are cut to fit between the top and bottom rails and the end pieces of the jig.

In use, both sides of the core blocks and the inner faces of the outside layers are coated with glue. They are assembled in the jig and clamped with cauls on both sides. After the glue has begun to set, the top rail is removed and the clamps are loosened so the bottom rail and separators can be pulled out of the laminated assembly. Then the clamps are retightened until the glue cures completely, usually a matter of several hours.

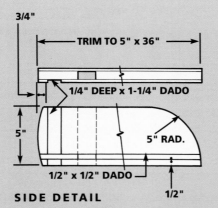

3/4"

TRIM TO 5" x 36"

1/4" DEEP x 1-1/4" DADO

5"

5" RAD.

1/2" x 1/2" DADO

1/2"

SIDE DETAIL

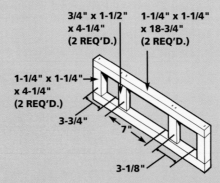

3/4" x 1-1/2"
x 4-1/4"
(2 REQ'D.)

1-1/4" x 1-1/4"
x 18-3/4"
(2 REQ'D.)

1-1/4" x 1-1/4"
x 4-1/4"
(2 REQ'D.)

3-3/4"

7"

3-1/8"

BACK LAMINATING JIG

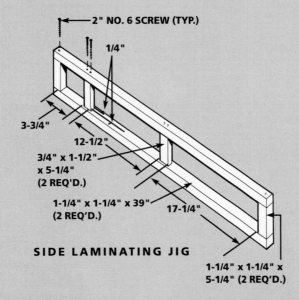

2" NO. 6 SCREW (TYP.)

1/4"

3-3/4"

12-1/2"

3/4" x 1-1/2"
x 5-1/4"
(2 REQ'D.)

1-1/4" x 1-1/4" x 39"
(2 REQ'D.)

17-1/4"

SIDE LAMINATING JIG

1-1/4" x 1-1/4" x
5-1/4" (2 REQ'D.)

Build the bed sides and back

● ● ● ● ● ● ● ● ● ● ● ● ● ● ● ● ● ● ●

1 ● To build the sides and back of the wagon bed you must laminate 1/4-inch thick outer layers to 3/4-inch thick core pieces. You build in pockets for the stake sides as you laminate the pieces, and then trim them to final size and shape afterward.

2 ● First make laminating jigs (see box at left) from scrap wood to hold the pieces in place for clamping. Also, cut flat boards to use as cauls to distribute the pressure of the clamps and protect the wood. Check the fit of the core pieces (F, G, J, K, L) in the jigs to make sure they don't bind. Then set each outside face (E, H) in place. It must fit between the top and bottom rails and the end pieces of the jig. Mark the positions of the jig separators on the back side of each outside piece. Those are the positions of the stake holes.

3 ● Start by laminating one side assembly. Use waterproof resorcinol glue—a dark, two-part glue that you must mix just before use. Apply it to both sides of the core pieces (J, K, L) and to the back sides of the two outer layers (H). Keep the glue 1/4 inch away from the stake hole positions to minimize any glue squeeze-out (Photo 3).

4 ● Assemble the pieces in the jig and put a caul over each side. Clamp the sandwich together for about 10 minutes. Then remove the screws in the top rail of the jig, loosen the clamps a bit, and pull the bottom rail down, moving the jig ends and separators out of the laminated assembly. Retighten the clamps. Allow the glue to cure for at least 10 hours before removing the clamps. Laminate the other side assembly and the back assembly (E, F, G) in the same way.

5 ● Rip the laminated back to 4 inches wide. Mark the ends of the back 2-7/8 inches from the outside edge of each stake hole; the finished length should be 15-3/4 inches. Cut the back to length.

6 • Rip the laminated sides to 5 inches wide. Mark the ends of each side 3-1/2 inches from the rear stake holes and 17 inches from the front stake holes. The finished length of the sides should be 36 inches, but don't cut them until Step 8.

7 • The sides are mirror images of each other. Label the bottom, top, back, and front of each side to avoid cutting mistakes. Cut a dado 1/2-inch wide by 1/2-inch deep along the inside face of each side, 1/2 inch up from the bottom (see Side Detail, page 132). Also cut dadoes 1-1/4 inch wide and 1/4 inch deep located 3/4 inch from the back edge of each side (Photo 4).

8 • Use a compass to draw the curves on the fronts and rears of the laminated side assemblies (Side Detail, page 132). Cut the curves with a saber saw or handsaw, and sand the cut faces to a smooth final shape.

Assemble the wagon bed

1 • The wagon bed consists of the floorboard assembly, the laminated sides and back, and a solid front (D). To build the floorboard assembly (see detail, below right), first lay out and drill all 3/16-inch and 1/4-inch holes in the cleats (C) and floorboards (A, B). Don't drill the 3/16-inch holes for the cleats completely through the floorboards.

2 • Finish-sand the side and back assemblies, floorboards, cleats, and front end (D).

3 • Glue and clamp the outer floorboards (A) into the long dadoes in the laminated sides and allow the glue to cure. Then glue and clamp the laminated back into the vertical dadoes at the rear of the sides. When you do this, clamp one of the cleats (C) to the front of the outer floorboards to hold the sides the proper distance apart. Check that everything stays square as you tighten the clamps.

4 • After the glue has cured, screw the front and rear cleats (C) to the underside of the outer floorboards (A) with No. 8 x 7/8-inch flathead screws. The middle two cleats are attached later. Also drive screws up through the cleats to fasten the two inner floorboards (B) in place. Then drive No. 8 x 1-1/2 inch flathead screws from below into the laminated back and the front (D). Finally, drill pilot holes and drive 2-1/2 inch finishing nails through the sides into the ends of the bed front.

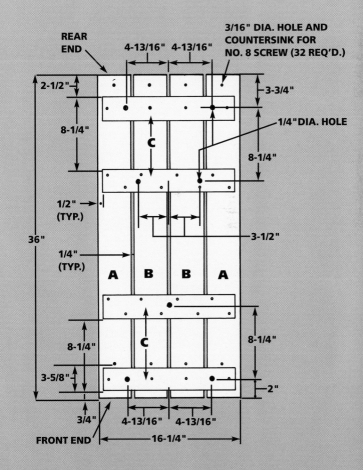

Floorboard Assembly — Bottom View

REAR END

4-13/16" 4-13/16"

3/16" DIA. HOLE AND COUNTERSINK FOR NO. 8 SCREW (32 REQ'D.)

2-1/2"

3-3/4"

8-1/4"

C

1/4"DIA. HOLE

8-1/4"

1/2" (TYP.)

3-1/2"

36"

1/4" (TYP.)

A B B A

8-1/4"

C

8-1/4"

3-5/8"

2"

3/4"

4-13/16" 4-13/16"

FRONT END 16-1/4"

BUILD THE BED SIDES AND BACK

Photo 3 • Apply resorcinol glue to all parts to be laminated. Keep the glue 1/4 inch away from the stake holes to keep squeeze-out to a minimum.

DADO FOR BACK

BLADE GUARD REMOVED FOR CLARITY (USE YOURS)

Photo 4 • Cut the long 1/2-inch dadoes in one pass. Cut each short, wide dado in several passes, until the width matches the thickness of the back.

Build the bolsters

1 • Lay out the top and bottom front bolster (U) and the rear bolster (T) on pieces of thick stock (see details, page 131). Rout axle grooves in the bottom edges of the rear and bottom front bolsters with a core box bit (Photo 5). Then cut the bolsters to their final shapes.

2 • Set the axles (AA) into their grooves, and position them so equal lengths extend at the bolster ends. Locate and drill 9/64-inch holes for the axle-positioning roll pins. Also locate and drill the 1/4-inch and 1/2-inch holes and the 7/8-inch counterbores that run vertically through the bolsters. Do not drill the 1/4-inch holes in the faces until you have the braces in position (Steps 4 and 5).

3 • Hammer a roll pin into the vertical axle (Z), and slip the axle into the hole in the top front bolster (U). Attach the top front and rear bolsters to the underside of the wagon bed with carriage bolts, washers, and nuts.

4 • Attach the rear bolster braces (EE) and rear axle hardware (AA, HH) to the rear bolster with 1/4-20 x 1-1/2-inch carriage bolts and nuts.

5 • Lay the front bolster brace (Y), and the top front bolster axle pivot plate (CC) over the front vertical axle. Drill the mounting holes for the bolster braces.

6 • Attach the inner cleats (C) to the floorboards (A, B) with No. 8 x 7/8-inch flathead screws (Photo 6). Bolt the bolster braces (Y, EE) to the cleats and floorboards with 1/4-20 x 1-1/2 inch carriage bolts, washers, and nuts.

7 • Assemble the yoke (DD) and axle hardware (AA, BB, HH) on the bottom front bolster (U) with carriage bolts and nuts (Photo 7).

8 • Assemble the handlebar (V, W, X) with 10-24 x 1-1/2 inch stove bolts, and attach it to the yoke with a 1/4-20 x 4-inch hex-head bolt. Trim the bolt to length with a hacksaw, file the threads clean, and attach a nylon locknut.

BUILD THE BOLSTERS

Photo 5 • Set up a router with a 1/2-inch core box bit in a router table to cut the axle grooves in the bolsters. Clamp a fingerboard to the router table to protect your hands.

Photo 6 • Use the bolster braces as guides for positioning the inner floorboard cleats. Drill holes through the braces and cleats, and into the mounting floorboards.

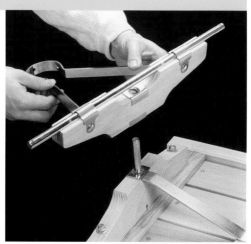

Photo 7 • Slip the bottom front bolster over the vertical shaft. Insert the cotter pin, but don't open it to lock the bolster in place until everything operates smoothly.

Complete the wagon

1 • To build the stake sides, place the stakes (Q) in their holes in the laminated sides and back. Wrap masking tape around the lower half of each stake so it sits firmly centered in its hole. Use 1/2-inch spacers as guides for positioning the side and back stake sides (M, N, P) and the side cleats (S).

2 • Glue and clamp the lower slats of the sides and back (M, P) to their stakes. Glue and clamp the short cleats (S) to the lower slats of the sides at the same time (Photo 8).

3 • Use 1/2-inch spacer blocks to position the upper slats (N, P) above the lower slats in the sides and back. Glue and clamp them in place.

4 • Reinforce all the joints where the slats cross the stakes or cleats with 1-inch finish nails.

5 • To decorate the wagon as shown in the finished photograph (page 128), use a straight-edge and pinstriping tool, available at auto-supply stores. Apply pinstripes to each slat in the stake sides and back, and to the laminated sides and back of the wagon bed (Photo 9). You can of course use other decorating schemes to suit your taste.

6 • Allow the pinstripes to dry overnight, then disassemble the wagon parts that are fastened with bolts. Do not remove any screws. Apply polyurethane varnish to all exposed surfaces. When the finish is dry, reassemble the wagon, and install the wheels and hubcaps.

7 • Take your favorite youngster for a joyride, or bring home a wagonload of groceries from the supermarket.

COMPLETE THE WAGON

SPACERS

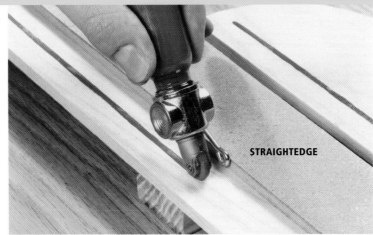

STRAIGHTEDGE

Photo 8 • Glue and clamp the slats to the side and back stakes and cleats. Allow the glue to cure, then nail the slats with 1-inch finish nails.

Photo 9 • Clamp a straightedge in place to guide the pinstriping tool. Practice the striping technique on scrap wood until you feel comfortable with it.

An easy-to-build little red wagon

This *little red wagon has the handsome look of toys from years gone by. The stake sides lift out to accommodate loads of various sizes or provide an open bed. The hardwood underbody construction, steel wheels, and hard-rubber tires ensure that the wagon will last and be treasured for years to come.*

Getting started

You don't have to be an expert woodworker to build this wagon and enjoy doing it. All you need are basic tools and some experience with simple projects. You can buy materials to make the metal parts at a hardware store or home center, and you can bend and shape the parts without having to be a blacksmith.

You'll need a circular saw and a portable saber saw. If you have a table saw or a band saw, cutting some parts will be even easier. A drum sanding attachment for your electric drill is helpful for smoothing curved edges, but a file and sandpaper also will work. Clamps are useful for gluing some parts together, but are not absolutely necessary.

Assembly Plan

2-1/4"

3/4" x 1-9/16"
STAKE SLOTS

USE AT BOLSTER ENDS

5-1/4"

1/2" x 6" CARRIAGE BOLT

1/2" DIA. HOLE

5-3/4"

1/4" SPACE

1-1/8"

5-3/4"

TYP.

TYP.

6"

9"

CC
U
CC

1/4" x 4"
MACHINE BOLT
AND LOCKNUT

1/4" x 2"
MACHINE BOLT
AND LOCKNUT
(2 OF EACH)

T

1/2" DIA. HOLE
1/2" DIA.
WASHER

5/8" DIA. HOLE

1/2" WASHER

N   P

3/8" X 4"
MACHINE BOLT,
WASHERS (4)
AND LOCKNUT

5/8" DIA. HOLE
1/2" DIA. WASHER
1/2" LOCKNUT

DD

CENTER
BRACE (S)

3/4" X 3/4"
PLASTIC
BUMPER

M

AA

BB

Labels: V, V, X, W, G, D, E, A, B, B, C, B, D, E, F, G, H, J, J, R, Q, Q, S, R, K, Z, L, Y, J, R, H, J, S, R

HARDWARE NOTES

① No. 6 x 3/4" pan-head
   screws

② 1-1/4" galv. deck screws

③ 1-5/8" galv. deck screws

④ 2-1/2" galv. deck screws

⑤ No. 8 finish washers

CONSTRUCTION TIP

When making the
metal fittings for this
wagon, take care
to avoid scratching
the surfaces or
damaging the edges.
Pad vise jaws with
1/4-inch plywood or
hardboard when you
clamp the metal for
bending. Tap care-
fully with the face
of the hammer flat
against the metal to
bend it. Round off all
sharp edges and
corners with a metal
file, and ream all
drilled holes to
remove any burrs
around the edges.

Cutting List

Key	Pcs.	Size and Description
A	2	3/4" x 1-1/2" x 34-1/2" pine (inner side rails)
B	2	3/4" x 1-1/2" x 14" pine (front and rear inner rails)
C	4	3/4" x 1-1/2" x 13-7/16" pine (side spacers)
D	2	3/4" x 1-1/2" x 10-15/16" pine (front and rear spacers)
E	4	3/4" x 1-1/2" x 1-1/2" pine (edge spacers)
F	2	3/4" x 2-1/4" x 36" pine (outer side rails)
G	2	3/4" x 2-1/4" x 17" pine (front and rear outer rails)
H	1	3/4" x 5-1/2" x 34-1/2" pine (center bed slat)
J	2	3/4" x 5-1/2" x 34-1/2" pine (side bed slats)
K	2	3/4" x 6-1/2" x 14-1/4" maple (rear bolster halves)
L	2	3/4" x 2" x 13-1/2" maple (upper front bolster)
M	2	3/4" x 4-1/2" x 14-1/4" maple (lower front bolster)
N	1	3/4" x 7-1/4" x 13-1/2" maple (upper yoke half)
P	1	3/4" x 7-1/4" x 12" maple (lower yoke half)

Key	Pcs.	Size and Description
Q	2	3/4" x 3" x 5" maple (rear bolster braces)
R	2	3/4" x 1-3/4" x 5" maple (front bolster braces)
S	1	3/4" x 2" x 7-1/4" maple (center brace)
T	1	1-1/2" x 1-1/2" x 30" pine (handle shaft)
U	1	3-7/16" x 1-1/4" diameter birch dowel (handle)
V	10	3/4" x 1-1/2" x 9-1/2" pine (stakes)
W	4	1/2" x 2-3/4" x 33-1/2" pine (side stake rails)
X	2	1/2" x 2-3/4" x 16" pine (end stake rails)
Y	4	1/8" x 1" x 6" aluminum (axle retainers)
Z	2	18" x 1/2" diameter steel (axle)
AA	4	1-3/4" x 10" diameter ball-bearing wheels
BB	4	1/2" stop caps (wheel retainers)
CC	2	1/8" x 1" x 6" steel (handle supports)
DD	1	2-1/2" x 1/2" diameter copper tubing (bushing)

Shopping List

Quantity	Item
1	1x6 x 10' clear pine
3	1x2 x 8' clear pine
1	1x4 x 10' clear pine
1	1x8 x 8' maple
2	1/2" x 2-3/4" x 12' clear pine
1	2x2 x 30" pine
1	1-1/4" diameter dowel
1	1/8" x 1" x 24" aluminum bar
1	1/2" x 36" round steel rod
1	1/8" x 1" x 12" steel bar
1	1/2" x 2-1/2" soft copper tubing
7	1/2" washers
1	1/2" locknut
1	1/2" x 6" carriage bolt
1	3/8" locknut
4	3/8" washers
1	3/8" x 4" machine bolt
1	1/4" x 4" machine bolt
2	1/4" x 2" machine bolts
3	1/4" locknuts
16	No. 6 x 3/4" pan-head screws
36	1-1/4" galvanized deck screws
74	1-5/8" galvanized deck screws
6	2-1/2" galvanized deck screws
32	No. 8 grommet washers (finish washers)
4	10" steel wheels with rubber tires (1-1/2" hub thickness)
4	1/2" stop caps (wheel retainers)
1	3/4" x 3/4" plastic bumper

Carpenter's glue; construction adhesive; spar varnish; paint thinner; exterior-grade primer; gloss enamel

Choose the lumber

1 • Most of the lumber used in this wagon is standard dimension stock. However, note the following exceptions, to be sure you get the proper size wood.

2 • The outside rails of the wagon bed (parts F and G) must be cut to width from 1x4 or wider stock. If you use 1x6 lumber, you can rip two rail widths from a single piece, but be sure the wood is free of flaws along all edges and across the entire width.

3 • The rails for the stake sides and back (parts W and X) are intended to be 1/2 inch thick by 2-3/4 inches wide. Not all home centers and lumber outlets carry 1/2-inch stock. If you can't find appropriate material, you can use standard 3/4-inch thick boards instead. Or you can have a cabinet shop plane stock to whatever thickness you require.

4 • The upper parts of the wagon are all pine, which keeps overall weight to a minimum. For greater durability you could use a hardwood. In that case, you may prefer to finish everything with varnish, rather than painting the rails of the stake sides.

5 • A hardwood is essential for the underbody parts of the wagon—the axle bolsters and the steering yoke. Maple or birch is perhaps the best choice for these parts. If you use oak, be sure to varnish it so it won't discolor if you leave the wagon outside.

Build the wagon bed

1 • The wagon bed consists of slats (J, H) for a platform, and rail assemblies (B–E) that form a frame for the platform. Cut these and the other upper pieces (U–W) to the dimensions in the Cutting List. Be sure to use straight-grained wood for the handle shaft (T).

2 • Assemble the outside frame of the platform using screws and waterproof carpenter's glue. Carefully position the side spacers (C) on each inner side rail (A) so the stakes will fit into their recesses. Place parts C 3-1/16 inches from each end of part A, locate and drill pilot holes, and glue and screw the parts together with 1-1/4 inch galvanized deck screws. For the front and rear inner rails (B), center parts D over parts B, locate and drill pilot holes, and glue and screw the parts together with 1-1/4 inch galvanized deck screws. Also, drill pilot holes into the ends of parts A and the edges of parts B, and then screw the parts together with 1-5/8 inch galvanized deck screws.

3 • Locate and drill pilot holes, and glue and screw the outer rail parts (F, G) to the inner frame with 1-5/8 inch galvanized deck screws. Immediately after assembly, make sure the frame is square and wipe off excess glue with a damp cloth.

4 • Glue and clamp the edge spacers (E) between the inner and outer rails, and set the frame assembly aside until the glue dries.

5 • Turn the frame assembly upside down, and lay in the bed slats (H, J) (Photo 1). Locate and drill pilot holes, and screw the slats to the inner rails of the frame with 1-5/8 inch galvanized deck screws (see the Assembly Plan).

OUTSIDE FRAME

BED SLATS

Photo 1 • Build the frame assembly for the wagon bed. Then position the bed slats, drill pilot holes, and screw the slats to the frame assembly.

Bolster, Yoke, and Hardware Plans

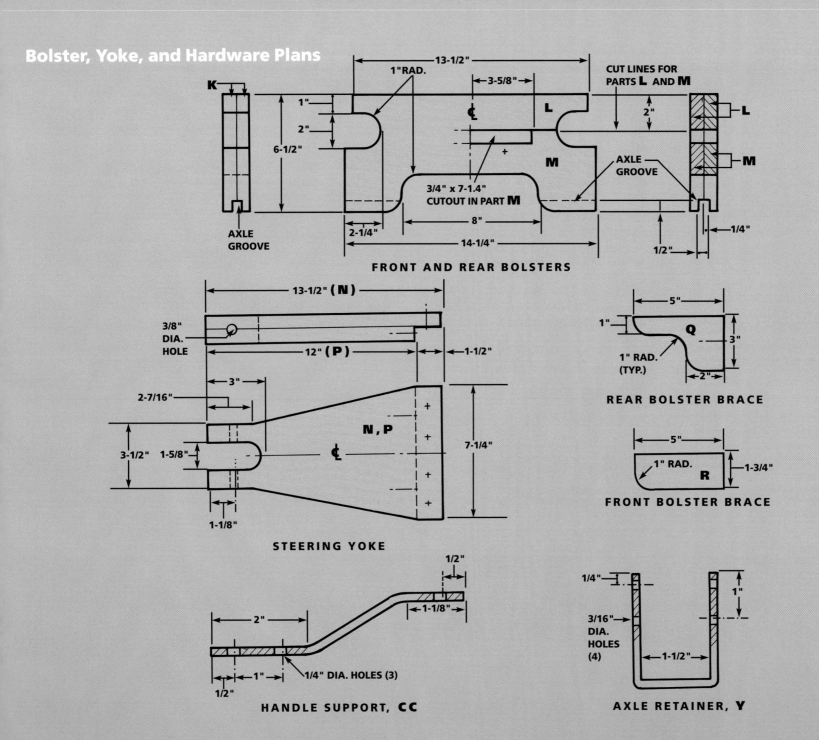

FRONT AND REAR BOLSTERS

- 13-1/2"
- 1" RAD.
- 3-5/8"
- CUT LINES FOR PARTS **L** AND **M**
- 1"
- 2"
- 6-1/2"
- **L**
- 2"
- **L**
- **M**
- AXLE GROOVE
- **M**
- 3/4" x 7-1.4" CUTOUT IN PART **M**
- 8"
- 2-1/4"
- 14-1/4"
- 1/2"
- 1/4"
- **K**
- AXLE GROOVE

STEERING YOKE

- 13-1/2" (**N**)
- 3/8" DIA. HOLE
- 12" (**P**)
- 1-1/2"
- 3"
- 2-7/16"
- 3-1/2"
- 1-5/8"
- **N, P**
- 7-1/4"
- 1-1/8"

REAR BOLSTER BRACE

- 5"
- 1"
- **Q**
- 3"
- 1" RAD. (TYP.)
- 2"

FRONT BOLSTER BRACE

- 5"
- 1" RAD.
- **R**
- 1-3/4"

HANDLE SUPPORT, CC

- 1/2"
- 2"
- 1-1/8"
- 1"
- 1/4" DIA. HOLES (3)
- 1/2"

AXLE RETAINER, Y

- 1/4"
- 1"
- 3/16" DIA. HOLES (4)
- 1-1/2"

Cut and mount the bolsters

1 • Draw the outlines of an axle bolster piece (K) onto 3/4-inch maple (see the bolster plans, opposite). Cut out this piece with a saber saw and use it as a template to trace the shape onto three more pieces of maple. Cut them out. You will glue these pieces together in pairs to make a rear and a front bolster (Step 2). And you will cut the front bolster into an upper and a lower section (Step 4).

2 • Lay out and cut 1/2-inch deep notches for the axles (Z) along the lower inside edge of each bolster piece with a hand saw (Photo 2). Position the bolster halves with their notches aligned, and glue and clamp them together. If you don't have clamps, drill pilot holes, and glue and screw the halves together with 1-1/4 inch galvanized deck screws.

3 • While the glue is drying, lay out and cut the yoke parts (N, P) with a saber saw, and glue them together (see the plans, opposite). Also lay out and cut the bolster braces (Q, R). Then cut the center brace (S) from the remaining waste. Set the parts aside.

4 • Draw a cutting line 2 inches from the top of the glued-up front bolster, dividing it into upper (L) and lower (M) sections. Cut these sections apart with a handsaw or table saw.

5 • Cut a notch 7-1/4 inches long and 3/4 inch deep in the lower front bolster (M) to accept the steering yoke.

6 • Locate and drill pilot holes for attaching the steering yoke to the lower front bolster (M). Screw the yoke to the bolster with four 1-5/8 inch galvanized deck screws. Also locate and drill two pilot holes through the bolster (M), into the back edge of the lower piece of the yoke. Drive 2-1/2 inch galvanized deck screws in these holes.

7 • Locate and drill pilot holes for the 1-1/4 and 1-5/8 inch screws that fasten the bed slats to the bolsters (see the Assembly Plan). Center the bolsters between the outside edges of the platform. For the front bolster, screw through the bed slats into the upper section (L), using the shorter screws on the outer holes. Attach the rear bolster (K) in the same way.

8 • Attach the rear bolster braces (Q) to the rear bolster, and the front bolster braces (R) to the front bolster. Locate the center brace (S) 1-1/2 inches behind the front bolster (Photo 3) and drive screws into it through the front bolster braces. Also drive screws through the slats of the wagon bed into all the braces (see Assembly Plan).

CUT AND MOUNT THE BOLSTERS

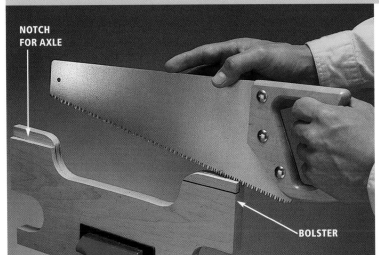

NOTCH FOR AXLE

BOLSTER

Photo 2 • Cut a notch for the axle in each bolster piece. When two pieces are glued together to make the entire bolster, the notches form a groove for the axle.

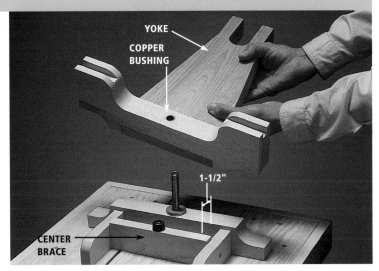

YOKE

COPPER BUSHING

1-1/2"

CENTER BRACE

Photo 3 • Attach the steering yoke and lower bolster assembly to the upper bolster. A copper bushing prevents the pivot from wearing the yoke.

Make the hardware and steering assembly

Working Tip

To cut the curved parts of the sled you need to draw them to size on the wood. Start by drawing 1-inch grids on your plywood or stock. Then, following the patterns shown here, mark the approximate spots on the wood where a pattern outline intersects each grid line. Smoothly connect the marks to create the cutting outline.

1 • Make the axle retainers (Y) from 1/8- x 1-inch aluminum, available at most hardware stores. Cut four 6-inch lengths, and mark bending lines 2-1/8 inches from each end.

2 • Clamp an axle retainer in a vise, aligning one bending line with the top of the vise jaws; use shims in the jaws to protect the aluminum. Hammer the retainer over to make a 90-degree bend (Photo 4). Reclamp the retainer in the vise and bend the other side in the same way to get a square U shape (see plans, page 140). Bend the other three retainers in the same way.

Photo 4 • Bend 1/8-inch thick aluminum bars to make axle retainers. Mark bending lines on the metal and clamp it in a vise. Tap with a hammer to make the bends.

3 • Use 1/8- x 1- x 6-inch steel strap to make the two handle supports (CC). Mark bending lines 2 inches from one end and 1-1/8 inches from the other end of each piece. Bend as shown in the plan (opposite) in the same way as with the retainers. Locate and drill 1/4-inch holes in the ends of the handle supports, and in the handle dowel (U). Test-fit the handle and handle supports with the handle shaft (T), and adjust the bends on handle supports if necessary. Set the supports aside for painting.

4 • Cut the bushing (DD) from 1/2-inch soft copper tubing using a hacksaw, and file or sand the ends smooth.

5 • Locate and drill a 5/8-inch hole through the steering yoke and the lower bolster (M). Enlarge the hole slightly by running the bit in and out a few times until the copper bushing (DD) fits snugly inside. Insert the bushing.

6 • Locate and drill a 1/2-inch hole through the center bed slat (H) and the middle of the upper front bolster (L).

7 • Turn the wagon upside down. Insert the 1/2 x 6-inch carriage bolt through the hole in the bed slat (H). Slip the washers over the bolt, and install the lower bolster and steering yoke assembly (Photo 3, page 141). Tighten the 1/2-inch locknut securely to the bolt, but make sure the yoke can turn.

8 • Cut 1/2- x 36-inch steel rod into two 18-inch axles (Z). This axle length is only for wheels with 1-1/2 inch hub thickness. If your wheels are a different size, adjust the axle length accordingly. While the wagon is still upside down, lay the axles in the bolster slots and slide on the washers and wheels to check their fit. The axles should protrude 1/2 inch from the wheels. (The wheels used have hubs that are 1-1/2 inches thick; if your wheels are different, adjust axle length accordingly.)

9 • Locate and drill 3/8-inch holes in the yoke tongue and the bottom of the handle shaft (T) (see the Assembly Plan). Bolt the handle shaft to the yoke with a 3/8- x 4-inch machine bolt and washers in the correct positions.

10 • Disassemble all parts that are held by bolts and nuts, for varnishing and painting.

Finish the wagon

1 • Sand all edges to round off sharp corners. Sand the faces of the stakes (V) so they slide easily into the slots in the frame assembly. Leave about a 1/32-inch clearance to allow for the thickness of the varnish.

2 • All wooden parts except the rails of the stake sides need three coats of spar varnish to protect them from water and the sun's ultraviolet rays. Seal the wood with a thin first coat—three parts spar varnish mixed with one part mineral spirits. Then apply two more unthinned coats of varnish. Follow the directions on the varnish label for drying time between the coats.

3 • Paint the rails of the stake sides, front and back. First apply exterior-grade primer. When it is dry, spray on a gloss enamel. Mask off the tires before you paint the wheels. You also can experiment with pinstriping or decals along the sides of the stake rails, or you can paint your child's name to personalize the wagon.

4 • Reassemble the steering assembly and the axles, wheels, and washers. Tap the stop caps—hat-shaped steel metal washers with internal teeth—onto the axles with a hammer until they lock in place. The stop caps are almost impossible to remove without ruining them, so make sure you've assembled all parts and washers correctly before you install them.

5 • Locate and drill pilot holes in the front and rear bolsters for attaching the axle retainers (Y); fasten the retainers with No. 6 x 3/4-inch pan-head screws (Photo 5). Screw the plastic bumper to the center brace (S); the bumper limits the turning radius of the wagon for safety (see detail in the Assembly Plan).

6 • Build each section of the stake sides with the stakes positioned in their slots to guarantee a good fit. Use 3/4-inch spacer blocks to maintain correct clearance between the wagon bed and the lower rails (Photo 6). Locate and drill pilot holes for the 1-1/4 inch galvanized deck screws. Attach rails with screws, grommet washers, and construction adhesive. Align the top edges of the upper rails with the tops of the stakes, and attach them in the same way.

7 • Turn the wagon over to a young person, and watch the fun.

FINISH THE WAGON

Photo 5 • After varnishing the parts, put the wheels and axles in place and screw the aluminum axle retainers to the bolsters. Add a bumper as a safety stop for steering.

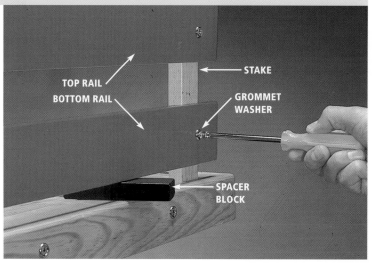

Photo 6 • Use 3/4-inch spacers on the bed frame to correctly position the lower rails when screwing them to the stakes. Attach the upper rails flush with the stake tops.

Furniture and Storage

Shelving Unit

Create plenty of open storage in any child's room with this clever and modern plywood-and-PVC design.

146

Lego Table

This colorful play table may *look* like it's made of Lego blocks, but sturdy construction guarantees it will hold up to years of building and stacking.

148

Heirloom Cradle

With heart-shaped cutouts in the head and foot, this walnut piece will cradle generations of infants in love and comfort.

152

Pine Cradle

The simplified construction of this reproduction doesn't interfere with its classic Colonial grace and charm.

156

Country Bench

Natural pine and simple heart cutouts add a country twist to this bench and storage chest.

162

Toy Storage Box

Teach your favorite child the ABC's of neatness with this delightful place to put away toys and treasures.

168

Bunk Beds

Kids sleep tight, and so will parents. These beds are safe and sturdy, *and* they're great space-savers.

176

Loft Bed

Make the most of even the smallest bedroom space. This combo bed, desk, and storage area does it all.

182

A *simple* shelving unit

This inexpensive, easy-to-build shelving unit can help organize any child's room. The spacious plywood shelves slide into slots cut in legs of PVC plumbing pipe. The whole structure is held together by apron blocks nailed and glued to the shelf edges. Paint the shelves to match the white plastic legs, or use a contrasting color.

Getting started

You'll need a minimum of skill and time to build this project, and only basic power tools: a circular saw or table saw, and a saber saw or jigsaw to cut the curved shelf ends and leg caps. A router with a round-over bit is helpful for shaping the leg caps and apron blocks, but a rasp and sandpaper also will work. Start the leg slots with a handsaw and use a coping saw or saber saw to finish making the notches.

Step-by-step instructions

1 • Cut four 3/4-inch birch plywood shelves to 13-1/2 x 60 inches with a circular saw or a table saw. Lay out the 6-3/4 inch radius ends, and cut them with a saber saw.

2 • Carefully locate and lay out slots for the shelves in all four PVC (polyvinyl chloride) legs. Draw a pencil line down the length of each leg and another on the other side, exactly opposite the first, to mark the bottoms of the slots. Lay out identical 3/4-inch wide slots on each leg, following the spacing intervals in the plans. Cut the slots with a handsaw, stopping exactly halfway through the pipes. Cut across the bottom of the slots with a coping saw or a saber saw, and file the corners square.

3 • Make four top caps for the legs. Each cap is two circles of 3/4-inch plywood held together with drywall screws. Cut the bottom circles slightly smaller than the inside diameter of the PVC pipe; cut the top circles to the outside diameter of the pipe, and round over their top edges with a router or a rasp and sandpaper.

4 • Cut eight shelf apron blocks 40-1/4 inches long. Cut one corner at each end to a 1-inch radius. Then cut off a piece 3-5/8 inches long at each end. This gives you eight apron blocks 33 inches long and 16 short end blocks. Cut 9-degree bevels on all edges that adjoin the legs (see plan detail).

5 • Prime and paint the leg end caps, the shelves, and the apron blocks.

6 • Assemble the unit: Lay the two rear legs flat on the floor and slip the shelves into their slots to hold them in position, then fit the front legs over the shelf edges. Position the legs so they're equidistant from the ends with a long apron block between them. Attach the long blocks with glue and 6d finish nails so they're tight against the legs and flush with the shelf tops; then nail and glue the end blocks on each shelf. Set all nailheads just below the surface. Turn the unit over, check the alignment of the legs, and glue and nail on the rear apron blocks.

7 • Stand the unit upright and glue the end caps to the tops of the legs with a bead of construction adhesive.

Assembly Plan

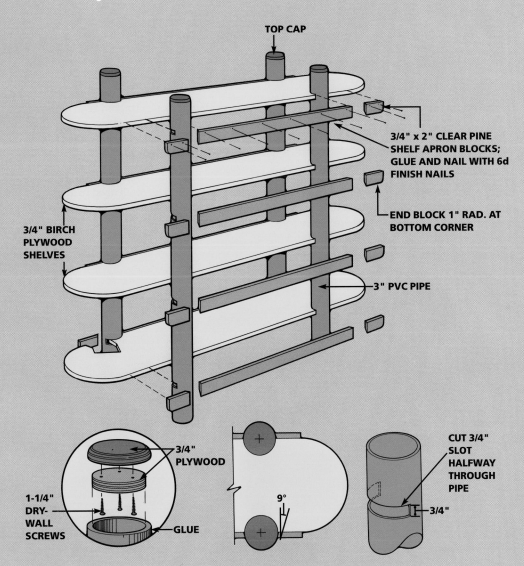

TOP CAP

3/4" x 2" CLEAR PINE SHELF APRON BLOCKS; GLUE AND NAIL WITH 6d FINISH NAILS

END BLOCK 1" RAD. AT BOTTOM CORNER

3/4" BIRCH PLYWOOD SHELVES

3" PVC PIPE

3/4" PLYWOOD

1-1/4" DRY-WALL SCREWS

GLUE

9°

CUT 3/4" SLOT HALFWAY THROUGH PIPE

3/4"

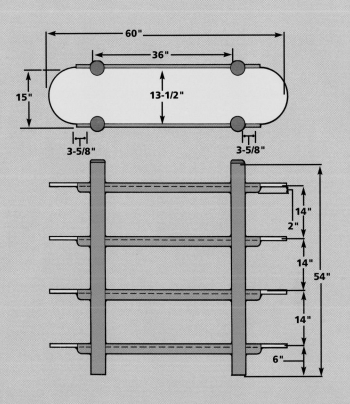

60"

36"

15"

13-1/2"

3-5/8"

3-5/8"

14"

2"

14"

54"

14"

6"

Materials List

Quantity	Description
1-1/2 sheets	4' x 8' x 3/4" birch plywood
28 feet	1x2 clear pine
4	54" lengths of 3" PVC pipe
	6d finish nails; 1-1/4" drywall screws
	Wood glue, construction adhesive, primer, paint

The perfect construction site—a Lego table

If your children play with Lego blocks, you've probably had the pleasure of helping corral lots of tiny pieces from the family room floor. This Lego-style table will help contain all the clutter.

The textured surface is made of Lego base plates that lift out so the table can be used for other toys or games as well.

Getting started

This table is designed around dimension lumber and is easy to build. If you have your lumberyard cut the plywood top, you can assemble the table in just a few hours using basic tools: a miter box, drill, hammer, nail set, and screwdriver. A router with a 3/16-inch round-over bit or a Surform tool are handy for rounding over the edges, but a rasp and sandpaper also will work.

The table legs look like stacked Lego blocks, but they are really one-piece columns, so they won't tumble apart. The top is screwed to the legs for maximum stability.

Plan to spend as much time painting the project as building it. You'll need to apply multiple coats to achieve the deep, glossy colors of Lego blocks.

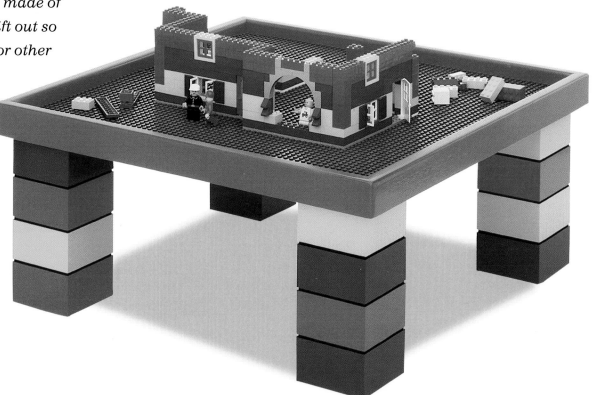

Assembly Plan

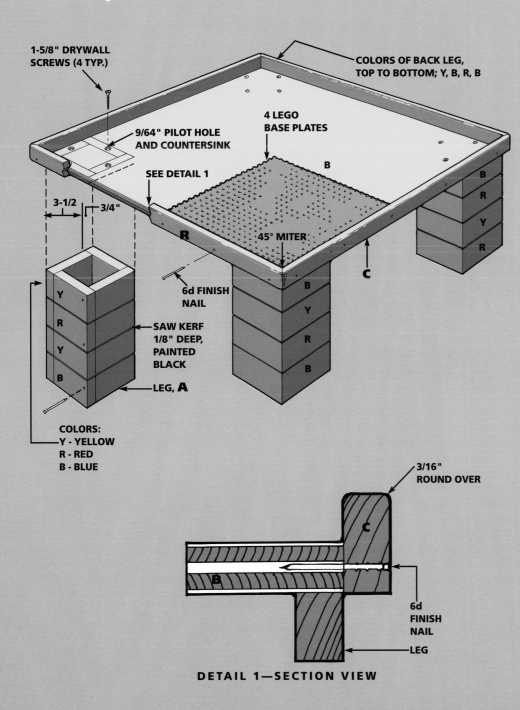

1-5/8" DRYWALL SCREWS (4 TYP.)

COLORS OF BACK LEG, TOP TO BOTTOM; Y, B, R, B

9/64" PILOT HOLE AND COUNTERSINK

4 LEGO BASE PLATES

SEE DETAIL 1

B

3-1/2

3/4"

45° MITER

R

C

6d FINISH NAIL

B

B

R

Y

R

B

Y

R

Y

B

Y

R

SAW KERF 1/8" DEEP, PAINTED BLACK

LEG, **A**

COLORS:
Y - YELLOW
R - RED
B - BLUE

3/16" ROUND OVER

C

B

6d FINISH NAIL

LEG

DETAIL 1—SECTION VIEW

Cutting List

Key	Pcs.	Size and Description
A	16	3/4" x 3-1/2" x 8" birch
B	1	3/4" x 20-1/8" x 20-1/8" birch plywood
C	4	3/4" x 21-5/8" x 1-1/2" birch

Materials List

1/4 sheet	3/4" birch plywood
2	1x4 x 6' birch
1	1x2 x 8' birch
	Carpenter's glue
	6d finish nails
	1-5/8" drywall screws
	Spackling compound
	Enamel primer
	Blue, yellow, red, and black enamel
	Fine artist's brush

Build the Lego table

1 • Cut the top (B) from 3/4-inch birch plywood. Make sure it is exactly square: 20-1/8 x 20-1/8 inches. When four 10-inch square Lego base plates (see Construction Tip with the Assembly Plan) are put in place, there will be 1/16 inch clearance around the outside edges—just enough to let you lift the base plates out when needed.

2 • Cut two 6-foot birch 1x4's in half. Build them into a box 4-1/4 inches square and 36 inches long. Butt one edge of each piece against the adjacent piece; let the other edge overlap the adjacent piece (see plan). Fasten the box edges with both carpenter's glue and 6d finish nails.

3 • When the glue is dry, cut the box into four 8-inch lengths. These are the legs (A). Make sure they are all exactly the same length so the table will not wobble. Set all nailheads below the wood surface with a nail set. Sand all joints flush and fill the porous end grain, the nail holes, and any surface imperfections with spackling compound. Sand again, and round over the sharp edges slightly.

4 • Draw lines 2 inches apart all the way around each leg, dividing it into four equal segments. Then saw shallow 1/8-inch grooves on the lines to simulate the joints between stacked blocks. If you use a handsaw, use a guide block to get straight cuts (Photo 1).

5 • Round over both edges along one narrow side of the 1x2's. These will be at the top of the table edging (C). Use a router with a 3/16-inch round-over bit, a Surform tool, or a rasp, followed by sandpaper.

6 • Now cut the edging (C) to length, one piece at a time. The corners have miter joints; cut them as follows: Cut one end at a 45-degree angle, then hold the piece in position against the edge of the table top (B) and mark the location of the miter at the other end. Cut that miter, then glue and nail the first piece to the top with 6d finish nails. Cut and attach the other three edging pieces in the same way.

7 • Round over the sharp corners at the miter joints with sandpaper to prevent injury.

8 • Set a leg in each corner on the tabletop and trace around it to mark its position. Lift the leg away and drill four 9/64-inch countersunk pilot holes in the top (see the plans). Position the legs under the table and the corners and drill corresponding pilot holes in the top edges of the legs.

9 • Paint the legs and the table edging with enamel primer. When it is dry, use tape to mask off the areas to be painted in various colors. Choose spray or brush-on enamel paints that match the colors of Lego blocks (Photo 2). Apply several coats to cover the wood grain. Follow the instructions on the label for drying time between coats. Let the final coat harden for several days.

10 • Paint the saw kerfs on the legs in black enamel with a fine artist's brush.

11 • Screw the legs to the top with 1-5/8 inch drywall screws (Photo 3) and lay the four Lego base plates onto the top.

12 • Turn your junior architect or contractor loose to build the city of the future.

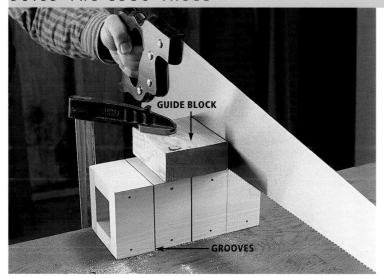

Working Tip

To save lots of time, cut the leg grooves (Photo 1) on a table saw. Set the blade to cut 1/8 in. deep and set the fence 2 in. from the blade. Run a leg through with one end against the fence four times, to cut a groove on each side. Turn the leg end for end and cut the set of grooves at the other end. Do the same with the other legs. Finally, set the fence 4 in. from the blade and run the legs through to cut the center grooves.

Photo 1 • Cut shallow grooves on all four sides of the legs to simulate the joints between blocks. Clamp a block to the leg to keep the saw blade straight and vertical.

Photo 2 • Mask off each section of the leg, then spray or brush on paint. When the legs are dry, paint the grooves black with a fine brush. Also paint the table edging.

Photo 3 • Screw the legs to the top with flathead screws after the paint has thoroughly hardened. Then lay the Lego base plates in place inside the edging.

A charming Pennsylvania Dutch **heirloom cradle**

This heirloom cradle design is based on a genuine antique, but it has been modified to make construction easier and the cradle safer. The heart-shaped cutouts and solid-walnut construction are especially emblematic of traditional Pennsylvania Dutch furniture.

Safety Tip

This cradle is intended only for young children who aren't yet able to sit or pull themselves up by the sides. Do not use it for active infants, and do not let older children use it as a toy for rocking "rides."

Getting started

Building this cradle is only a moderately difficult project. There are just seven parts—most of them duplicates—and they fit together with simple screw-and-plug joints. You'll need a table saw or radial arm saw; a jigsaw or saber saw; a router with a 1/2-inch cove bit; and a 3/8-inch plug-cutting bit fitted in a drill press or a portable electric drill with a drilling guide.

The cradle shown here has a rich oil finish, but a varnish would be just as appropriate.

Assembly Plan

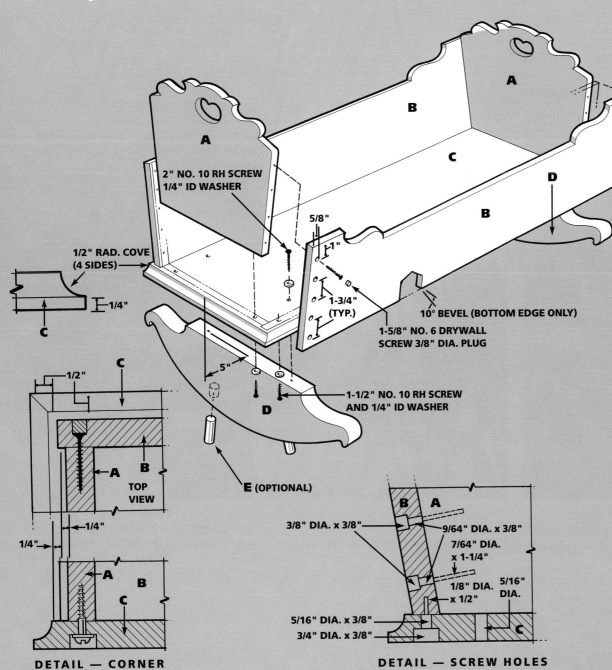

2" NO. 10 RH SCREW
1/4" ID WASHER

1/2" RAD. COVE
(4 SIDES)

1/4"

C

5/8"

1"

1-3/4"
(TYP.)

10° BEVEL (BOTTOM EDGE ONLY)

1-5/8" NO. 6 DRYWALL
SCREW 3/8" DIA. PLUG

5"

1-1/2" NO. 10 RH SCREW
AND 1/4" ID WASHER

E (OPTIONAL)

DETAIL — CORNER

1/2"

C

A   B

TOP
VIEW

1/4"

1/4"

A

B

A

C

DETAIL — SCREW HOLES

3/8" DIA. x 3/8"

B   A

9/64" DIA. x 3/8"

7/64" DIA.
x 1-1/4"

1/8" DIA.
x 1/2"

5/16"
DIA.

5/16" DIA. x 3/8"

3/4" DIA. x 3/8"

C

Cutting List

Key	Pcs.	Size and Description
A	2	3/4" x 12-1/2" x 18" walnut (ends)
B	2	3/4" x 9" x 35" walnut (sides)
C	1	3/4" x 17-1/2" x 36-1/2" walnut (bottom)
D	2	1-1/2" x 6" x 30" walnut (rockers)
E	2	2" x 3/4" diameter walnut (optional legs)

Shopping List

1	15" x 33" cradle mattress
12 board feet	3/4" walnut
4 board feet	1-1/2" walnut
14	No. 10 x 1-1/2" round-head screws
4	No. 10 x 2" round-head screws
18	1/4" flat washers
1	4" x 3/4" diameter walnut dowel
	Hide glue or shellac sticks
	Tack cloth
	Oil or varnish finish

Build the cradle

1 • Cut all boards to their rough lengths (see the Cutting List), and edge-glue stock to get the widths you need for the ends (A), the sides (B), the bottom (C), and the rockers (D). Carefully select your lumber; avoid boards that contain lighter walnut sapwood.

2 • Fill small knotholes or imperfections with hide glue and walnut dust or melted drops from a shellac stick used for furniture repair. Plane and sand the glued-up blanks flat and smooth. If you must use stock with imperfections, try to reserve it for the bottom (C).

3 • Cut the glued-up boards into blanks on which you will mark the final shapes. Cut the sides (B) to 9 x 35 inches, and cut a 10-degree bevel on their bottom edges. Cut the ends (A) to 12-1/2 x 18 inches with a table saw or radial-arm saw (see the End pattern, opposite); save the cut-off scraps to use later as clamping pads. Cut the bottom (C) to 17-1/2 x 36-1/2 inches. Sand both sides of all parts with 180-grit sand-paper, except for the outside faces of the sides (B); you'll sand those after gluing in the screw plugs. Rout the cove on the edges of the bottom (C), making several light passes with a 1/2-inch radius cove bit (Photo 1).

4 • Lightly draw a grid of 1-inch squares on your glued-up blanks. For each square in the gridded pattern, find the corresponding square on your wood, and draw a line on the wood that matches the line in the pattern square. Lightly draw corresponding lines in all squares, then connect them with a single smooth line to make the final outline. (Or enlarge the patterns and transfer them onto heavy paper, cut out the shapes, and trace them onto the wood.) In either case, you'll need to flop the half-patterns given for the ends (A), sides (B), and rockers (D) in order to obtain the full shapes.

Working Tip

You can enlarge patterns onto the wood as described in Step 4, or you can photocopy the patterns printed on the opposite page at an enlarged scale. You may need to recopy in two or three steps to get to the final full size of each grid square equal to 1 inch.

BUILD THE CRADLE

Photo 1 • Rout the edges of the cradle bottom with a 1/2-inch self-piloted cove bit, making several light cuts.

Photo 2 • Transfer and enlarge the patterns onto the wood, then cut the scrollwork with a saber saw or jigsaw.

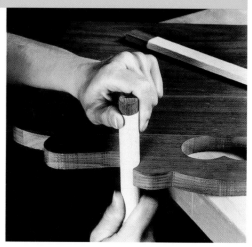

Photo 3 • Sand the curved edges with sandpaper taped to a dowel, or use a sanding drum mounted in an electric drill or a drill press.

5 • Shape the scrollwork with a jigsaw or a saber saw (Photo 2), cutting directly on the outline marked on the wood. Use a fine-tooth blade to minimize sanding on the cut edges.

6 • Sand all the cut edges. To speed work on the curves, chuck a sanding drum in your electric drill or drill press, or use a dowel wrapped with sandpaper (Photo 3).

7 • Cut 24 walnut plugs with a 3/8-inch plug-cutting bit. Test the first plug in a sample counterbored plug hole you've drilled in scrap wood. If the fit isn't snug, choose a different bit for the plug holes.

8 • Locate and drill the plug holes and 9/64-inch screw shank holes in the sides (B). Use a drill press, or a guide for your portable electric drill, to keep all holes vertical. Then, on a flat surface, clamp the sides to the ends (A) with a 1/4-inch overhang at each end; use the cut-off end scraps you saved earlier for clamp pads. Make sure the holes in the sides are centered on the edges of the ends and drill matching pilot holes in the ends (A).

9 • Glue and screw the sides to the ends with No. 6 x 1-5/8 inch drywall screws, then glue in the walnut plugs. Orient the plugs so the grain matches and blends in with the grain on the surface of the sides. Cut the plugs to within 1/8 inch of the sides with a small saw, then plane or chisel the ends flush. Finish-sand the plugs and sides with 180-grit sandpaper.

10 • Lay out the locations of the holes for the rockers (D) and the side-end assembly on the underside of the bottom (C). Note that these holes are drilled oversize to allow the bottom to shrink and expand without cracking. Drill the 3/4-inch holes first, then drill the 5/16-inch shank holes. Clamp the side-end assembly to the bottom (C) and drill matching pilot holes in the bottom edges of the sides and ends (see the Screw Holes detail in the plans).

11 • Locate and drill four 5/16-inch holes in the bottom corresponding to the 1/8-inch pilot holes in the rockers. Screw the bottom to the rockers using No. 10 x 2-inch roundhead screws and 1/4-inch flat washers. (See the Screw Holes and Rocker details in the plans.)

12 • Locate and drill two 3/4-inch holes in one of the rockers (D) for the optional short dowel legs (E). If you install these legs, they will keep the cradle from rocking, which may be a desirable safety precaution. Drill the holes to a consistent 1-inch depth so the dowels will be interchangeable. Cut the dowels to length and sand them smooth.

13 • Finish-sand all surfaces with 180-grit sandpaper. Remove sanding dust with a tack cloth.

14 • Apply an oil finish. Oil is the perfect finish for a hardwood project like this: It soaks into the wood to bring out its color, and its resins leave a low gloss.

15 • Let the wood soak up as much of the first coat of oil as it can. Reapply oil to any dull spots. After an hour, wipe off the oil, and continue wiping it off at hourly intervals several more times as more oil bleeds to the surface. Let the wood dry for 24 hours, then dry-sand any raised grain with 600-grit sandpaper.

16 • Apply two additional coats of oil in the same way, wiping it off as before. For best results, never let excess oil dry on the surface. After wiping off the last coat, buff all surfaces with 0000 steel wool.

Pattern Pieces

Each square = 1"

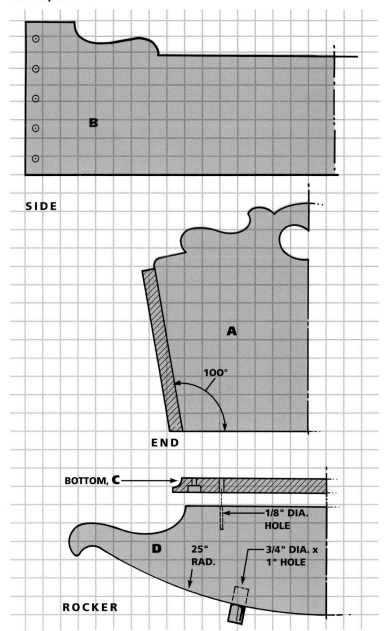

An Early American pine cradle

Although squarely in the Colonial tradition, this updated cradle is easier to construct than many similar reproductions. When you build it, you'll be creating a family heirloom that will be cherished for generations.

Getting started

Even a beginning woodworker should be able to build this cradle in two or three weekends. You'll need a table saw, a jigsaw or saber saw, a router, a belt sander, an orbital sander, a 3/8-inch plug-cutting bit for your drill, and three or more 30-inch long pipe or bar clamps. A band saw and a drill press would speed the work but aren't essential.

All the parts are cut from clear pine and go together with nails and screws. For the wider parts, you'll need to edge-glue 1x10 boards (actual width 9-1/2 inches) to get the widths you need. Make these blanks slightly longer and wider than the dimensions given in the Cutting List, and then cut them down to their finished sizes later.

This cradle is designed to accept a standard 2- x 18- x 36-inch cradle mattress, but measure the bedding you plan to use before you begin the project and adjust the length and width of the cradle as necessary. For sources of mattresses, look under Furniture—Children's in the Yellow Pages.

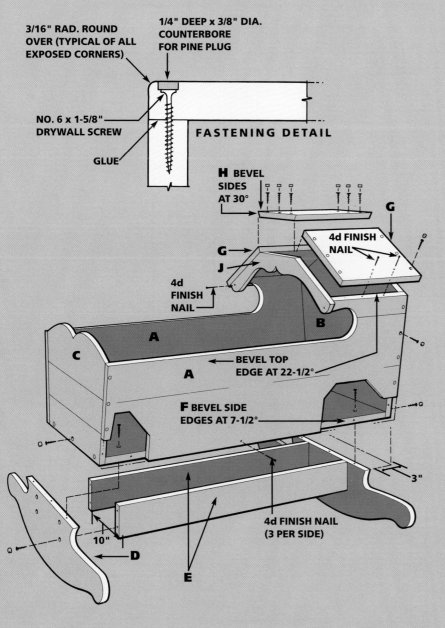

3/16" RAD. ROUND OVER (TYPICAL OF ALL EXPOSED CORNERS)

1/4" DEEP x 3/8" DIA. COUNTERBORE FOR PINE PLUG

NO. 6 x 1-5/8" DRYWALL SCREW

GLUE

FASTENING DETAIL

H BEVEL SIDES AT 30°

G

4d FINISH NAIL

G

J

4d FINISH NAIL

A

B

C

A

BEVEL TOP EDGE AT 22-1/2°

F BEVEL SIDE EDGES AT 7-1/2°

4d FINISH NAIL (3 PER SIDE)

3"

10"

D

E

Cutting List

Key	Pcs.	Size and Description
A	2	3/4" x 17-3/4" x 37-1/2" pine (sides)
B	1	3/4" x 22" x 24" pine (head end)
C	1	3/4" x 14" x 22" pine (foot end)
D	2	3/4" x 8" x 36" pine (rocker)
E	2	3/4" x 4" x 30" pine (cross supports)
F	1	3/4" x 18-1/4" x 36" pine (bottom)
G	2	3/4" x 10" x 11" pine (roof sides)
H	1	3/4" x 8-7/8" x 11" pine (roof center)
J	1	3/4" x 6-1/2" x 26" pine (roof front)

Shopping List

7	1x10 x 8' pine
56	No. 6 x 1-5/8" drywall screws
10	4d finish nails
1	3/8" diameter plug cutter
1 pint	Early American wood stain
1 pint	Danish oil finish
1	2" x 18" x 36" cradle mattress pad
	Carpenter's glue
	Wood putty

CONSTRUCTION TIP

To form smooth, symmetrical curves on the cradle pieces, do not lay out grid patterns directly on the pine blanks. Instead, make templates of 1/4-inch plywood, which is easy to sand for fine-tuning the shape. Then trace the template outlines on to the cradle wood. Do not use hardboard for templates; it will rapidly dull your saw blade.

Pattern Pieces

Each square = 1 "

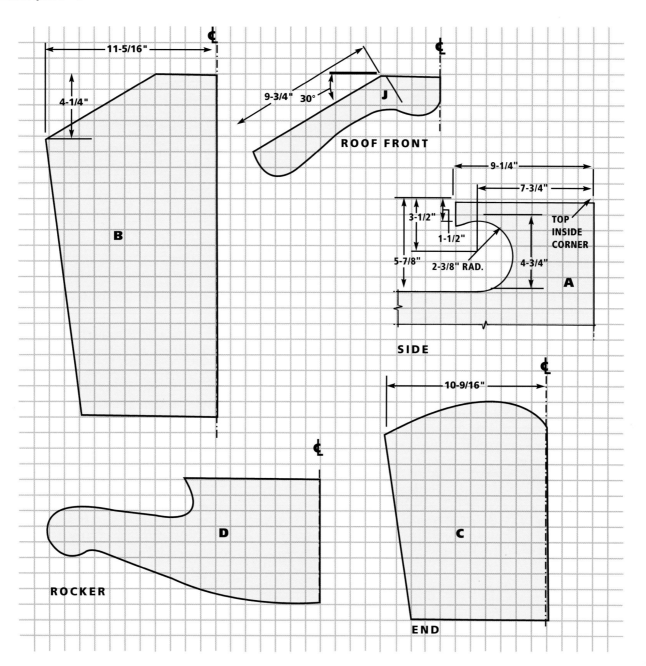

11-5/16"

4-1/4"

B

9-3/4" 30°

J

ROOF FRONT

9-1/4"

7-3/4"

3-1/2"

1-1/2"

**TOP
INSIDE
CORNER**

5-7/8"

2-3/8" RAD.

4-3/4"

A

SIDE

10-9/16"

C

D

ROCKER

END

Glue-up and cut the blanks

1 • Choose the lumber for the cradle carefully. Buy the straightest, flattest clear pine 1x10's you can find, and make sure they're thoroughly dry. To minimize warping and cracking, and to get the width required for most of the pieces, you need to resaw and edge-glue the boards; see Edge-gluing Boards, at right.

2 • Glue-up at least three pieces of resawn pine to make a blank for each side (A). Glue and clamp one joint at a time and let the glue dry. Add more pieces one at a time until the glued-up panel is just over 18 inches wide (Photo 1). Next, edge-glue at least three resawn pieces to make the head end (B) and bottom (F), and at least two pieces to make the foot end (C) and the roof sides (G).

3 • Cut pieces A through J to the sizes in the Cutting List. The sides (A) are mirror images of each other, so label the inside, outside, top, bottom, head, and foot of each piece to make sure you cut them correctly.

4 • Cut the beveled edges on parts A, H, and F. For the top edges of the sides (A), set your table saw blade to cut at 22-1/2 degrees. Remember that the sides are mirror images of each other, so cut the bevels to slant to the outside face of each side. Cut 30-degree bevels on the long edges of the roof center (H), which adjoin the roof sides (G). Cut 7-1/2 degree bevels on the side edges of the bottom (F).

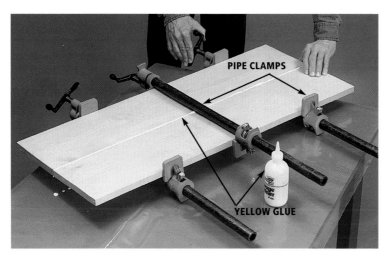

PIPE CLAMPS

YELLOW GLUE

Photo 1 • Glue narrow stock together to make wider pieces. Start at one end and get the joint flush as you clamp it. Continue to the other end, putting clamps on alternate sides of the assembly.

Edge-gluing Boards

The edges of the 1x10's you buy probably won't be in perfect condition. Cut clean, square outside edges with a table saw and a smooth-cutting planer blade. Then rip the boards into two pieces straight down the middle. If you have a jointer, rip the boards in half first, then joint both long edges of both pieces.

Pine warps and cups easily. To minimize these problems in glued-up pieces, alternate the direction of the growth rings on adjacent boards (see figure below). Turn over one board of each ripped pair end for end. That changes the grain direction but keeps the boards with their center ripped edges facing each other.

Apply a bead of carpenter's glue to both edges of a joint, press the edges together and slide them back and forth a bit to distribute the glue. Pull the boards apart briefly and inspect them to make sure both surfaces are completely covered with a thin layer of glue.

Reassemble the joint and apply clamps spaced about 12 inches apart as shown in Photo 1. Pad the clamp jaws with scrap wood to avoid denting the edges of the boards. Wipe off any squeezed-out glue immediately with a damp cloth. Proceed as described in the text (Step 2) to get blanks of the required width.

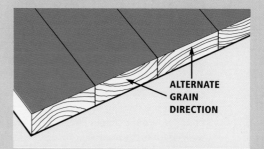

ALTERNATE GRAIN DIRECTION

Alternate the direction of the growth rings when edge-gluing pine boards.

Mark and cut the shaped pieces

1 Make 1/4-inch plywood templates for all shaped parts (A, B, C, D, J). Cut pieces of plywood a bit larger than the outside dimensions of the pattern grids (page 158). The grids represent 1-inch squares. Draw 1-inch squares on the plywood pieces, then transfer the points where the pattern outlines intersect the grid lines. Connect the dots to complete the outlines (Photo 2). Note that most patterns cover just half of the finished shape; you need only this much of a template (next step). Note also that no overall pattern is given for the sides (A).

You can lay out the curved shape that is shown on a 12-inch square of plywood. Cut out the plywood templates with a saber saw and sand the edges smooth.

2 Draw center lines on the glued-up blanks for the ends, rockers, and roof front (B, C, D, J). Align the center edge of each plywood template with its respective center line and trace the half shape onto the blank (Photo 3). Then flop the template to the other side of the center line and trace the second half of the shape.

3 To mark the sides (A), first cut the blanks to rectangles of overall finished size, 17-3/4 x 37-1/2 inches. Then align the partial template for the curve at the head end with the top inside corner of each side and trace the shape. Use a straightedge to extend the line of the top edge of the side all the way to the foot.

4 Cut out the shaped pieces with a saber saw (Photo 4), following the lines as closely as possible. Sand the sawn edges smooth. A small drum sanding attachment mounted in a drill or drill press will speed sanding the curves. In order to ensure symmetry, clamp matching parts together so you can sand the edges to shape at the same time.

MARK AND CUT THE SHAPED PIECES

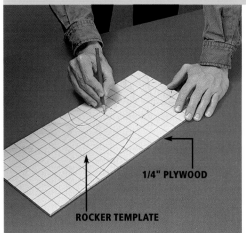

1/4" PLYWOOD

ROCKER TEMPLATE

Photo 2 Draw 1-inch grids on plywood for templates. Following the pattern plans, mark the points where the shapes intersect the grid lines, then connect the marks.

CENTER LINE

Photo 3 Line up the template for a half-shape with the centerline of the blank and trace the outline. Flop the template to the other side of the centerline to complete the outline.

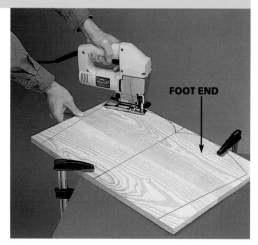

FOOT END

Photo 4 Cut out the shapes with a saber saw. Cut slowly, and follow the outlines closely to reduce the amount of sanding you'll need to do later.

Finish building the cradle

1 • Lay out the locations of all screw holes except for those that attach the bottom to the rockers (see the Assembly Plan). Drill pilot holes for the screws and counterbore 3/8-inch holes for plugs that will cover the screw heads, then drill the 1/8-inch pilot holes (see Fastening Detail in the plans). Test-fit the parts, and locate and drill pilot holes in the edges of mating pieces.

2 • Round over the curved edges of the rockers (D), the foot end (C), and the roof front (J). Also round over the bottom edges of the cross supports (E), the outside bottom edges of the roof sides (G), and the cut-out edges of the sides (A). Do not round over the last 3/4 inch of any inside edges where they overlap the foot end. Use a router and a 3/16-inch round-over bit, and sand the routed edges smooth. You'll round over the remaining edges after you assemble the cradle.

3 • Sand the faces of all pieces with a belt sander and a 120-grit sanding belt. Then use an orbital sander to finish-sand all inside surfaces and the outside surfaces of the cross supports. Use successively finer papers: 150-grit first, then 180- and 220-grit.

4 • Glue and screw the rockers (D) to the cross supports (E) with No. 6 x 1-5/8 inch drywall screws. Align the top edges of the sides (A) with the top edges of the ends (B, C) and glue and screw them together, one corner at a time. Finally, attach the bottom (F) to the ends with No. 6 x 1-5/8 inch drywall screws, and to the sides with 4d finish nails. Use a nail set to drive the nailheads slightly below the surface.

5 • Cut pine plugs to cover the screw heads. Use a 3/8-inch plug-cutting bit in an electric or hand-powered drill (Photo 5). Gently twist the blade of a screwdriver in the cuts to remove the plugs from the board. Glue and hammer the plugs into the counterbored plug holes in the rockers, sides, and ends. When the glue is dry, trim the protruding plug ends and sand with 120-grit sandpaper. Use an orbital sander to finish-sand the sides and rockers.

6 • Glue and nail the roof front (J) to the sides (A) so it overhangs equally at both sides. Glue and screw the roof center (H), and the roof sides (G) to the roof front and head end. Glue plugs into the screw holes and trim and sand them as before. Nail the bottom edge of the roof sides to the cradle sides with 4d finish nails. Fill all nail holes with wood putty.

7 • Sand all edges flush with their mating surfaces using a belt sander. Round over all remaining exposed edges, and finish-sand any unsanded outside surfaces.

8 • Test the stain for the cradle on scrap pine for color and depth (Photo 6). A medium-light stain is typical of Colonial furniture; for pine, use an oil-base stain. If the test pieces appear blotchy, apply a stain controller—available at paint stores—before using the stain. Follow the label instructions for applying both the controller and the stain application.

9 • Wipe a Danish oil finish over the stain. Let this finish dry for at least a week, and make sure no odor remains before completing the assembly and using the cradle.

10 • Turn the cradle upside down and center the rocker assembly on the bottom. Mark the positions of the rockers, then lift the assembly off. Mark and drill pilot holes for three screws inside each rocker position on the bottom; make sure the end screw locations will clear the screws that hold the rockers to their cross supports. Turn the cradle over, position the rocker assembly under it, and drill matching pilot holes in the edges of the rockers. Then screw the cradle to the rockers with No. 6 x 1-5/8 inch drywall screws.

FINISH BUILDING THE CRADLE

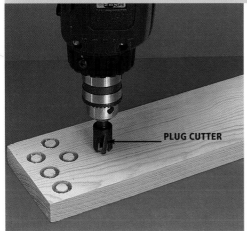

PLUG CUTTER

Photo 5 • Cut plugs to cover the screws using a 3/8-inch plug-cutting bit. To keep the bit from wandering, position it against the wood, then start drilling.

COTTON RAG

Photo 6 • Make tests on scraps of pine to find how to stain to the depth of color you want. Use oil-base stain, with a stain controller to avoid blotching if necessary.

A knotty-pine **country bench**

This combined bench and storage chest is equally suitable for a young person's playroom or bedroom. For a young child it's a great place to keep toys and games. When he or she grows older, it can hold sweaters, shoes, tapes and CD's, or keepsakes. The hinged seat lifts and stays safely up to provide access to whatever personal treasures are kept inside.

Getting started

The bench is easy to build even for a beginning woodworker. It's little more than a hinged box made from inexpensive lumberyard pine. The whitewashed finish is durable and easy to apply, but you could use a natural finish or stain and varnish if you wish.

You'll need a table saw or circular saw, a jigsaw or saber saw, a router with a 3/16-inch round-over bit, and a drill press or electric drill with a 3/8-inch plug-cutting bit. Pipe clamps also are necessary for edge-gluing boards to obtain wider stock.

Assembly Plan

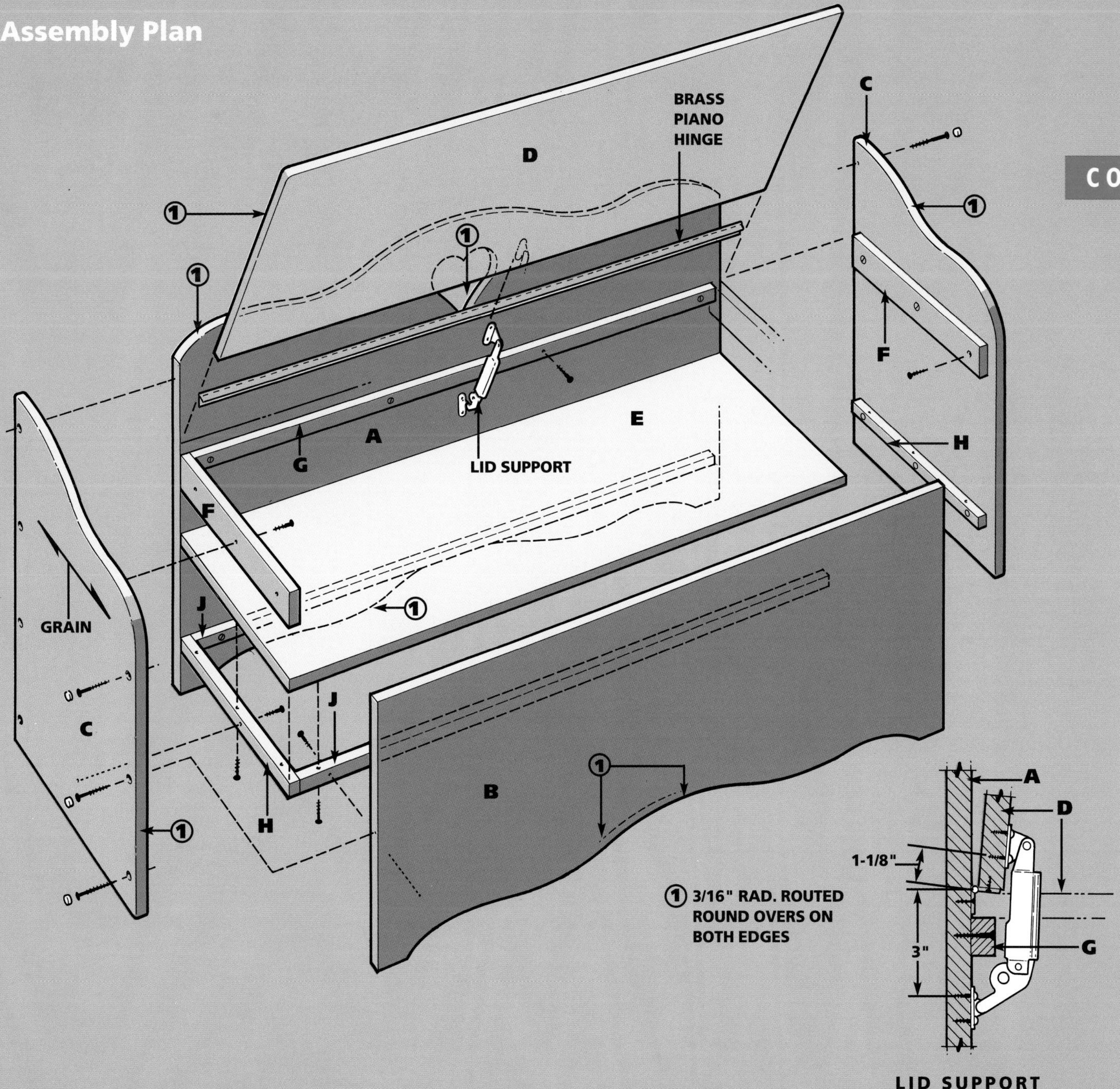

BRASS
PIANO
HINGE
D
C
①
①
①
①
A
G
LID SUPPORT
E
F
F
H
GRAIN
J
J
①
C
H
B
①
①
① 3/16" RAD. ROUTED
ROUND OVERS ON
BOTH EDGES
A
D
1-1/8"
3"
G

LID SUPPORT MOUNTING

CONSTRUCTION TIP

The lid support for this bench is listed in some catalogs as a Toy Box Lid Support. In other catalogs it is an Internal Spring Counterbalance Support or a Back-mounted Counter-balance Support. Orient and attach the support as shown in the Assembly Plans, not according to the instructions that come with it. However, the dimensions given in the manufacturer's instructions for screw-hole spacing and edge setback are correct.

Pattern Pieces

Each square = 2"

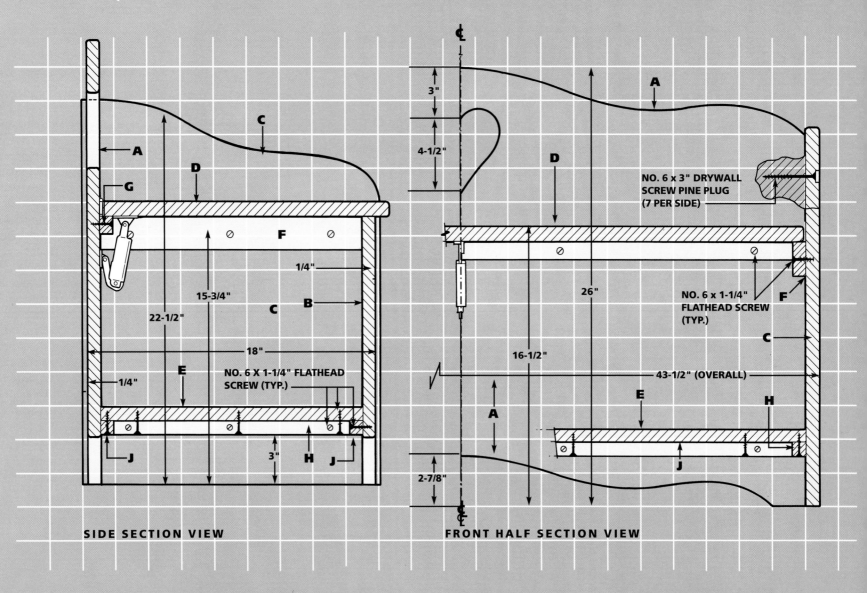

SIDE SECTION VIEW

A

C

D

G

F

1/4"

B

C

15-3/4"

22-1/2"

18"

E

NO. 6 X 1-1/4" FLATHEAD
SCREW (TYP.)

1/4"

J

3"

H

J

FRONT HALF SECTION VIEW

C̸ (C.L.)

3"

4-1/2"

A

D

NO. 6 x 3" DRYWALL
SCREW PINE PLUG
(7 PER SIDE)

26"

NO. 6 x 1-1/4"
FLATHEAD SCREW
(TYP.)

F

C

16-1/2"

43-1/2" (OVERALL)

E

H

A

2-7/8"

J

Cutting List

Key	Pcs.	Size and Description
A	1	3/4" x 26" x 42" pine (back)
B	1	3/4" x 15-3/4" x 42" pine (front)
C	2	3/4" x 22-1/2" x 18" pine (sides)
D	1	3/4" x 17-1/2" x 41-7/8" pine (seat)
E	1	3/4" x 16" x 42" pine (shelf)
F	2	3/4" x 2" x 16" pine (seat supports)
G	1	3/4" x 1" x 40-1/2" pine (seat support)
H	2	3/4" x 3/4" x 16" pine (shelf cleats)
J	2	3/4" x 3/4" x 40-1/2" pine (shelf cleats)

Shopping List

Quantity	Item
16	1x6 x 8' pine
14	No. 6 x 3" drywall screws
38	No. 6 x 1-1/4" flathead screws
1	1-1/2" x 72" brass piano hinge
1	Toy box lid support (see Construction Tip with the Assembly Plan)
1 pint	White or other wood stain
1 quart	Clear, low-luster urethane acrylic finish

Glue-up and cut the blanks

1 • You must edge-glue 1x6 boards to get stock for all the wide pieces of the bench—the back (A), the front (B), the sides (C), the seat (D), and the shelf (E). Choose your lumber carefully to avoid large, unsound knots. If the board edges are imperfect, resaw them for a tight joint when you glue and clamp them together (Photo 1). Then cut the individual boards slightly long so you can trim them to finished size after they're glued together. For specific information about joining boards in this way, see the box Edge-gluing Boards on page 159.

2 • Mark off the sections on the glued-up stock that you can use for each of the wide parts. Try to get an even distribution of knots, for good appearance, and plan ahead for the shapes you will cut. You need to avoid cutting through knots on any edges—especially the shaped edges and the heart cutout.

3 • Cut the marked sections to the dimensions given for the wide pieces in the Cutting List. These are blanks on which you will draw the shaped forms shown in the patterns.

4 • Cut the shelf cleats (H, J) and the seat supports (F, G) to the finished sizes given in the Cutting List, at left.

GLUE-UP AND CUT THE BLANKS

Photo 1 • Use bar clamps on both sides of the assembly to hold boards together as the glue dries. Wipe off squeezed-out glue on both sides of the board with a damp cloth immediately after tightening the clamps.

Lay out and cut the curved shapes

1 • Lay out and draw grids with 2-inch squares on the top and bottom of the blank you have cut for the back (A) and the top of the blank for one side (C) (Photo 2).

2 • Refer to the patterns. Mark each grid line on the wood at the point where it intersects the part outline in the pattern. Also mark all points between grid lines that you can locate by calculating dimensions from the patterns (Photo 3). Connect the marked points with a smooth line, using a French curve or a flexible drafting curve (Photo 4). These drawing tools are available at art supply stores.

3 • Cut out the marked shapes with a fine-tooth blade in a jigsaw or saber saw. Then use the bottom contour of the back (A) to trace the shape for the bottom of the front (B). Similarly, use the side (C) to trace a second side on another glued-up blank. Cut out these pieces. Also cut out the heart-shaped hole in the back (Photo 5).

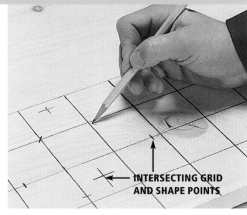

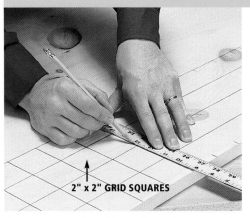

Photo 2 • Draw the grids on the back and top of one side. Use a soft-lead pencil and light pressure to avoid gouging the soft pine.

Photo 3 • Mark all points at which the pattern outlines intersect the grid lines. This produces a dotted outline of the pattern piece.

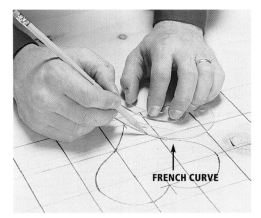

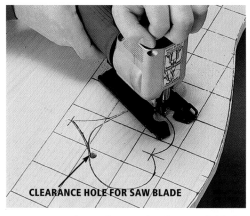

Photo 4 • Connect the dots to complete the pattern outline. Drawing aids such as French curves and a flexible drafting curve are helpful.

Photo 5 • Cut the outlines with a fine-tooth blade in your saber saw. Drill a hole inside the heart outline to start the cut.

Build the bench

1 • Check that all pieces are cut to the proper final size, then sand the cut edges smooth. Use a belt sander or sandpaper wrapped around a long sanding block for straight edges. Use a sanding drum chucked in a drill press or a portable electric drill for curved edges (Photo 6).

2 • Lay out and drill pilot holes and counterbored 3/8-inch plug holes in the sides (C). (See the Assembly Plan and the patterns for screw locations. Also lay out, countersink, and drill pilot holes in the shelf cleats (H, J) and seat supports (F, J).

3 • Use a 3/16-inch round-over bit in a router on the top and front edges of the sides (C); the top, curved bottom, and heart edges of the back (A); the curved bottom edges of the front (B); and the side and front edges of the seat (D).

4 • Finish-sand all surfaces, and sand any sharp edges. Be sure there are no raised edges along the glued joints in the wide pieces.

5 • Position the side seat supports and shelf cleats (F, H) on the sides (C), and drill corresponding pilot holes in the sides. Screw the supports and cleats to the sides with No. 6 x 1-1/4 inch flathead screws.

6 • Clamp the front (B) and back (A) in position against the sides (C). Make sure they are tight against the ends of the seat supports and the shelf cleats. Locate and drill pilot holes through the sides into the edges of the front and back. Screw the sides to the front and back with No. 6 x 3-inch drywall screws (Photo 7).

7 • Screw the remaining shelf cleats (J) to the front (B) and back (A) with No. 6 x 1-1/4 inch flathead screws. Place the shelf (E) inside the bench and locate, drill, and countersink pilot holes in the cleats and shelf. Screw the shelf to the cleats from underneath with No. 6 x 1-1/4 inch flathead screws.

8 • Position the rear seat support (G) on the back (A) and drill pilot holes through it into the back. Then fasten the support to the back with No. 6 x 1-1/4 inch flathead screws.

9 • Cut 14 pine plugs with a 3/8-inch plug-cutting bit. Glue and lightly hammer the plugs into their holes in the sides (C). Cut the plugs flush with the sides and sand them smooth.

10 • Drill three 1-inch diameter ventilation holes in the back for safety (see tip at right). Locate them about 4 inches below the rear slot support (F) and equally spaced across the back.

11 • Cut the piano hinge 41-7/8 inches long with a hacksaw. File the cut edges smooth. Screw the hinge to the back edge of the seat (D). Set the bench on its back, and attach the piano hinge and seat assembly to the back (A). Install the toy box lid support (see detail in the Assembly Plan).

12 • Unscrew the lid support, piano hinge, seat supports (F, G), shelf (E), and shelf cleats (H, J). Apply stain to all exposed surfaces.

13 • When the stain is dry, brush on three coats of latex urethane finish. Allow each coat to dry completely before applying the next coat, and sand lightly between coats. When the finish is dry, reassemble the bench.

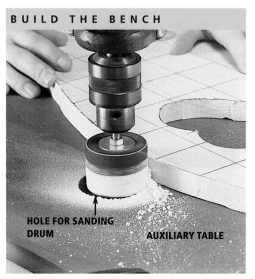

HOLE FOR SANDING DRUM   AUXILIARY TABLE

Photo 6 • Sand the curved cut edges with a sanding drum in an electric drill. An auxiliary table with a large hole lets you move the drill up and down to use the full length of the drum.

Safety First

Do not fail to drill ventilation holes in the back (Step 10) to prevent suffocation if a child should get trapped inside the bench.

Photo 7 • Screw the sides to the front and back with 3-inch drywall screws. Although the pine is soft, drill pilot holes at all screw locations, especially into end grain.

A *letter-perfect* toy storage box

Safety Tip

To help make this toy storage box as safe as possible, use only self-balancing lid supports. These supports keep the top open in any position to prevent entrapment, and help protect little fingers as well.

There will be no more excuses for a cluttered room with this stylish store-all. The giant building block rolls about on casters, comes with a "secret drawer" in back, and even has a self-balancing lid that stays put for an extra measure of safety.

Getting started

Plan to spend several weekends on this showpiece project. You'll need these power tools: a table saw with a dado blade; a router with 1/4- and 1/2-inch round-over bits and a 3/4-inch flush-trimming bit; a belt sander and a 150-grit sanding belt; an orbital sander; a drill press; a portable electric drill; a 1-inch diameter sanding-drum attachment for a drill and 80-grit sleeves; a 1-1/2 inch diameter hole saw for a drill; a jigsaw or a saber saw; a hacksaw; and at least four 30-inch or longer bar or pipe clamps.

Assembly Plan

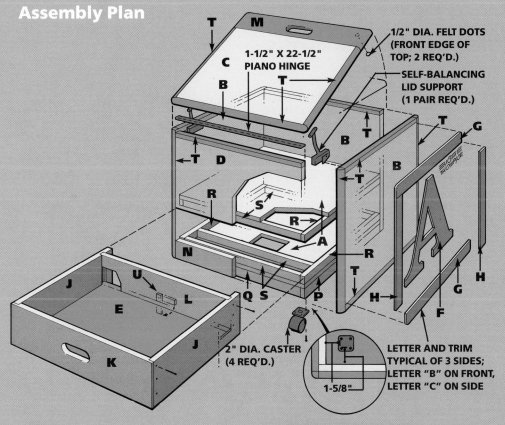

1/2" DIA. FELT DOTS (FRONT EDGE OF TOP; 2 REQ'D.)

SELF-BALANCING LID SUPPORT (1 PAIR REQ'D.)

1-1/2" X 22-1/2" PIANO HINGE

2" DIA. CASTER (4 REQ'D.)

1-5/8"

LETTER AND TRIM TYPICAL OF 3 SIDES; LETTER "B" ON FRONT, LETTER "C" ON SIDE

CASTER LOCATION

Shopping List

15 board feet	1x6 birch (quantity allows for 50% waste)
1 sheet	3/4" x 4' x 8' birch plywood
1 sheet	1/4" x 2' x 8' hardboard
79	No. 6 x 1-1/4" drywall screws
12	1-1/2" brads
4	2" diameter casters
1	1-1/2" x 36" brushed-brass piano hinge
2	Self-balancing lid supports (mounting dimensions shown in details, page 170)
2	1/2" diameter felt dots
2 cans	Spray enamel primer
1 can ea.	Red, white spray enamel
1 pint	Polyurethane clear satin brush-on finish
1 can	Polyurethane clear satin spray finish

Cutting List

Key	Pcs.	Size and Description
A	2	3/4" x 22-1/2" x 22-1/2" birch plywood (bottoms)
B	3	3/4" x 21-3/4" x 22-1/2" birch plywood (sides and front)
C	1	3/4" x 19-3/4" x 22-1/2" birch plywood (top)
D	1	3/4" x 12-3/8" x 22-1/2" birch plywood (back)
E	1	1/4" x 21-5/8" x 21-5/8" hardboard (drawer bottom)
F	3	1/4" x 16" x 16" hardboard (letters)
G	6	1/4" x 2" x 22-1/2" hardboard (letter frame tops and bottoms)
H	6	1/4" x 2" x 18-1/2" hardboard (letter frame sides)
J	2	3/4" x 5-15/16" x 23" birch (drawer sides)
K	1	3/4" x 5-15/16" x 22-3/8" birch (drawer front)
L	1	3/4" x 5-3/16" x 21-3/8" birch (drawer back)
M	1	3/4" x 3-9/16" x 24-1/2" birch (top front)
N	1	3/4" x 3-3/16" x 22-1/2" birch (lower back)
P	2	3/4" x 1-9/16" x 22-1/2" birch (cleats)
Q	2	3/4" x 1-9/16" x 21" birch (cleats)
R	4	3/4" x 1" x 22-1/2" birch (drawer runners)
S	5	3/4" x 1" x 21" birch (drawer runners and drawer stop)
T	15	3/4" x 3/4" x 24-1/2" birch (edging)
U	1	1/4" x 3/4" x 3" birch (drawer stop latch)

Construction Details

TOP

PIANO HINGE

SELF-BALANCING LID SUPPORT

1"

1-7/8"

5/8"

1-7/16"

2-1/2"

2-13/16"

SIDE

BACK

LID SUPPORT MOUNTING

1/4" RAD. ROUND OVER (TYP.)

NO. 10 x 1-1/4" PAN HEAD SCREW, WASHER

U

4-1/2"

1-1/2"

L

U

1-1/4"

HANDHOLD CUTOUT

STOP LATCH

E

L

1/2" DEEP x 3/4" RABBET IN FRONT

1/4" DEEP x 3/4" DADO

K

1-1/2" BRAD (TYP.)

J

1-1/4"

K

1/4" x 3/8" DEEP GROOVE (FRONT AND SIDES)

L

E

J

1/2"

U

DRAWER ASSEMBLY

NO. 6 x 1-1/4" DRYWALL SCREW (4 REQ'D.)

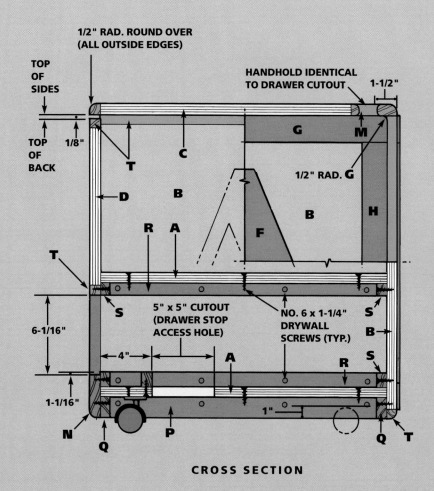

1/2" RAD. ROUND OVER (ALL OUTSIDE EDGES)

HANDHOLD IDENTICAL TO DRAWER CUTOUT

1-1/2"

TOP OF SIDES

TOP OF BACK

1/8"

T

C

G

M

1/2" RAD. G

D

B

B

H

R

A

F

T

S

S

S

B

6-1/16"

5" x 5" CUTOUT (DRAWER STOP ACCESS HOLE)

NO. 6 x 1-1/4" DRYWALL SCREWS (TYP.)

4"

A

R

S

1-1/16"

N

Q

P

1"

Q

T

CROSS SECTION

Make the sides and top

1 • Cut pieces A through U to the dimensions given in the Cutting List. Parts M, P, Q, and T are cut oversize to allow for trimming later, during assembly.

2 • Glue and clamp the edging pieces (T) to the top and bottom edges of the sides and front (B), to the top and bottom edges of the back (D), and to the side edges of the top (C). (See box, Edging Plywood, at right.)

3 • Trim off the overhanging ends, then glue and clamp the remaining edging pieces (T) to the sides (B) and top (C). Also glue and clamp the top front piece (M) to the top. Then draw a pencil line even with the edge of the plywood and trim off the ends with a saber saw.

4 • Sand the edging pieces (T) flush with the faces of the plywood on all sides. Use a belt sander and a 150-grit sanding belt.

5 • Finish-sand the inside surfaces of the sides, front, back, and top (B, C, D), using an orbital sander. Start with 150-grit sandpaper; finish with 180-grit paper.

6 • Glue and clamp the edge-trimmed back (D–T), lower back (N), and edge-trimmed front assembly (B–T) to one side assembly (B–T). Make sure the front and back are at exact right angles to the side as you tighten the clamps. Also make sure that the top edge of the back assembly is 1/8 inch below the top edge of the side assembly, and that the drawer opening is 6-1/16 inches tall (see Cross Section in the Construction Details, opposite). Use only a 1/8-inch diameter bead of glue near the outside edge of the joint to avoid the accumulation of any glue squeeze-out on the inside corners. Wipe off any spilled or squeezed-out glue immediately with a damp cloth.

7 • When the glue for the first assembly is dry, glue and clamp the remaining edge-trimmed side (B–T) in place.

GLUING TECHNIQUES
Edging Plywood

Before you assemble the toy box, you'll have plenty of edge-gluing to do. Here's how.

• Cut the edging pieces about 1/32 inch thicker and 1 inch longer than the plywood.

• Apply a bead of glue near each edge of one edging piece. Align and clamp the piece to one end of the plywood. Put another clamp 4 to 6 inches away and apply a little pressure. Lay a finger over the joint near the clamp. Move the other end of the edging piece up or down until you can feel with your finger that the piece overhangs each face of the plywood equally. Then tighten the clamp. Continue aligning and clamping all along the length of the edging piece.

• Dampen a rag with hot water and wipe off the glue squeeze-out.

• Let the glue joint dry, then attach the opposite edging piece in the same way. Trim off the overhanging ends, then attach the remaining edging pieces to the plywood.

• Sand the edging pieces flush with the faces of the plywood. Use a 150-grit belt in a belt sander, taking care not to sand through the face veneer of the plywood.

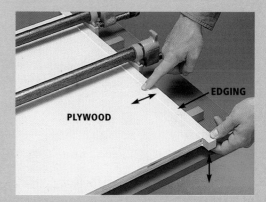

EDGING

PLYWOOD

Add the interior components

1 • Mark the outline of the drawer stop access hole in the lower bottom (A). It is 5 inches square, centered between the side edges and hole 4 inches from the back edge of the bottom piece (see Cross Section detail in the construction details, page 170). Cut the hole with a saber saw.

2 • Lay out, countersink, and drill pilot holes for the No. 6 x 1-1/4 inch drywall screws in the bottoms (A), drawer bottom (E), cleats (P, Q), drawer runners and stop (R, S), and drawer stop latch (U). Screw locations are shown in the Cross Section detail.

3 • Mount the lower bottom (A). Trim the width of the cleats (P, Q) so they're equal to 2-1/4 inches minus the thickness of the lower

bottom (see the plans). Glue and screw the pieces to the inside of the box in this order: Cleats (P) to the side assemblies; cleats (Q) to the front assembly and lower back (N); lower bottom (A) to cleats (P, Q); lower drawer runners (R) to the side assemblies; lower drawer runners (S) to the front assembly and lower back (N); and finally, the drawer stop (S) to the lower bottom (A).

4 • Glue and screw the upper drawer runners (R, S) to the side, front, and back assemblies. Use a temporary 6-inch spacer to align the runners as you screw them in place (Photo 1).

5 • Finish-sand the top of the upper bottom (A) with an orbital sander; start with 150-grit sandpaper, and finish with 180-grit paper. Glue and screw the upper bottom to the upper drawer runners (see Cross Section in the Construction Details).

Mount the top and assemble the drawer

1 • Cut the piano hinge to length with a hacksaw so the hinge fits on the top edge of the back assembly. Smooth both ends of the hinge with a fine metal file. Screw the hinge to the box, then screw the hinge to the top assembly (see Mounting the Piano Hinge, at right.)

2 • Clamp the top to the box. Trim off the edges of the top that overhang the sides and front with a router and a flush-trimming bit. Remove the piano hinge; it will interfere with routing the back edges. Align and clamp the top to the box again, and round the top's corners with a router and a 1/2-inch round-over bit (Photo 2). Remove the top and round over the outside edges of the top and box.

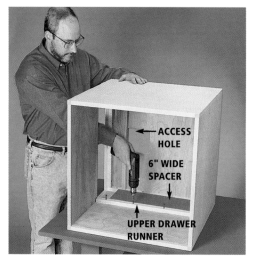

Photo 1 • Use a 6- x 20-in. piece of 3/4-in. thick plywood as a spacer to align the upper drawer runners as you glue and screw them to the box.

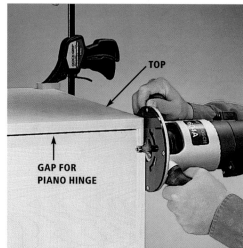

Photo 2 • Round the corners of the top this way. It will prevent accidentally rounding over the bottom edges of the top or tearing out the wood.

3 • Lay out the handhold in the drawer front (K). Center it top to bottom and side to side (see Handhold Cutout in the Construction Details). Lay out the same size handhold in the top front (M), located 1-1/2 inches back from the front edge and centered between the sides. Cut the ends of the handholds with a 1-1/2 inch diameter hole saw; finish the cut with a saber saw. Use a 1-inch sanding drum to smooth the sawn edges, then round over the top and bottom edges of the holes with a router and a 1/4-inch round-over bit.

4 • Cut the rabbets and dado grooves in the drawer sides (J) and front (K) (see Drawer Assembly detail in the plans). Finish-sand the insides of the drawer sides, front, and back (L), then glue and clamp the pieces together. Drill pilot holes and drive in 1-1/2 inch brads. Fill the brad holes with wood filler, and finish-sand the rest of the drawer. Don't install the drawer bottom until after you apply the finish.

Mounting the Piano Hinge

Although you could build this toy box with the piano hinge mounted on the outside surfaces of the top and back, mounting the hinge so its flaps are concealed when the top is closed gives the box a much neater appearance. Here are a few tips to make concealing the hinge a bit easier.

• Align the hinge so the bottoms of the hinge knuckles are flush with the outside edge of the back assembly. Locate and drill pilot holes, then screw the hinge to the back assembly (Figure A).

• Screw the hinge to the top next. When the hinge is mounted properly, the edges of the top will slightly overhang the box sides and front. You'll trim off these overhanging edges later. Cut two riser blocks that are 7/8 inch tall and 26 inches long from scrap wood. Set the back of the box on the riser blocks and slide the top under the hinge. Visually align the sides of the top with the sides of the box, and the bottoms of the hinge knuckle openings with the back edge of the top. Drill a pilot hole and drive a screw at one end of the hinge (Figure B).

• Close the top and check its alignment. If you need to make an adjustment, remove the screw, realign the top, drill a pilot hole through the adjacent hinge hole and drive a screw there instead.

• After aligning one side, do the other side. Fill any unused screw holes with short pieces of toothpicks and glue. Then drill pilot holes and drive the rest of the hinge screws.

PIANO HINGE

Figure A

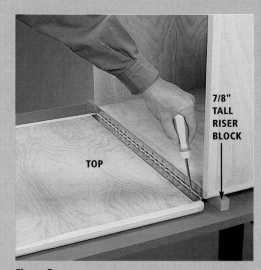

7/8" TALL RISER BLOCK

TOP

Figure B

Complete the toy box

Make the letters and letter frames

1 • Round the outside corners of the letter frame tops and bottoms (G) with a router and a 1/2-inch round-over bit (Photo 3). To save time and make all pieces exactly the same shape, gang-rout the pieces: Cut two pieces of scrap wood the same size as the hardboard frame pieces; sandwich the frame pieces between the scrap, aligning the ends. Clamp everything to a work surface, and rout all the ends at the same time.

2 • Transfer and enlarge the letter shapes from the gridded patterns (opposite page) to the hardboard pieces (F). Cut out the letters with a jigsaw (Photo 4), and sand the sawn edges. If possible, use a 1-inch diameter sanding drum

chucked in a drill press with an auxiliary table (Photo 5). Otherwise, work carefully with a sanding block and file.

3 • Finish-sand the surfaces of the letters and all exposed sharp edges. Use 120- or 150-grit paper in your orbital sander.

Apply the finish and complete the assembly

4 • Align the letter frame pieces and letters on the box, and trace around them with a pencil. Cover the areas inside the letter tracings with masking tape to within 1/4 inch of the penciled outlines. Also use newspaper and masking tape to cover the other unpainted surfaces of the box. The unpainted bare wood will ensure a permanent glue bond for the letters and for the letter frame pieces.

5 • Apply aerosol primer to the box sides and front (Photo 6) and to the tops and edges of the letters and letter frame pieces; don't paint the backs of the letters or frame pieces. Apply at least two coats of primer to the porous edges of the hardboard pieces. Let the primer dry completely between coats.

6 • Apply white spray enamel to the box sides and front. Spray-paint the letters and letter frame pieces with red enamel—or use a different color for each panel. After the paint is dry, remove the masking tape and newspaper.

7 • Align and glue the letter frame pieces and letters to the box one side at a time. With the side you're working on facing up, apply carpenter's glue to the back of a letter frame top piece. Align it and press it in place with your hands; no clamping is necessary. Glue on the other three frame pieces and the letter. Let the glue dry completely before turning the box to work on the next surface.

Letter Tip

This box calls for the letters A, B, and C to be 14-1/2 inches tall. Rather than transferring patterns as described in the text, you may be able to find templates of a suitable size at a professional art supply store. For sources of precut letters, look under "Letters—Sign" in the Yellow Pages.

Letter Patterns

Each square = 2"

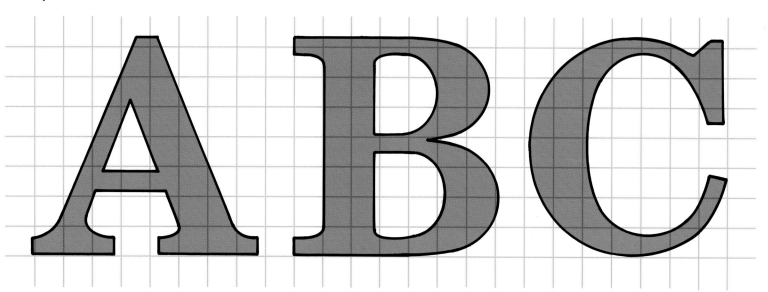

8 • Brush two coats of polyurethane on all unpainted birch surfaces. Let each coat dry as specified in the product directions.

9 • Apply spray polyurethane to all painted surfaces. Do one side at a time, with the surface horizontal; spray lightly to avoid drips. Let the finish dry before doing the next side. When the last surface is done, let the finish cure for at least one week.

10 • Mount the casters to the box bottom. Remount the piano hinge and top, and mount the two lid supports (see the Lid Support Mounting in the Construction Details). Follow the directions that come with the lid supports carefully. Adjust the tension of the lid supports so they hold the top open in any position. Stick felt dots on the front corners of the underside of the top to protect the surface.

11 • Insert the drawer bottom, and attach the drawer stop latch (U). Rub a little paraffin on the drawer runners for smooth operation. Turn the stop latch on the back of the drawer horizontal so you can insert the drawer in its opening, then reach up through the access hole in the bottom of the box and turn the stop latch down so it will hit the drawer stop (S) and prevent the drawer from being pulled all the way out.

COMPLETE THE TOY BOX

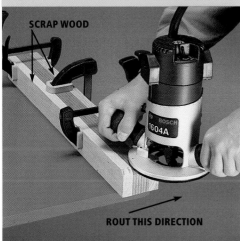

SCRAP WOOD

ROUT THIS DIRECTION

Photo 3 • Gang the hardboard frame pieces between two pieces of scrap for routing, to make all pieces exactly the same shape. Use a 1/2-in. diameter round-over bit.

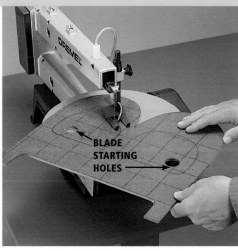

BLADE STARTING HOLES

Photo 4 • Cut the outside shapes of the letters with a jigsaw. Then drill starting holes in the letters "A" and "B" to insert the blade for cutting out the inside shapes.

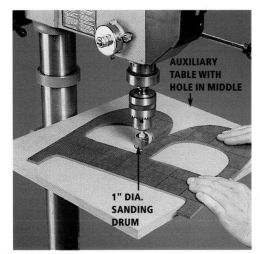

AUXILIARY TABLE WITH HOLE IN MIDDLE

1" DIA. SANDING DRUM

Photo 5 • Smooth the sawn edges of the letters with a 1-in. diameter sanding drum mounted in a drill press. Use an auxiliary table with a hole just a bit larger than the drum.

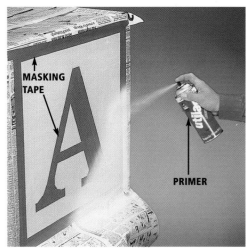

MASKING TAPE

PRIMER

Photo 6 • Use masking tape and newspaper to cover all surfaces that must remain unpainted for gluing later. Apply the primer, let it dry, then apply white enamel.

Working Safety

Whenever you use spray paint, work in a well-ventilated area and wear a paint respirator.

Double-deck bunk beds

Double-deck bunk beds can effectively double bedroom space. The design shown here is simple, economical, good looking, sturdy and, most important, safe. It's also versatile: By making only minor changes to the plans, you can build a bed-and-desk unit instead of a double-deck bunk.

Getting started

You'll need only basic power tools to build this bunk bed: an electric drill with a bit for driving screws, a saber saw, and a sander. If you own a circular saw with a fine-tooth blade, use it to speed the straight cuts. You'll also need simple hand tools, including a wood file and a square to use as a saw guide. A clamp with padded jaws is handy for holding the pieces in position when you assemble the bed.

You can build the bed from economical construction-grade lumber as specified in the Shopping List, or choose more expensive clear grades for the pieces that show.

To finish the wood, you can use paint, stain and varnish, or Danish oil. An oil finish is particularly easy to touch up, and it lets the pine age gracefully to a warm, mellow color. On the bunk shown here the parts that don't get a lot of wear are painted, and the others are finished with a nontoxic oil.

Double-deck Bed Assembly Plan

1-3/4" RAD. (TYP.)

F, E, A, F, E

K J

L L M

10"

G

H

41-1/2"

10"
10-1/2" (TYP.)
4-1/2"
2" SPACING (TYP.)
7-1/4"
8"
8"

H, F, E, B, C, A, D, 3/4", 4", 2", 2", 2", 2", 7-1/4"

Cutting List

Key	Pcs.	Size and Description
A	4	2x4 x 71" pine (corner posts; from 12' boards)
B	4	2x6 x 32" pine (end rails; from 12' boards)
C	4	2x4 x 36" pine (end support rails; from 14' boards)
D	4	2x4 x 76" pine (side support rails; from 14' boards)
E	4	1x8 x 41" pine (end face boards; from 14' boards)
F	8	1x4 x 39-1/2" pine (end guard rails; from 14' boards)
G	4	1x8 x 79" pine (side face boards; from 14' boards)
H	16	1/2" x 7-3/4" x 39" BC plywood (slats)
J	2	2x4 x 71" pine (ladder rails; from 12' board)
K	6	2x4 x 15-1/2" pine (ladder steps; from 8' board)
L	2	1x4 x 27-1/2" pine (side guard rails; from 6' board)
M	2	2x2 x 16" pine (guard rail posts; from cutoff)

Shopping List

1	2x4 x 8' pine
3	2x4 x 12' pine
3	2x4 x 14' pine
1	2x6 x 12' pine
1	1x4 x 6' pine
2	1x4 x 14' pine
3	1x8 x 14' pine
1-1/2 sheets	1/2" BC plywood
88	2" brass-colored deck screws
40	3" brass-colored deck screws
88	Brass finish washers to fit 2" screws
48	2-1/2" drywall screws
70	1-5/8" drywall screws
2	1/4" x 2-1/2" round-head brass bolts
4	1/4" flat brass washers
2	1/4" cap (acorn) nuts
4	5/16" x 3-1/2" lag bolts
4	5/16" flat washers

Hardware Notes

① 3" brass-colored deck screw

② 2-1/2" drywall screws

③ 2" brass-colored deck screw and finish washer

④ 1-5/8" drywall screw

⑤ 1/4-20 x 2-1/2" round head brass bolt, washer, and acorn nut

⑥ 5/16" X 3-1/2" lag bolt and washer

DETAIL 1—TYPICAL CORNER

TOE SCREW TOP AND BOTTOM

WALL STUD

A, G, E, B, C, D

DETAIL 2

E, F, A, A

1/4" RAD. (TYP.)

DRILLING PATTERNS

1/8" DIA. HOLES (TYP.)

3/4", 3/4"
F
2"
2-3/4"
1-1/2"
2"
2"
E
1-3/4"

G
1"
2-5/8"
2-5/8"
1"
3/4"

Using Bunk Beds Safely

This unit is designed to comply with federal safety recommendations for bunk beds. Be sure to follow these important tips for installing and using it:

• Install a smoke detector in the bedroom where the bunk bed is located. If a fire breaks out, the child in the upper bunk will be at greater risk of smoke inhalation.

• Bolt the bed to the wall. This bed is not designed to be freestanding.

• Do not allow children under the age of six to use the upper bunk.

• Do not allow horseplay on the beds or the ladder.

• Do not allow more than one child at a time on the upper bunk.

• Do not let your children jump from the upper bunk. Insist that they use the ladder.

• Make sure the mattresses fit tightly against the bed sides, and that their tops are at least 5 inches below the tops of the guard rails.

Assembly Plan–Bed-and-desk Unit

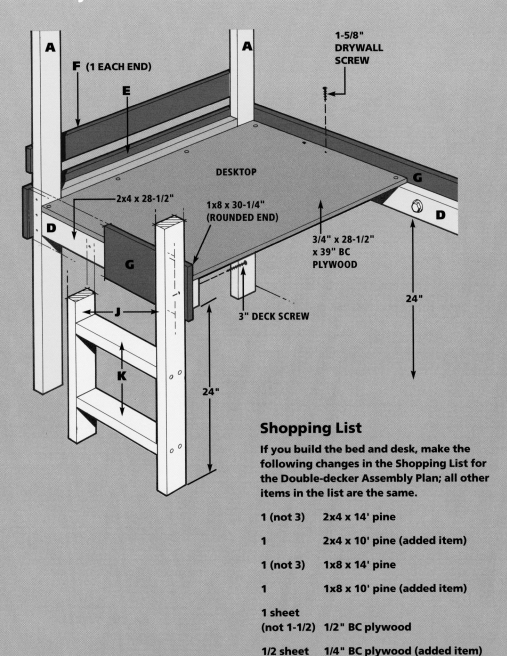

Shopping List

If you build the bed and desk, make the following changes in the Shopping List for the Double-decker Assembly Plan; all other items in the list are the same.

1 (not 3)	2x4 x 14' pine
1	2x4 x 10' pine (added item)
1 (not 3)	1x8 x 14' pine
1	1x8 x 10' pine (added item)
1 sheet (not 1-1/2)	1/2" BC plywood
1/2 sheet	1/4" BC plywood (added item)

Prepare the pieces

1 • Before buying or cutting wood, buy twin mattresses. For this bed, each mattress must fit tightly into a 39- x 76-inch space and be less than 8 inches thick. If your mattresses are larger, adjust the Cutting List dimensions.

2 • Choose your lumber carefully. Be sure the 1x4's are free of weak knots that might cause them to break, and try to select 1x4's and 1x8's with at least one good face.

3 • Lay out all the parts on the lumber and ply-wood; see the Cutting List with the plan and the layout tip at right. The Cutting List indi-cates what length boards to use for various parts for the most economical layout. When you lay out the 16 slats (H) on the plywood, make sure the grain of the best surface runs lengthwise on each slat. For easy identification in cutting and assembly, label each part by writ-ing its key letter on a piece of masking tape.

4 • Cut all boards to length, making sure to get square ends (Photo 1). An easy way to cut the plywood is to put it on the floor over a sheet of scrap plywood, or support it on scrap boards with one always placed under the cut line. Set the circular saw blade to barely cut through the thickness of the workpiece, and tack down a long straight board to guide the saw.

5 • Use a compass to mark 1-3/4 inch radius curves on the ends of the corner posts (A), the ladder rails (J), and the side guard rails (L). Cut the curves with a saber saw (Photo 2). Smooth the cut faces with a file or sander, then sand a 1/4-inch round over on the edges of the curves and all along the long edges of the pieces. To prevent the newly cut ends of the 2x4's from cracking as they dry, cover them with a plastic bag for 24 hours.

6 • File and sand 1/4-inch round overs on the ends of the end face boards (E) and the end guard rails (F) (see Detail 2 in the plan).

7 • Sand all surfaces that will show when the parts are assembled. This includes all surfaces of parts A, J, K, L, and M. Be sure to sand the ladder rails and steps (J, K) free of splinters.

8 • Drill screw pilot holes in parts E, F, G, J, K, and L (Photo 3). The holes should be predrilled, because the parts are painted or finished before assembly. Hole locations are shown in the overall Assembly Plan and the Drilling Patterns detail with the plan.

9 • Apply paint or oil finish, as appropriate, to the parts. For the painted parts, first fill all flaws with wood putty and sand smooth. If the wood has knots, use shellac or a shellac-based primer as a first coat, to keep sap from oozing out and showing through the paint. Follow that with three coats of paint. For the oiled surfaces, apply three coats of Danish oil. With both paint and oil, sand lightly with 120-grit sandpaper between coats.

PREPARE THE PIECES

Photo 1 • Use a square as a saw guide to crosscut square ends on boards. Use a straight board as a guide for longer cuts.

Photo 2 • Cut rounded ends with a saber saw and a fine-tooth blade. Smooth the cut faces with a file or belt sander.

Photo 3 • Drill pilot holes for all screws to prevent splitting the wood. Use a piece of scrap wood underneath each board.

Assemble the project

Double-deck bed

1 • Put the bed together in the room where it will be used. First, make end rail assemblies by attaching the end support rails (C) to the end rails (B) with 2-1/2 inch drywall screws. Make sure the bottom edges are flush and that part C overlaps B by 2 inches at each end.

2 • Now build end frames: Lay two corner posts (A) on the floor and put two end rail assemblies between them with the ends of C overlapping the posts. Position the lower end assembly 8 inches from the bottom of the posts; the upper assembly is 41-1/2 inches from the bottoms. Drill two pilot holes through each C end and drive 2-1/2 inch drywall screws into A. Build a second frame in the same way. Then stand the frames up, drill angled pilot holes through the top and bottom edges of the end rails (B), and drive 3-inch deck screws through them into the corner posts (A) (Photo 4).

3 • Have a helper hold a long side support rail (D) between the lower end assemblies of the end frames. Drill pilot holes through the corner posts into the ends of the side rail and attach them with 3-inch deck screws (see the plans and Photo 5). Attach the upper support rail (D) on this side in the same way, then add the corresponding support rails on the other side of the bed frame.

4 • Attach the end face boards (E), end guard rails (F), and side face boards (G) to the corner posts (A) with 2-inch deck screws and finish washers (Photo 6). Brass-colored deck screws have a zinc chromate finish and are harder than brass; they can be driven with a power drill. If you can't find deck screws, substitute ordinary No. 8 or No. 10 slotted brass screws and drive them with a screwdriver. You can also use silver-colored screws and chrome-plated finish washers. Finish washers (Photo 7) fit screw heads that are beveled rather than flat on their undersides. They eliminate the need to countersink screw heads in the wood, distribute the pressure of the screw head, and cover the sharp edges of the screw head to prevent possible injury.

5 • Assemble the ladder with 3-inch deck screws driven through the rails (J) into the ends of the steps (K). In this case, countersink the screw heads into the wood to get the maximum amount of screw shaft extending into the steps for support. Then position the ladder against the side face boards (G) 10 inches from the inside face of one corner post. Drill pilot holes through the bed rails into the ladder rails (J), and attach the ladder to the bed with 2-1/2 inch deck screws from inside the frame.

6 • Assemble the side guard rail (L, M) with 2-inch deck screws and finish washers. Position it as shown in the Assembly Plan, and attach it to the bed frame with 1/4-20 x 2-1/2 inch round-head bolts (Photo 8). Use washers under each bolt head and nut. Be sure to use an acorn or cap nut over the end of the bolt on the inside of the frame, to avoid tearing the side of the mattress when it is in place.

7 • Locate two studs in the wall against which you'll place the bed. To find the first stud near one end, use an inexpensive magnetic or electronic stud finder, or probe the wall with a small nail or drill bit in an area that will be covered by the side face rail. Then measure over at 16-inch intervals and locate a second stud near the other end of the bed.

8 • Bolt the bed in place with 5/16- x 3-1/2 inch lag bolts and washers. Drill pilot holes and drive the bolts with a hex-head or open-end wrench through the upper side face board (G) into the stud (see Detail 1 in the Assembly Plan, page 177). Do not skip this step. It is essential for safety as children climb around on the bed.

9 • Put the end slats (H) in position at the head and foot of the lower bunk and space six more slats equally between them. Attach them to the support rails (C, D) with 1-5/8 inch drywall screws (Photo 9). Install the slats for the upper bunk in the same way. Put the mattresses in place and add sheets and blankets.

Bed-and-desk unit

10 • If you prefer to build just the upper bunk and put a desk below, refer to the bed-and-desk plan (page 178) and make the following variations in the project instructions.

11 • When you lay out and cut the parts (Prepare the Pieces, Steps 3 and 4), make one rail (D) only 28-1/2 inches long. Make one side face board (G) only 30-1/4 inches long. Cut six end guard rails (F) instead of eight.

12 • When you build the end frames (Assemble the Project, Step 2), attach the lower end rail assemblies (C–B) 24 inches above the bottom of the corner posts.

13 • When you install the side support rails (assembly, Step 3), put long rails (D) at both levels on the back of the bed frame and at the top (bunk) level on the front. Attach the short front rail at the lower (desk) level, at one end.

14 • When you attach the end guard rails (F) (assembly, Step 4), put only one rail at the lower level of each end frame.

15 • Instead of slats on the lower level (assembly, Step 9), install a desktop of 3/4-inch BC plywood measuring 28-1/2 x 39 inches. Before installation, fill, sand, and round over the front, exposed edge and finish the desktop. Polyurethane or enamel paint is a better choice than an oil finish for this piece. Attach the desktop to the support rails with 1-5/8 inch drywall screws (see plan, page 178).

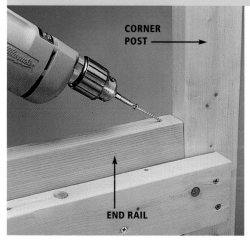

Photo 4 • Toe-screw the 2x6 rails to the 2x4 corner posts with 3-in. deck screws driven in angled pilot holes top and bottom.

Photo 5 • Attach the long side support rails to the uprights with 3-in. deck screws driven through the corner posts into their ends.

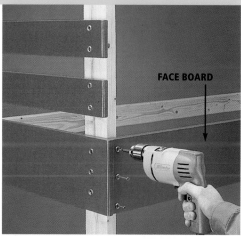

Photo 6 • Screw the side and end face boards to the rails of the bed frame with 2-inch deck screws and finish washers.

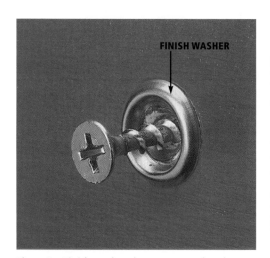

Photo 7 • Finish washers have structural and protective functions, as well as making a decorative feature of the screws used for assembly.

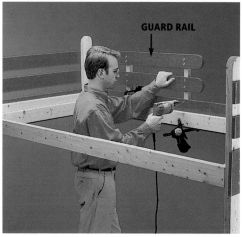

Photo 8 • Clamp the assembled guard rail in position to drill 1/4-in holes for its mounting bolts. Use washers and acorn nuts on the bolts.

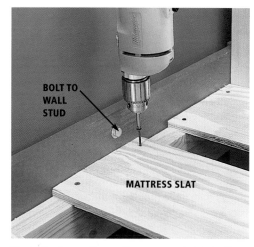

Photo 9 • Screw the mattress support slats to the bed frame. Bolt the bed to wall studs at two points on the upper level.

All-purpose loft bed

More than a bed, this unit is also a desk and a walk-in storage closet. A shelf above the desk holds books and other treasures. The U-shaped shelves in the storage area are wide enough to accommodate wire baskets, so there are no drawers to build.

Getting started

The bed frame is sized to hold a standard twin-size foam mattress with lots of room to spare; for other sizes, measure the mattress you'll use and adjust the overall dimensions accordingly. Removable guard rails on one side and the end permit easy bed-making.

The design shown here tucks the desk under the right end of the bed. But if it would work better under the left end for your room layout, simply reverse the plan, keeping all the dimensions the same.

The unit is built from 2x6's, 2x4's, and 3/4-inch plywood. Cedar boards and birch plywood are recommended. These materials cost a bit more than some others but usually are straighter, need less sanding and filling of holes, and are easier to paint. If you don't mind the additional sanding, you could use less-expensive spruce or fir boards and fir plywood.

In any case, there are no tricky joints to make, and all the parts fit together with screws. You'll need a circular saw, a jigsaw, an electric drill that you also can use to drive screws, and a few simple hand tools.

To build the bunk bed, cut out all the parts and make a trial assembly in your workshop. Then disassemble the base, shelves, and desk; finish-sand and paint all the parts; and re-assemble the whole unit in the bedroom.

Assembly Plan

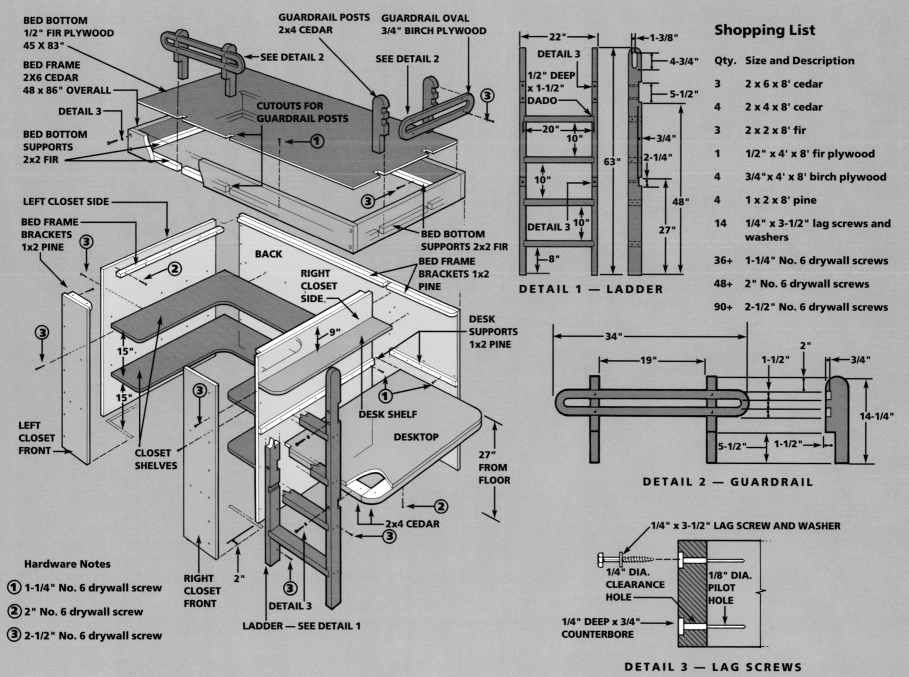

BED BOTTOM
1/2" FIR PLYWOOD
45 X 83"

BED FRAME
2X6 CEDAR
48 x 86" OVERALL

DETAIL 3

BED BOTTOM
SUPPORTS
2x2 FIR

GUARDRAIL POSTS
2x4 CEDAR

SEE DETAIL 2

GUARDRAIL OVAL
3/4" BIRCH PLYWOOD

SEE DETAIL 2

CUTOUTS FOR
GUARDRAIL POSTS

③

①

③

LEFT CLOSET SIDE

BED FRAME
BRACKETS
1x2 PINE

③

③

②

BACK

RIGHT
CLOSET
SIDE

BED BOTTOM
SUPPORTS 2x2 FIR

BED FRAME
BRACKETS 1x2
PINE

DESK
SUPPORTS
1x2 PINE

9"

15"

15"

LEFT
CLOSET
FRONT

CLOSET
SHELVES

③

①

DESK SHELF

DESKTOP

27"
FROM
FLOOR

2x4 CEDAR

②

③

RIGHT
CLOSET
FRONT

2"

③

③

DETAIL 3

LADDER — SEE DETAIL 1

Hardware Notes

① 1-1/4" No. 6 drywall screw

② 2" No. 6 drywall screw

③ 2-1/2" No. 6 drywall screw

22"

DETAIL 3

1-3/8"

4-3/4"

1/2" DEEP
x 1-1/2"
DADO

5-1/2"

20"

10"

3/4"

63"

2-1/4"

10"

48"

DETAIL 3

10"

27"

8"

DETAIL 1 — LADDER

Shopping List

Qty.	Size and Description
3	2 x 6 x 8' cedar
4	2 x 4 x 8' cedar
3	2 x 2 x 8' fir
1	1/2" x 4' x 8' fir plywood
4	3/4"x 4' x 8' birch plywood
4	1 x 2 x 8' pine
14	1/4" x 3-1/2" lag screws and washers
36+	1-1/4" No. 6 drywall screws
48+	2" No. 6 drywall screws
90+	2-1/2" No. 6 drywall screws

34"

19"

2"

1-1/2"

3/4"

14-1/4"

5-1/2"

1-1/2"

DETAIL 2 — GUARDRAIL

1/4" x 3-1/2" LAG SCREW AND WASHER

1/4" DIA.
CLEARANCE
HOLE

1/8" DIA.
PILOT
HOLE

1/4" DEEP x 3/4"
COUNTERBORE

DETAIL 3 — LAG SCREWS

Plywood Cutting Patterns

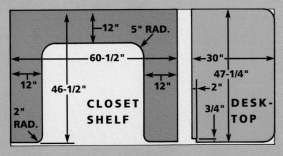

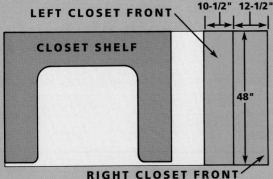

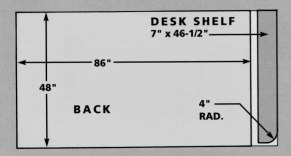

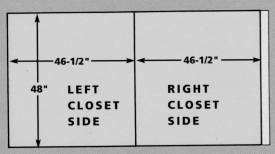

Build the bed and desk

Bed frame

1 • Cut the 2x6's to length: two pieces 86 inches long, and two pieces 45 inches long. Drill the pilot holes, clearance holes, and countersink holes (see Detail 3 in the Assembly Plan); also drill 3/4-inch counterbore holes to provide clearance for the socket wrench you'll use to install the lag screws.

2 • Screw the frame together with lag screws (Photo 1). Cut 2x2's to support the bottom and screw them inside the frame, flush with the bottom edge (see the Hardware Notes in the plans for screw sizes). Cut the bed bottom from 1/2-inch fir plywood, put it in place (Photo 2), and screw it to the 2x2 supports.

Base

3 • Cut out all of the 3/4-inch plywood parts for the base, as shown in the Plywood Cutting Patterns at left. Lay the full sheets of plywood with the good face down across four 2x4's, and cut them with a circular saw. Use a straight board as a saw guide (Photo 3). For clean cuts, use only a sharp carbide-tip saw blade.

4 • Stand the base panels upright on a level floor and tack them together with 4d finish nails. Then drill pilot holes, countersinking them for the screw heads. Screw the base together with 2-1/2 inch drywall screws (Photo 4). Make sure all top edges align and that the right closet side is positioned to allow an inside dimension of exactly 60-1/2 inches so the U-shaped shelves will fit snugly.

5 • Cut out the U-shaped shelves (Photo 5). Set them in place inside the base, using 15-inch temporary spacers to hold them in position (Photo 6). When the shelves are properly positioned, mark along their tops and bottoms.

Then remove the shelves and drill holes for screws in the back, side, and front panels. Reposition the shelves and drive 1-1/2 inch drywall screws into the edges of each shelf.

6 • Cut 1x2 brackets to hold the bed frame to the base. Roundover the three visible ends, and screw the brackets flush with the top edges of the base. Drill pilot holes for drywall screws in the brackets, spacing them 2 inches from bracket ends and 8 inches apart.

7 • With a helper, lift the assembled bed frame and lay it on top of the base. Drill pilot holes in the bed bottom supports to match those in the bed frame brackets. Attach the bed frame to the base with 2-inch No. 6 drywall screws driven up through the brackets on the base into the supports on the bed frame.

Desk

8 • Cut the desktop to size. Use 2-inch drywall screws to attach 2x4's flat to the underside of the desktop so they're flush with the front and left edges. Then mark and cut the rounded corners, cutting through both the plywood and the 2x4's (Photo 7). Check that no screws are in the path of your cuts.

9 • Screw the 1x2 support cleats in place at a height that places the surface of the desktop 27 inches above the floor. Lay the desktop in place, and mark and drill pilot holes in the base sides and the desktop 2x4's. Then screw the desktop to the base.

10 • Now cut the desk shelf and mark its position on the base sides. Locate and drill screw holes in the base sides and the shelf edge, and screw the shelf in place.

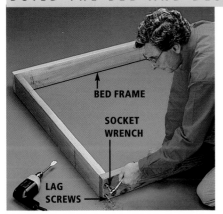

Photo 1 • Assemble the 2x6 bed frame on a level floor with lag screws and washers. Predrill the screw holes, and counterbore them with a 3/4-inch spade bit.

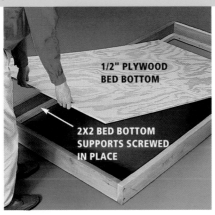

Photo 2 • Lay the 1/2-inch plywood bed bottom inside the frame on the 2x2 bottom supports. Fasten the bottom to the supports with screws.

Photo 3 • Cut 3/4-inch plywood to size for the base, shelves, and desk. Lay the plywood face down on four 2x4's for cutting; use a straight board for a saw guide.

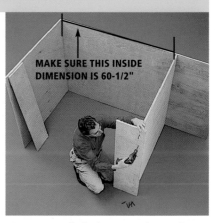

Photo 4 • Tack the base panels together with 4d finish nails. Predrill and counter-sink holes, then assemble the base with 2-1/2 inch drywall screws.

Photo 5 • Cut the U-shaped shelves with a saber saw. The corner radiuses in the cutting patterns are approximate; mark them with a can or lid about that size.

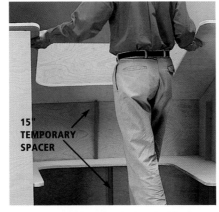

Photo 6 • Position the shelves inside the base using six 15-inch spacers. Then mark the shelf locations, drill holes, and drive screws into the shelf edges.

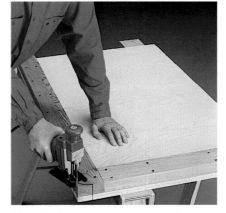

Photo 7 • Cut rounded corners on the desktop after screwing 2x4's under the front and left sides. Set the 2x4's flat and flush with the edges of the plywood.

Build the ladder and guardrails

Ladder

1 • Cut the two vertical rails to length. Shape the rounded tops with a jigsaw. Form the handhold slots by drilling two 1-3/8 inch diameter holes at each end of the slot and cutting out the center section with a saber saw.

2 • Cut 1/2-inch deep dadoes—notches for the ends of the ladder steps—in the vertical rails (Photo 8). To make them accurately, clamp both rails edge-to-edge, mark the cut locations, and make repeated cuts 1/2 inch deep with a circular saw. Hold a square in place to guide the saw. Clean out the remaining wood with a sharp chisel.

3 • Using a saber saw, make 3/4-inch notches in the ladder rails to fit over the bed frame and the edge of the desk.

Guardrails

4 • Cut the four vertical posts for the guard rails to size and shape. Then clamp the posts together side-by-side and cut notches for the oval guardrails using the same method as for the ladder-step dadoes.

5 • Make cutouts in the 1/2-inch plywood bed bottom and the 2x2 supports to accept the posts (Photo 9). You may need to reposition a few screws holding the supports. Slide the posts into position.

6 • Cut the oval guardrails from the remaining pieces of 3/4-inch plywood; cut the rounded ends and oval cutouts with a saber saw.

7 • Fit the rails into the notches while the posts are in place; center them, and attach with lag screws (Photo 10).

BUILD THE LADDER AND GUARDRAILS

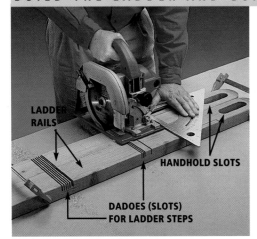

LADDER RAILS

HANDHOLD SLOTS

DADOES (SLOTS) FOR LADDER STEPS

Photo 8 • Cut matching dadoes 1/2 inch deep in the ladder rails for the ladder steps. Make multiple cuts, then chisel out the waste.

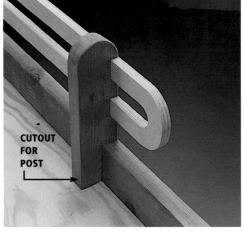

CUTOUT FOR POST

Photo 9 • Notch the plywood bed bottom to accommodate the guardrail posts and help hold them in place.

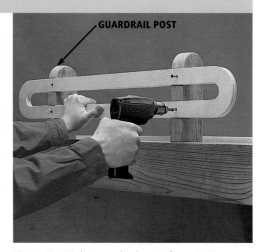

GUARDRAIL POST

Photo 10 • Make guardrail posts from 2x4's; cut oval rails from 3/4-inch birch plywood, fit them into notches in the posts, and attach with screws.

Finish the unit

Filling, sanding, and painting

1 • Fill any imperfections in the wood with wood filler. Pay special attention to the plywood edges. Then remove the bed frame from the base and partially disassemble the unit—the shelves, desk, and base.

2 • Do a thorough finish-sanding with 100-grit sandpaper. Pay special attention to smoothing out the rounded corners (Photo 11). Also round over all edges—especially on pieces that will be touched often, such as the guardrails.

3 • Paint all parts with an oil-base primer. For easier coverage with your final coat, ask the paint store to tint the primer to the same shade as your final paint color. Apply two coats of oil-base semigloss enamel. Use a foam roller for a smooth finish, and lightly sand all surfaces between coats. Oil-base paint is a bit more work to use and clean up than latex paint, but it's far more durable and well worth the trouble for a hard-use piece of furniture.

4 • When the paint is dry, reassemble the unit in the bedroom. Cover all of the countersunk screw heads in the closet front panel with wood filler, then sand them smooth and touch them up with paint. Paint all other screw heads, including the lag screws, but leave them unfilled so that you are able to disassemble the unit later.

Final details

5 • To run wires neatly for a desk lamp, computer, or other electrical items, drill a hole in the back corner of the desktop that's large enough for a plug to pass through. Then drill another hole in the back side panel underneath the desktop to route a cord to an outlet. You can mount a covered plug-in fluorescent light in the closet area the same way.

Tips for Painting

• **Wear a dust mask when sanding.** Disposable masks are inexpensive and they help protect your lungs from dust particles.

• **Work in a well-ventilated area.** If you're sensitive to paint fumes, wear a respirator. Do not rely on a dust mask; it does not provide any protection against fumes.

• **Make sure the room is as dust-free as possible.** Dust in the air will settle on the wet painted surfaces, so vacuum the room thoroughly before starting to paint.

• **Don't skip the priming step.** An unprimed surface requires more coats of paint, and the paint won't cover as evenly or go as far.

• **Surfaces must be clean** or every imperfection will show. Wipe them with a tack cloth or solvent-dampened cloth after each sanding, and again just before applying each coat of paint.

FINISH THE UNIT

ROUND OVER
ALL EXPOSED EDGES

Photo 11 • Sand all surfaces, edges, and rounded ends before painting. It's easiest to partially disassemble the unit beforehand.

Photo 12 • Reassemble the unit in the bedroom after it's painted, and slide it into the corner. A socket wrench will speed installing the lag screws.

Index

Sources

for specialized items

Cherry Tree Toys, Inc.
PO Box 369-318, Belmont, OH 43718
(614) 484-4363.

Craftsman Wood Service
1735 West Cortland Ct., Addison, IL 60101
(800) 543-9367.

Meisel Hardware Specialties
PO Box 70, Mound, MN 55364.

Wisconsin Wagon Co., Inc.
507 Laurel Ave., Janesville, WI 53545
(608) 754-0026.

The Woodworker Store
21801 Industrial Blvd., Rogers, MN 55374
(800) 279-4441.

Project, Item, and Source

Advent Calendar (p. 26); **knobs;**
The Woodworker Store.

Toy Minivan (p. 34); **wheels, axle pins;**
Cherry Tree Toys, Inc.

Race Car (p. 38); **wheels, axle, driver, gas cap;**
Meisel Hardware Specialties.

School Bus (p. 50); **5-1/2 inch diameter wheels;**
The Woodworker Store.

Marble Hockey Game (p. 86); **knobs;**
The Woodworker Store.

Chinese Checkers (p. 90); **colored marble sets;**
Meisel Hardware Specialties.

Jigsaw Puzzles (p. 98); **basswood plywood;**
Craftsman Wood Service.

Tabletop Soccer Game (p. 104); **rubber feet, hand grips, mesh netting;** Meisel Hardware Specialties.

Thoroughbred Rocking Horse (p. 122); **1-1/2 inch diameter birch balls, dowel rod, plug cutter;**
The Woodworker Store.

Stake-Side Wagon (p. 128); **hardware;**
Wisconsin Wagon Co.

Toy Storage Box (p. 168); **casters, hinges, lid supports, felt dots;** The Woodworker Store.

Acknowledgments:

Ron Chamberlain, Elaine Carney, John Emmons, Bill Faber, Jon Frost,
Duane Johnson, Bruce Kieffer, Mike Krivit, Phil Leisenheimer, Don Mannes,
Caryl Marshall, Norm Marshall, Doug Oudekerk, Don Prestly, Dave Radtke,
Art Rooze, Mike Smith, Dan Stoffel, Theodora Briggs Sweeney, Bert Taylor,
Eugene Thompson, Mark Thompson, Bob Ungar, Alice Wagner, Gregg
Weigand, Annette Weir, Gary Wentz, Michaela Wentz, Gordy Wilkinson,
Marcia Williston, Donna Wyttenbach, Bill Zuehlke.

This book was produced by Roundtable Press, Inc.,
for the Reader's Digest Association
in cooperation with *The Family Handyman* magazine.

If you have any questions or comments, please feel free to write us at:

The Family Handyman
Eagan Business Commons, Suite 700
2915 Commers Drive
Eagan, MN 55121